Objectivity, relativism, and truth

Objectivity, relativism, and truth
Philosophical papers

VOLUME I

RICHARD RORTY
University Professor of Humanities
University of Virginia

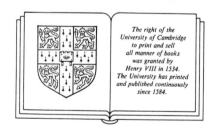

The right of the
University of Cambridge
to print and sell
all manner of books
was granted by
Henry VIII in 1534.
The University has printed
and published continuously
since 1584.

CAMBRIDGE UNIVERSITY PRESS

CAMBRIDGE

NEW YORK   PORT CHESTER   MELBOURNE   SYDNEY

Published by the Press Syndicate of the University of Cambridge
The Pitt Building, Trumpington Street, Cambridge CB2 1RP
40 West 20th Street, New York, NY 10011, USA
10 Stamford Road, Oakleigh, Melbourne 3166, Australia

© Cambridge University Press 1991

First published 1991

Printed in the United States of America

Library of Congress Cataloging-in-Publication Data

Rorty, Richard.

Objectivity, relativism, and truth / Richard Rorty.

p.   cm. – (Philosophical papers ; 1)

ISBN 0-521-35369-6. – ISBN 0-521-35877-9 (pbk.)

1. Representation (philosophy).   2. Truth.   3. Objectivity.
4. Relativity.   5. Postmodernism.   I. Title.   II. Series: Rorty,
Richard. Philosophical papers ; 1.

B945.R52   1991   vol. 1
[B945.R523023]
191 s – dc20

[191]   90-41632
                                                          CIP

British Library Cataloguing in Publication Data

Rorty, Richard

Objectivity, relativism, and truth : philosophical papers
I.

1. Knowledge. Objectivity
I. Title
121.4

ISBN 0-521-35369-6 hardback (volume 1)
ISBN 0-521-35877-9 paperback (volume 1)
ISBN 0-521-35370-X hardback (volume 2)
ISBN 0-521-35878-7 paperback (volume 2)
ISBN 0-521-40476-2 hardback (set)
ISBN 0-521-40915-2 paperback (set)

To Patricia

Contents

Acknowledgments   *page* ix

Introduction: Antirepresentationalism, ethnocentrism, and liberalism   1

Part I

Solidarity or objectivity?   21

Science as solidarity   35

Is natural science a natural kind?   46

Pragmatism without method   63

Texts and lumps   78

Inquiry as recontextualization: An anti-dualist account of
   interpretation   93

Part II

Non-reductive physicalism   113

Pragmatism, Davidson and truth   126

Representation, social practise, and truth   151

Unfamiliar noises: Hesse and Davidson on metaphor   162

Part III

The priority of democracy to philosophy   175

Postmodernist bourgeois liberalism   197

On ethnocentrism: A reply to Clifford Geertz   203

Cosmopolitanism without emancipation: A response to Jean-François
   Lyotard   211

Index of names   223

Acknowledgments

"Solidarity or Objectivity?" was first given as a Howison Lecture at Berkeley. I read a revised version at Nanzan University, which appeared in *Nanzan Review of American Studies*. A still later version, the one which apppears here, was published in *Post-Analytic Philosophy*, John Rajchman and Cornel West, eds. (New York: Columbia University Press, 1985), pp. 3–19.

"Science as Solidarity" was written for a conference at the University of Iowa, and appeared in *The Rhetoric of the Human Sciences*, John S. Nelson, A. Megill, and D. N. McCloskey, eds. (Madison: University of Wisconsin Press, 1987), pp. 38–52. Some paragraphs of the original version duplicated or paralleled paragraphs in "Solidarity or Objectivity?" These paragraphs have been omitted or replaced in the present version.

"Is Natural Science a Natural Kind?" was written for a symposium held at the University of Notre Dame in honor of Professor Ernan McMullin, and was published in *Construction and Constraint: The Shaping of Scientific Rationality*, Ernan McMullin, ed. (Notre Dame, Ind.: Notre Dame University Press, 1988), pp. 49–74.

"Pragmatism Without Method" appeared in *Sidney Hook: Philosopher of Democracy and Humanism*, Paul Kurtz, ed. (Buffalo: Prometheus Books, 1983), pp. 259–73.

"Texts and Lumps" was published in *New Literary History* 17 (1985), pp. 1–15. It is reprinted here by permission.

"Inquiry as Recontextualization: An Anti-Dualist Account of Interpretation" was written for the Summer Institute on "Interpretation" organized by Hubert Dreyfus and David Hoy and held, under the sponsorship of the National Endowment for the Humanities, in the summer of 1988 at the University of California at Santa Cruz. It will appear in a collection of papers which stemmed from that Institute, to be edited by David Hiley and others.

"Non-Reductive Physicalism" was written for presentation at the Institute of Philosophy of the Chinese Academy of Social Sciences. It originally appeared in Chinese translation, and later (in English) in *Theorie der Subjectivität*, a Festschrift for Dieter Henrich, Konrad Cramer et al., eds. (Frankfurt: Suhrkamp Verlag, 1987), pp. 278–96.

"Pragmatism, Davidson and Truth" was published in *Truth and Interpretation: Perspectives on the Philosophy of Donald Davidson,* Ernest LePore, ed. (Oxford: Blackwell, 1986), pp. 333–68.

"Representation, Social Practise, and Truth" was written for a conference held at the University of Pittsburgh to honor Wilfrid Sellars on his seventy-fifth birthday, and was published in *Philosophical Studies* 54 (1988), pp. 215–28. It is reprinted by permission of Kluwer Academic Publishers.

"Unfamiliar Noises: Hesse and Davidson on Metaphor" was a contribution to a symposium on metaphor (with Mary Hesse and Susan Haack) held at the Joint Session of the Mind Association and the Aristotelian Society in Cambridge in the summer of 1987. It was published in *Proceedings of the Aristotelian Society* Suppl. Vol. 61 (1987), pp. 283–96.

"The Priority of Democracy to Philosophy" was written for a conference at the University of Virginia, held in 1984 to celebrate the two-hundredth anniversary of the Virginia Statute of Religious Freedom. It was published in *The Virginia Statute of Religious Freedom,* Merrill Peterson and Robert Vaughan, eds. (Cambridge: Cambridge University Press, 1988), pp. 257–88.

"Postmodernist Bourgeois Liberalism" was a contribution to a symposium on "the social responsibility of intellectuals" held at the 1983 annual meeting of the Eastern Division of the American Philosophical Association. It was published in *The Journal of Philosophy* 80 (Oct. 1983), pp. 583–9. It is reprinted here with permission.

"On Ethnocentrism: A Reply to Clifford Geertz" was written as a comment on Professor Geertz's Tanner Lecture, "The Uses of Diversity," given at the University of Michigan in 1985. It was published in *Michigan Quarterly Review* 25 (1986), pp. 525–34. It is reprinted here with permission.

"Cosmopolitanism Without Emancipation" was written in reply to a paper by Jean-François Lyotard given at a symposium at Johns Hopkins University in which we both participated. The original version was published in French in *Critique* 41 (May 1985), pp. 569–80. A revised version of the English original appears here and in *Modernity and Identity,* Scott Lash and Jonathan Friedman, eds. (Oxford: Blackwell, 1990).

I am grateful to the organizers of the conferences, institutes, and symposia at which various of these papers were presented, and to the publishers of the various journals and collections in which they appeared. I should also like to express my continuing gratitude to the John D. and Catherine T. MacArthur Foundation. The majority of the papers in this and the following volume were written while I held a MacArthur Fellowship.

Introduction:
Antirepresentationalism, ethnocentrism,
and liberalism

This is the first volume of a collection of papers written between 1980 and 1989. The papers in this volume take up, for the most part, issues and figures within analytic philosophy. Those in the second volume deal mostly with issues arising out of the work of Heidegger, Derrida, and Foucault.

The six papers that form Part I of this volume offer an antirepresentationalist account of the relation between natural science and the rest of culture. By an antirepresentationalist account I mean one which does not view knowledge as a matter of getting reality right, but rather as a matter of acquiring habits of action for coping with reality. These papers argue that such an account makes it unnecessary to draw Dilthey-like distinctions between explaining "hard" phenomena and interpreting "soft" ones. They offer an account of inquiry which recognizes sociological, but not epistemological, differences between such disciplinary matrices as theoretical physics and literary criticism.

The antirepresentationalism I advocate here harks back to my 1979 book, *Philosophy and the Mirror of Nature*. Although the figures looming in the background of that book were Wittgenstein, Heidegger, and Dewey, my most proximate intellectual debts at the time I was writing it were to Wilfrid Sellars and Willard van Orman Quine. In the subsequent ten years, I have come to think of Donald Davidson's work as deepening and extending the lines of thought traced by Sellars and Quine. So I have been writing more and more about Davidson – trying to clarify his views to myself, to defend them against actual and possible objections, and to extend them into areas which Davidson himself has not yet explored. The four chapters which make up Part II of this volume are a mixture of exposition of Davidson and commentary on him.

The remaining four chapters in the volume – those which make up Part III – are about political liberalism, rather than about antirepresentationalism. The connection between Part III and the first two parts is the one Dewey saw between the abandonment of what he called the "spectator theory of knowledge" and the needs of a democratic society. I read Dewey as saying that it suits such a society to have no views about truth save that it is more likely to be obtained in Milton's "free and open encounter" of opinions than in any other way. This thought, characteristic of Peirce and Habermas as well as Dewey, is the one which I try to develop in "The Priority of Democracy to Philosophy" and in the three shorter pieces which follow it.

The remainder of this introduction has two aims. In the first two-thirds of it, I try to clarify the relations between antirepresentationalism and antirealism. I claim that the representationalism-vs.-antirepresentationalism issue is distinct from the realism-vs.-antirealism one, because the latter issue arises only for representationalists. In the final third, I use the notion of ethnocentrism as a link between antirepresentationalism and political liberalism. I argue that an antirepresentationalist view of inquiry leaves one without a skyhook with which to escape from the ethnocentrism produced by acculturation, but that the liberal culture of recent times has found a strategy for avoiding the disadvantage of ethnocentrism. This is to be open to encounters with other actual and possible cultures, and to make this openness central to its self-image. This culture is an *ethnos* which prides itself on its suspicion of ethnocentrism – on its ability to increase the freedom and openness of encounters, rather than on its possession of truth.[1]

Philosophers in the English-speaking world seem fated to end the century discussing the same topic – realism – which they were discussing in 1900. In that year, the opposite of realism was still idealism. But by now language has replaced mind as that which, supposedly, stands over and against "reality." So discussion has shifted from whether material reality is "mind-dependent" to questions about which sorts of true statements, if any, stand in representational relations to nonlinguistic items. Discussion of realism now revolves around whether only the statements of physics can correspond to "facts of the matter" or whether those of mathematics and ethics might also. Nowadays the opposite of realism is called, simply, "antirealism."

This term, however, is ambiguous. It is standardly used to mean the claim, about some particular true statements, that there is no "matter of fact" which they represent. But, more recently, it has been used to mean the claim that *no* linguistic items represent *any* nonlinguistic items. In the former sense it refers to an issue within the community of representationalists – those philosophers who find it fruitful to think of mind or language as containing representations of reality. In the latter sense, it refers to antirepresentationalism – to the attempt to eschew discussion of realism by denying that the notion of "representation," or that of "fact of the matter," has any useful role in philosophy. Representationalists typically think that controversies between idealists and realists were, and controversies between skeptics and antiskeptics are, fruitful and interesting. Antirepresentationalists typically think both sets of controversies pointless. They diagnose both as the results of being

---

1 On this point, see my exchange with Thomas McCarthy about the Habermasian claim that truth-claims are claims to universal, intercultural validity. McCarthy's criticism of me, "Pragmatism and the Quest for Truth," appeared in *Critical Inquiry* 16 (1990), as did my "Truth and Freedom: A Reply to Thomas McCarthy" and his "Ironist Theory as Vocation: A Response to Rorty's Reply."

held captive by a picture, a picture from which we should by now have wriggled free.[2]

The term "antirealism" was first put in circulation by Michael Dummett, who used it in the first sense. He formulated the opposition between realism and antirealism in the following terms:

> Realism I characterise as the belief that statements of the disputed class possess an objective truth-value, independently of our means of knowing it: they are true or false in virtue of a reality existing independently of us. The anti-realist opposes to this the view that statements of the disputed class are to be understood only by reference to the sort of thing which we count as evidence for a statement of that class.[3]

Dummett believes that much of the history of philosophy, including the battles between realists and idealists, can be usefully reinterpreted by deploying this distinction. He also believes that "philosophy of language is first philosophy," for he views the difference between the realist and the antirealist as a difference about the *meaning* of the disputed class of statements. So he thinks the theory of meaning philosophically fundamental.

In taking this stance, Dummett turned away from the "therapeutic" conception of philosophy familiar from Wittgenstein's *Philosophical Investigations,* and from such earlier books as James's *Pragmatism* and Dewey's *Reconstruction in Philosophy.* In this respect, Dummett is typical of the majority of English-speaking philosophers of the last two decades. These decades have seen a gradual repudiation of the Wittgensteinian conception of philosophy as therapy, and a gradual return to systematic attempts to solve traditional problems. The trouble with the later Wittgenstein, Dummett says, is that he cannot "supply us with a *foundation* for future work in the philosophy of language or in philosophy in general."[4] Wittgenstein gave us no "systematic theory of meaning," and hence nothing on which to build. Indeed, he thought such a theory impossible, since (in Dummett's words) he rejected his earlier view that "the meanings of our sentences are given by the conditions that render them determinately true or false" and substituted the view that "meaning is to be explained in terms of what is taken as *justifying* an utterance."[5]

This latter view is typical of antirepresentationalist philosophers, for their concern is to eliminate what they regard as representationalism's pseudo-problems,

---

2 Colin McGinn provides a nice illustration of the way in which his own representationalism and Donald Davidson's antirepresentationalism are at cross-purposes. After noting that Davidson's "principle of charity" makes it possible to simply shrug off the skeptic rather than answering him, he adds "I had the idea of using the anti-sceptical consequences of the principle of charity as a *reductio* before I learned that Davidson regards this as a *virtue* of his account of interpretation." McGinn, "Radical Interpretation and Epistemology," in Ernest LePore, ed., *Truth and Interpretation: Perspectives on the Philosophy of Donald Davidson* (Oxford: Blackwell, 1986), p. 359n.

3 Michael Dummett, *Truth and Other Enigmas* (Cambridge, Mass.: Harvard University Press, 1978), p. 146.

4 Ibid., p. 453.

5 Ibid., p. 452.

rather than to build systems or to solve problems.[6] The later Wittgenstein, Heidegger, and Dewey, for example, would all be as dubious about the notion of "truth-makers" – nonlinguistic items which "render" statements determinately true or false – as they are about that of "representation." For representationalists, "making true" and "representing" are reciprocal relations: the nonlinguistic item which makes S true is the one represented by S. But antirepresentationalists see both notions as equally unfortunate and dispensable – not just in regard to statement of some disputed class, but in regard to all statements.

Representationalists often think of antirepresentationalism as simply transcendental idealism in linguistic disguise – as one more version of the Kantian attempt to derive the object's determinacy and structure from that of the subject. This suspicion is well stated in Bernard Williams's essay "Wittgenstein and Idealism." Williams says there that a Wittgensteinian view of language seems committed to the following chain of inference:

(i) 'S' has the meaning we give it.

(ii) A necessary condition of our giving 'S' a meaning is Q.

Ergo

(iii) Unless Q, 'S' would not have a meaning.

(iv) If 'S' did not have a meaning, 'S' would not be true.

Ergo

(v) Unless Q, 'S' would not be true.

Since the values of Q will typically include human social practices, the conclusion of this set of inferences is, indeed, reminiscent of transcendental idealism. But the antirepresentationalist will reply that (v) merely says that unless certain social practices are engaged in, there will be no statements to call "true" or "false." Williams, however, rejoins that "it is not obvious that for the later Wittgensteinian view . . . we can so easily drive a line between the sentence 'S' expressing the truth, and what is the case if S." His point is that antirepresentationalists typically do not think that, behind the true sentence S, there is a sentence-shaped piece of nonlinguistic reality called "the fact that S" – a set of relations between objects which hold independently of language – which makes 'S' true. So, Williams concludes, antirepresentationalists, and in particular the later Wittgenstein, are committed to the idea that "the determinacy of reality comes from what we have decided or are prepared to count as determinate."[7]

---

6 See Robert Brandom's contrast between representationalist theorists and social-practice theorists in his "Truth and Assertibility," *Journal of Philosophy* LXIII (1976), p. 137 – a contrast I discuss in more detail in "Representation, Social Practise, and Truth," in Part II.

7 These quotes from Williams are from his *Moral Luck* (Cambridge: Cambridge University Press, 1981), pp. 162–3. For an example of the sort of thing which makes Williams nervous, see Martin Heidegger, *Being and Time*, Macquarrie and Robinson, trans. (New York: Harper and Row, 1962), p. 269: "Newton's laws, the principle of contradiction, any truth whatever – these are true only as long as Dasein *is*."

The trouble with this conclusion is that "comes from" suggests causal dependence. The picture called up by Williams's terminology is of some mighty immaterial force called "mind" or "language" or "social practice" – a force which shapes facts out of indeterminate goo, constructs reality out of something not yet determinate enough to count as real. The problem for antirepresentationalists is to find a way of putting their point which carries no such suggestion. Antirepresentationalists need to insist that "determinacy" is not what is in question – that neither does thought determine reality nor, in the sense intended by the realist, does reality determine thought. More precisely, it is no truer that "atoms are what they are because we use 'atom' as we do" than that "we use 'atom' as we do because atoms are as they are." *Both* of these claims, the antirepresentationlist says, are entirely empty. Both are pseudo-explanations.

It is particularly important that the antirepresentationalist insist that the *latter* claim is a pseudo-explanation. For this is a claim which the typical realist can, sooner or later, be counted upon to make. He or she will say that we achieve *accurate* representation because, sometimes, nonlinguistic items cause linguistic items to be used as they are – not just in the case of particular statements within social practices (as when the movement of a tennis ball causes the referee to cry "Out!") but in the case of social practices as wholes. On this account, the reason why physicists have come to use "atom" as we do is that there really are atoms out there which have caused themselves to be represented more or less accurately – caused us to have words which refer to them and to engage in the social practice called microstructural physical explanation. The reason why such explanation meets with more success than, say, astrological explanation, is that there are no planetary influences out there, whereas there really *are* atoms out there.

The antirepresentationalist is quite willing to grant that our language, like our bodies, has been shaped by the environment we live in. Indeed, he or she insists on this point – the point that our minds or our language could not (as the representationalist skeptic fears) be "out of touch with the reality" any more than our bodies could. What he or she denies is that it is explanatorily useful to pick and choose among the contents of our minds or our language and say that this or that item "corresponds to" or "represents" the environment in a way that some other item does not. On an antirepresentationalist view, it is one thing to say that a prehensile thumb, or an ability to use the word "atom" as physicists do, is useful for coping with the environment. It is another thing to attempt to *explain* this utility by reference to representationalist notions, such as the notion that the reality referred to by "quark" was "determinate" before the word "quark" came along (whereas that referred to by, for example, "foundation grant" only jelled once the relevant social practices emerged).

Antirepresentationalists think that attempt hopeless. They see no way to explain what "determinate" means in such a context except by chanting one of a number of equally baffling words, and so they see the realist's use of "determinate" as merely incantatory. Just as Quine suggests that we throw out the whole cluster of concepts (e.g., "synonomous," "conceptual") which are invoked to make us think that we understand what "analytic" meant, so antirepresentationalists suggest that we throw out the whole cluster of concepts (e.g., "fact of the matter," "bivalence,") which are used to make us think we understand what "the determinacy of reality" means.

Antirepresentationalists think this latter cluster dispensable because they see no way of formulating an *independent* test of accuracy of representation – of reference or correspondence to an "antecedently determinate" reality – no test distinct from the success which is supposedly explained by this accuracy. Representationalists offer us no way of deciding whether a certain linguistic item is usefully deployed because it stands in these relations, or whether its utility is due to some factors which have nothing to do with them – as the utility of a fulcrum or a thumb has nothing to do with its "representing" or "corresponding" to the weights lifted, or the objects manipulated, with its aid. So antirepresentationalists think "we use 'atom' as we do, and atomic physics works, because atoms are as they are" is no more enlightening than "opium puts people to sleep because of its dormitive power."

This point that there is no independent test of the accuracy of correspondence is the heart of Putnam's argument that notions like "reference" – semantical notions which relate language to nonlanguage – are internal to our overall view of the world. The representationalists' attempt to explain the success of astrophysics and the failure of astrology is, Putnam thinks, bound to be merely an empty compliment unless we can attain what he calls a God's-eye standpoint – one which has somehow broken out of our language and our beliefs and tested them against something known without their aid. But we have no idea what it would be like to be at that standpoint. As Davidson puts it, "there is no chance that someone can take up a vantage point for comparing conceptual schemes [e.g., the astrologer's and the astrophysicist's] by temporarily shedding his own."[8]

From the standpoint of the representationalist, the fact that notions like representation, reference, and truth are deployed in ways which are internal to a language or a theory is no reason to drop them. The fact that we can never *know* whether a "mature" physical theory, one which seems to leave nothing to be desired, may not be entirely off the mark is, representationalists say, no reason to deprive ourselves of the notion of "being off the mark." To think otherwise, they add, is to be "verificationist," undesirably anthropocentric in the same way in which nineteenth-century idealism was undesirably anthropocentric. It is to fall under the influence of what Thomas Nagel calls "a significant strain of idealism in

8 Donald Davidson, *Inquiries into Truth and Interpretation* (Oxford: Oxford University Press, 1984), p. 185.

contemporary philosophy, according to which what there is and how things are cannot go beyond what we could in principle think about."[9] Nagel thinks that to deprive ourselves of such notions as "representation" and "correspondence" would be to stop "trying to climb outside of our own minds, an effort some would regard as insane and that I regard as philosophically fundamental."[10]

Antirepresentationalists do not think such efforts insane, but they do think that the history of philosophy shows them to have been fruitless and undesirable. They think that these efforts generate the sort of pseudo-problems which Wittgenstein hoped to avoid by abandoning the picture which held him captive when he wrote the *Tractatus*. Wittgenstein was not insane when he wrote that book, but he was right when he later described himself as having been buzzing around inside a fly-bottle. His escape from the bottle was not, as Williams suggests, a matter of buzzing off in the direction of transcendental idealism, but rather of refusing any longer to be tempted to answer questions like "Is reality intrinsically determinate, or is its determinacy a result of our activity?" He was not suggesting that we determine the way reality is. He was suggesting that questions which we should have to climb out of our own minds to answer should not be asked. He was suggesting that both realism and idealism share representationalist presuppositions which we would be better off dropping.

Nagel thinks that if we follow Wittgenstein we must "acknowledge that all thought is an illusion," for "the Wittgensteinian atttack on transcendent thoughts depends on a position so radical that it also undermines the weaker transcendent pretensions of even the least philosophical of thoughts."[11] Pretty much the same view is found in David Lewis's reply to Putman's suggestion that we be content to remain intratheoretical, content not to seek a God's-eye view. Lewis grants that if theories of reference are "made true by our referential intentions," then Putnam's internalism is inescapable. But, he says, "What we say and think not only doesn't settle what we refer to, it doesn't even settle the prior question of *how* it is to be settled what we refer to."[12] So, he continues, we need a constraint on theories of reference which is something other than our referential intentions, and we can get it by "taking physics . . . at face value." "Physics," according to Lewis, "professes to discover the elite properties," where "elite" means the ones whose "boundaries are established by objective sameness and difference in nature."[13]

9 Thomas Nagel, *The View from Nowhere* (New York: Oxford University Press, 1986), p. 9.
10 Ibid., p. 11.
11 Ibid., p. 107.
12 David Lewis, "Putnam's Paradox," *Australasian Journal of Philosophy*, 1983, p. 226.
13 "Among all the countless things and classes that there are, most are miscellaneous, gerrymandered, ill-demarcated. Only an elite minority are carved at the joints, so that their boundaries are established by objective sameness and difference in nature. . . . Physics discovers which things and classes are the most elite of all; but others are elite also, though to a lesser degree. . . ." (ibid., pp. 227–8).

Lewis thus builds representationalism into the "face value" of physics.[14] This is characteristic of representationalists who are realists rather than skeptics. For they see physics as the area of culture where nonhuman reality, as opposed to human social practices, most obviously gets its innings. The representationalist believes, in Williams's words, that "we can select among our beliefs and features of our world picture some that we can reasonably claim to represent the world in a way to the maximum degree independent of our perspective and its peculiarities".[15] By contrast, antirepresentationalists see no sense in which physics is more independent of our human peculiarities than astrology or literary criticism. For them, various areas of culture answer different human needs, but there is no way to stand outside of all human needs and observe that some of them (e.g., our need for predictions of what will happen in various circumstances, our need for simple and elegant ways of saving the phenomena) are gratified by detecting "objective sameness and difference in nature" whereas others are gratified by whomping up what Lewis calls "miscellaneous, gerrymandered, ill-demarcated"[16] objects. The human need which is gratified by the attempt thus to stand outside all human needs – the need for what Nagel calls "transcendence" – is one which antirepresentationalists think it culturally undesirable to exacerbate. They think this need eliminable by means of a suitable moral education – one which raises people up from the "humility" which Nagel recommends. Such an education tries to sublimate the desire to stand in suitably humble relations to nonhuman realities into a desire for free and open encounters between human beings, encounters culminating either in intersubjective agreement or in reciprocal tolerance.

When we turn away from the contrast Dummett draws between realist and antirealist views about various classes of statements, we find "antirealism" being used in the second of the two senses I distinguished earlier. In this sense, the sense in which it is a synonym for what I have been calling "antirepresentationalism," Donald Davidson has come to be thought of, in recent years, as the arch antirealist.

Dummett originally portrayed Davidson as an archetypal *realist,* but Davidson

---

14 Not all philosophers of physics share Lewis's view of what physics professes to do. Arthur Fine, for example, attributes to the physicist only what he calls "the natural ontological attitude," abbreviated as "NOA." Fine writes as follows: "Does science aim at truth, or does science merely aim at empirical adequacy? This is the springboard for the realism/instrumentalism controversy. NOA wants to pull back a bit from the question to ask, more fundamentally, whether science 'aims' at all." Fine sums up his own antirepresentationalism when he says "NOA does not think that truth is an explanatory concept, or that there is some general thing that makes truths true." (Fine, "Unnatural Attitudes: Realist and Instrumentalist Attachments to Science," *Mind* XCV [1986], pp. 173, 175.)

15 Bernard Williams, *Ethics and the Limits of Philosophy* (Cambridge, Mass.: Harvard University Press, 1985), pp. 138–9.

16 Lewis, "Putnam's Paradox," p. 227.

has subsequently said things which have made clear that this was a misleading description of his view. He says, for example:

> Beliefs are true or false, but they represent nothing. It is good to be rid of representations, and with them the correspondence theory of truth, for it is thinking that there are representations that engenders thoughts of relativism.[17]

Davidson has argued, in papers stretching over the last twenty years, that if we once adopt the "scheme-content" distinction – the distinction between determinate realities and a set of words or concepts which may or may not be "adequate" to them – we shall, needlessly, find ourselves worried about relativism-vs.-absolutism – about whether our knowledge is merely "relative" to what Williams calls "our perspective and its peculiarities" or whether it is in touch with what Lewis calls "objective sameness and difference in nature." So he urges that we drop that distinction, and with it the notion that beliefs represent a content according to the conventions of a scheme. Davidson has no *parti pris* in favor of physics, and does not think that it, or any natural science, can provide a skyhook – something which might lift us out of our beliefs to a standpoint from which we glimpse the relations of those beliefs to reality. Rather, he takes us to be in touch with reality in all areas of culture – ethics as well as physics, literary criticism as well as biology – in a sense of "in touch with" which does not mean "representing reasonably accurately" but simply "caused by and causing."

In an attempt to circumvent this attempt to change the terms of controversy and rise above the old battles, David Papineau has invented some new definitions of the term "antirealist," definitions tailored to fit Davidson. At one point Papineau defines the term as follows: "Anti-realism is the thesis that the analysis of representation yields an a priori argument for holding that at some level judgement and reality must fit each other."[18] At another point he writes: "Anti-realists are philosophers who deny that it makes sense to think of reality as it is in itself in abstraction from the way it is represented in human judgement."[19]

Neither of Papineau's definitions avoids the misleading imputation of a belief in representations to philosophers who protest their lack of any such belief. Still, the latter definition, if not the former, catches something important in Davidson's view. For Davidson argues that "beliefs are by nature generally true," and claims that

17 Donald Davidson, "The Myth of the Subjective," in *Relativism: Interpretation and Confrontation,* Michael Krausz, ed. (Notre Dame, Ind.: University of Notre Dame Press, 1989), pp. 165–6.
18 David Papineau, *Reality and Representation* (Oxford: Blackwell, 1987), p. xii.
19 Ibid., p. 2. Compare Nagel, *The View from Nowhere,* p. 93, where "idealism" is defined as "the position that what there is must be possibly conceivable by us, or possibly something for which we could have evidence." Nagel notes that "an argument for this general form of idealism must show that the notion of what *cannot* be thought about by us or those like us makes no sense," and then launches into an argument against Davidson, whom he presumably counts as an idealist in the specified sense.

the agent has only to reflect on what a belief is to appreciate that most of his basic beliefs are true, and among his beliefs, those most securely held and that cohere with the main body of his beliefs are the most apt to be true.[20]

But for Davidson, of course, reflection on what a belief is is not "the analysis of representation." Rather, it is reflection on how a language-using organism interacts with what is going on its neighborhood. Like Dewey, Davidson takes off from Darwin rather than from Descartes: from beliefs as adaptations to the environment rather than as quasi-pictures. Like Bain and Peirce, he thinks of beliefs as habits of acting rather than as parts of a "model" of the world constructed by the organism to help it deal with the world.

This non-Cartesian, antirepresentationalist approach is, in both Dewey and Davidson, holist through and through. Both men see no need for, or possibility of, a theory which starts off by specifying which bits of language tie up with which bits of reality — what Davidson calls a "building-block" theory. For Dewey, the paradigm of such a theory was sense-datum empiricism. For Davidson, it is attempts such as Kripke's and Field's to make such concepts as reference susceptible to "an independent analysis or interpretation in terms of non-linguistic concepts."[21] By contrast with such attempts, Davidson suggests "that words, meanings of words, reference and satisfaction are posits we need to implement a theory of truth,"[22] where a theory of truth is neither an attempt to explain the meaning of the word "true" nor an attempt to analyze such notions as "corresponds to" or "makes true."

Such a theory is, instead, an account of how the marks and noises made by certain organisms hang together in a coherent pattern, one which can be fitted into our overall account of the interaction between these organisms and their environment. Davidson's argument that we must interpret the beliefs of any such organism (including ourselves) as true, and most of any organism's concepts as concepts which we ourselves also possess, boils down to the claim that we shall not take ourselves to have found such a coherent pattern unless we can see these organisms as talking mostly about things to which they stand in real cause-and-effect relations. Since our theory of how to correlate another organism's marks and noises with our own has to take its place within a general theory of our and their similar relation to relevant environments, there is no room for the sort of wholesale slippage between organism and environment which the Cartesian notion of "inner representation of the environment" is capable of producing. More generally, there is no room for the notion of "thought" or "language" as capable of being mostly out of phase with the environment — for there is no way to give sense to

20 Donald Davidson, "A Coherence Theory of Truth and Knowledge," in *Truth and Interpretation: Perspectives on the Philosophy of Donald Davidson*, Ernest LePore, ed. (Oxford: Blackwell, 1986), p. 319.
21 Davidson, *Inquiries*, p. 219.
22 Ibid., p. 222.

the notion of "out of phase." So Papineau is right, in a sense, in saying that for Davidson "judgment and reality must fit together." But this is not to say that, for Davidson, most of our representations must be accurate. For judgments – habits of action, including habitual productions of certain marks or noises – are not representations. He is also right in saying that for Davidson it "does not make sense to think of reality as it is in itself in abstraction from the way it is represented in human judgment."

By contrast, Papineau's "teleological theory of representation" is designed precisely to let us think of reality in this way. His defense of "realism" against what he thinks of as Davidson's "antirealism," depends upon the idea that we can use biology to give us just the sort of building-blocks Davidsonian holism suggests we cannot get. Because Papineau thinks of organisms as building models of the environment, he takes the notion of "truth condition" for the attribution of an observational predicate like "tree" to be that of "that state of affairs that the bearer of a given causal role is biologically supposed to represent."[23] He then goes on to argue that there is no reason to think that, for *non*observational concepts, there is any such tight biological tie, and thus (since, as he rightly says, "all concepts are to some degree non-observational") no reason to think that "the concepts of different communities must answer alike to objectively available referents."[24] So, he concludes, there is no reason to doubt that many, perhaps most, of our assertions have *no* truth conditions.

Here Papineau puts himself in the same dialectical position vis-à-vis Davidson as Lewis is in vis-à-vis Putnam. Papineau and Lewis share the conviction that there are "objective," theory-independent and language-independent matter-of-factual relationships, detectable by natural science, holding or failing to hold between individual bits of language and individual bits of nonlanguage. When these relations (e.g., "being caused by," "biologically supposed to represent") do hold they cause us to "accurately represent" some item which belongs within what Putnam calls "a certain domain of entities [the ones which are there regardless of

---

23 Papineau, *Reality and Representation*, p. 92. The difficulty which holists see in notions like "biologically supposed to" emerges when one asks whether visual systems good at responding to bilateral symmetry are "supposed to" recognize such symmetry or are "supposed to" recognize that, as Daniel Dennett puts it, "someone is looking at you." (See Dennett's discussion of this example in his *The Intentional Stance* [Cambridge, Mass.: MIT Press, 1987], pp. 303–4.) It is exactly as hard for the biologist to figure out what (anthropomorphized) Nature wants as for the radical interpreter to figure out what the native wants, and for the same reasons.

For a more detailed and sophisticated development of the notion of "biologically supposed to" than Papineau offers, see Ruth Garrett Millikan, *Language, Thought and Other Biological Categories* (Cambridge, Mass.: Bradford/MIT Press, 1984). We antirepresentationalists agree with Millikan when she says (p. 240) that "If language has its powers because it maps the world, then the identity or selfsameness of the significant variables of the affairs it maps must be an objective or thought-independent sameness – one that explains rather than being explained by the operations of language and thought." So we deny that that is why language has its powers.

24 Papineau, *Reality and Representation*, p. 93.

what we do or say] such that all ways of using words referentially are just different ways of singling out one or more of those entities."[25]

The antirepresentationalism common to Putnam and Davidson insists, by contrast, that the notion of "theory-independent and language-independent matter-of-factual relationships" begs all the questions at issue. For this notion brings back the very representationalist picture from which we need to escape. With William James, both philosophers refuse to contrast the world with what the world is known as, since such a contrast suggests that we have somehow done what Nagel calls "climbing out of our own minds." They do not accept the Cartesian-Kantian picture presupposed by the idea of "our minds" or "our language" as an "inside" which can be contrasted to something (perhaps something very different) "outside." From a Darwinian point of view, there is simply no way to give sense to the idea of our minds or our language as systematically out of phase with what lies beyond our skins.

The essays in Parts I and II below spell out my hope that issues about realism and antirealism (in Dummett's senses of those terms) will become as obsolete as the realism-vs.-idealism issue now seems. I should like to think that English-speaking philosophy in the twenty-first century will have put the representationalist problematic behind it, as most French- or German-speaking philosophy already has. In Volume II of these collected papers – *Essays on Heidegger and Others* – I discuss some "Continental" thinkers who have turned their back on this problematic and tried to break new ground. But the essays in this volume do not break such ground, nor do they offer new arguments which complement or underwrite those which have been offered by Davidson, Putnam, and others. Rather, they answer some objections to these latter arguments, and they enlarge on how various areas of culture (particularly science and politics) look from a nonrepresentationalist perspective. My principal motive is the belief that we can still make admirable sense of our lives even if we cease to have what Nagel calls "an ambition of transcendence." So I try to show how a culture without this ambition – a Deweyan culture – would be preferable to the culture of what Heidegger calls "the onto-theological tradition." I try to show how we might throw away a set of ladders which, though once indispensable, have now become encumbrances.

The lead essay in this volume – "Solidarity or Objectivity?" – announces a theme which is repeated with variations in most of the other essays. There I urge

25 Putnam, *Reality and Representation* (Cambridge, Mass.: MIT Press, 1988), p. 120. Putnam says that we should reject the idea of such a domain, and with it the picture which suggests that "what an 'object' of reference is is fixed once and for all at the start, and that the totality of objects in some scientific theory or other will turn out to coincide with the totality of All the Objects There Are." For Putnam, "there is no such totality as All the Objects There Are, inside or outside science."

that whatever good the ideas of "objectivity" and "transcendence" have done for our culture can be attained equally well by the idea of a community which strives after both intersubjective agreement and novelty – a democratic, progressive, pluralist community of the sort of which Dewey dreamt. If one reinterprets objectivity as intersubjectivity, or as solidarity, in the ways I suggest below, then one will drop the question of how to get in touch with "mind-independent and language-independent reality." One will replace it with questions like "What are the limits of our community? Are our encounters sufficiently free and open? Has what we have recently gained in solidarity cost us our ability to listen to outsiders who are suffering? To outsiders who have new ideas?" These are political questions rather than metaphysical or epistemological questions. Dewey seems to me to have given us the right lead when he viewed pragmatism not as grounding, but as clearing the ground for, democratic politics.

If you give up on the project of escaping from "human peculiarities and perspectives," then the important question will be about what sort of human being you want to become. If you accept the distinction between the public and the private realms which I draw in *Contingency, Irony, and Solidarity,* then this question will divide into two sub-questions. The first is: with what communities should you identify, of which should you think of yourself as a member? The second is (to adapt Whitehead's definition of religion): what should I do with my aloneness? The first is a question about your obligations to other human beings. The second is about your obligation to, in Nietzsche's words, become who you are.

The essays in this first volume are relevant to the former question, whereas many of those in the second veer toward the latter. The first and the last essay in this volume dwell on the topic of ethnocentrism. That is because one consequence of antirepresentationalism is the recognition that no description of how things are from a God's-eye point of view, no skyhook provided by some contemporary or yet-to-be-developed science, is going to free us from the contingency of having been acculturated as we were. Our acculturation is what makes certain options live, or momentous, or forced, while leaving others dead, or trivial, or optional.[26] We can only hope to transcend our acculturation if our culture contains (or, thanks to disruptions from outside or internal revolt, comes to contain) splits which supply toeholds for new initiatives. Without such splits – without ten-

---

26 Here I invoke the terminology of William James's "The Will to Believe," an essay whose argumentative force I, like Putnam, think has been greatly underestimated. James's point was not that you can *will* yourself to believe something against the evidence, but that there are situations in which the notion of "evidence" is not in point. One such situation is when you are not sure about the relevance of what you have previously taken to be evidence – a situation in which the past practices that dictated a sense of relevance are in question, and where you know of no super-practice to which questions of relevance can be referred. For the place of "The Will to Believe" in James's overall outlook, see Hilary and Ruth Anna Putnam, "William James' Ideas," *Raritan* VIII (1989), pp. 27–44 as well as their forthcoming book on James.

sions which make people listen to unfamiliar ideas in the hope of finding means of overcoming those tensions – there is no such hope. The systematic elimination of such tensions, or of awareness of them, is what is so frightening about *Brave New World* and *1984*. So our best chance for transcending our acculturation is to be brought up in a culture which prides itself on *not* being monolithic – on its tolerance for a plurality of subcultures and its willingness to listen to neighboring cultures. This is the connection which Dewey saw between antirepresenta- tionalism and democracy – the connection which I discuss in the papers that make up Part III of this volume.

In these papers I turn from criticisms of the notion of "language-independent determinate reality" to criticisms of the use of universalistic notions like "the nature of the self" or "our essential humanity" as fulcrums for criticism of current moral convictions or social institutions. I urge that, rather than trying to climb out of our own minds – trying to rise above the historical contingencies that filled our minds with the words and beliefs they presently contain – we make a virtue of necessity and rest content with playing off parts of our minds against other parts. For us antirepresentationalists, this is just to say that we should not try to do the impossible: we should not look for skyhooks, but only for toeholds.

This way of looking at proposals for moral or social change seems to many people, especially people who think of themselves as political radicals, a counsel of despair, an apologia for the powers that be. But it is not. It is just a way of saying that the activity of "climbing out of our own minds" which Nagel recom- mends is, in the only sense in which it *is* possible, not a process of setting aside our old vocabularies, beliefs, and desires but rather of gradually adding to and modifying them by playing them off against each other.[27] This is a process of reformation and enlargement rather than revolution. So the image of climbing out of our minds – to something external from which we can turn and look at them – needs to be replaced. The alternative image is that of our minds gradually growing larger and stronger and more interesting by the addition of new options – new candidates for belief and desire, phrased in new vocabularies. The principal means of such growth, as I argue in *Contingency, Irony, and Solidarity* and below in "Unfamiliar Noises," is the gradual enlargement of our imagination by the metaphorical use of old marks and noises.

Part of the hostility and suspicion which some of the essays in this volume – notably "The Priority of Democracy to Philosophy" and "Postmodernist Bour-

---

27 I take this to be the force of Dewey's claim that "Unless progress is a present reconstructing, it is nothing; if it cannot be told by qualities belonging to the movement of transition it can never be judged. . . . Progress means increase of present meaning, which involves multiplication of sensed distinctions as well as harmony, unification. . . . Till men give up the search for a general formula for progress they will not know where to look to find it." (*Human Nature and Conduct*, vol. 14 of *The Middle Works of John Dewey* [Carbondale, Ill.: Southern Illinois University Press, 1988], pp. 195–6.)

geois Liberalism" – have aroused in people to my political left may be due to my misleadingly ambiguous use of "ethnocentrism."[28] This ambiguity has made me appear to be attempting a transcendental deduction of democratic politics from antirepresentationalism premises. I should have distinguished more clearly between ethnocentrism as an inescapable condition – roughly synonymous with "human finitude" – and as a reference to a particular *ethnos*. In the latter usage, "ethnocentrism" means loyalty to the sociopolitical culture of what the Marxists used to call "bourgeois democracies" and what Roberto Unger calls, more neutrally, "the rich North Atlantic democracies."

Most of my critics on the left are fairly well disposed toward the antirepresentationalism I advocate, for this view is Nietzsche's and Foucault's as much as Dewey's or Davidson's. But they think of themselves as standing outside of the sociopolitical culture of liberalism with which Dewey identified, a culture with which I continue to identify. So when I say ethnocentric things like "our culture" or "we liberals," their reaction is "who, we?" I, however, find it hard to see them as outsiders to this culture; they look to me like people playing a role – an important role – within it. I do not see them as having developed an alternative culture, nor even as having envisaged one. I see the culture of the liberal democracies as still providing a lot of opportunities for self-criticism and reform, and my critics on the left as fellow citizens taking advantage of these opportunities. They, however, sometimes seem to see themselves as inhabiting a prison-house, one from which they must escape before starting to tear it down.[29]

28 For examples of such hostility and suspicion, see Richard Bernstein, "One Step Forward, Two Steps Back," *Political Theory*, November 1987 (together with my "Thugs and Theorists: A Reply to Bernstein" in the same issue); Christopher Norris, "Philosophy as a Kind of Writing: Rorty on Post-Modern Liberal Culture," in his *The Contest of the Faculties* (London: Methuen, 1986); Rebecca Comay, "Interrupting the Conversation: Notes on Rorty," *Telos* 60 (Fall 1986); Nancy Fraser, "Solidarity or Singularity: Richard Rorty Between Romanticism and Technocracy," in her *Unruly Practices* (Minneapolis: Minnesota University Press, 1989); Frank Lentricchia, "Rorty's Cultural Conversation," *Raritan* 3 (1983), and his *Criticism and Social Change* (Chicago: University of Chicago Press, 1983), pp. 15–19; and Milton Fisk, "The Instability of Pragmatism," *New Literary History* 17 (1985).

29 This is not to say that there is any particular reason for optimism about America, or the rich North Atlantic democracies generally, in the year in which I write (1990). Several of these democracies, including the United States, are presently under the control of an increasingly greedy and selfish middle class – a class which continually elects cynical demagogues willing to deprive the weak of hope in order to promise tax cuts to their constituents. If this process goes on for another generation, the countries in which it happens will be barbarized. Then it may become silly to hope for reform, and sensible to hope for revolution. But at the present time the United States is still a functioning democratic society – one in which change occurs, and can be hoped for, as a result of persuasion rather than force. When Frank Lentricchia, one of my critics to the left, says that "our society is mainly unreasonable," I can only ask "unreasonable by comparison to what other society?" For Lentricchia's remarks about pragmatism, see the opening pages of his *Criticism and Social Change* (Chicago: University of Chicago Press, 1983); the "mainly unreasonable" passage comes at p. 2. For comment on the line of thought which Lentricchia represents, see my "Two Cheers for the Cultural Left," *South Atlantic Quarterly* 89 (1990), pp. 227–34.

The contemporary post-Marxist left seems to me to differ from the earlier Marxist one mainly in that the latter had a specific revolution in mind – one in which selective replacement of public by private ownership of capital would bring about far-reaching desirable consequences, and in particular increasingly participatory democracy. From the point of view of that earlier left, it was plausible to claim that Dewey-style reformist tinkering had become merely an obstacle to the required revolution. But contemporary radicals have no such specific revolution to support. So I find it hard to see their purported nonmembership in the culture of the liberal democracies, and their vehement anti-Americanism, as more than a wistful desire that there be *some* sort of revolution, *any* sort. This desire is, perhaps, the result of an understandable rage at the very slow extension of hope and freedom to marginal social groups, and at the frequent betrayals of past promises. But I do not think that the over-theoretical and over-philosophized form this rage is currently taking is of much use.

In particular, I think that a lot of the energy of leftist intellectuals in the contemporary American academy is being wasted, just insofar as they hope that work within such disciplines as philosophy and literary criticism can be geared in with political action in some direct way (as opposed to a long-term, atmospheric, indirect way). One symptom of this hope is the conviction that it is politically useful to "problematize" or "call into question" traditional concepts, distinctions, and institutions. My own view is that it is not much use pointing to the "internal contradictions" of a social practice, or "deconstructing" it, unless one can come up with an alternative practice – unless one can at least sketch a utopia in which the concept or distinction would be obsolete. After all, *every* social practice of any complexity, and every element of such a practice, contains internal tensions. Ever since Hegel we intellectuals have been busy winkling them out. But there is little point in exhibiting such tensions unless you have some suggestions about resolving them. The Deweyan liberal left and the Marxist radical left of my youth both tried to work out utopian visions – to suggest practices which would minimize the tensions in question. My doubts about the contemporary Foucauldian left concern its failure to offer such visions and such suggestions.

In these last few pages I have tried to sketch the connections between anti-representationalism, ethnocentrism, and the virtues of the sociopolitical culture of the liberal democracies. As I have repeatedly suggested, I view the position developed in these essays as continuous with Dewey's – the figure who, in the decade since I wrote *Philosophy and the Mirror of Nature*, has, in my imagination, gradually eclipsed Wittgenstein and Heidegger. My position differs from Dewey's mainly in offering a somewhat different account of the relation of natural science to the rest of culture, and in stating the problematic of representationalism vs. antirepresentationalism in terms of words and sentences rather than in terms of ideas and experiences. But I do not see these differences as very great.[30]

What seems to me most worth preserving in Dewey's work is his sense of the gradual change in human beings' self-image which has taken place in recorded history – the change from a sense of their dependence upon something antecedently present to a sense of the utopian possibilities of the future, the growth of their ability to mitigate their finitude by a talent for self-creation. Dewey saw religious tolerance, Galileo, Darwin, and (above all) the rise of democratic governments and literate electorates, as central episodes in this story. His own effort to overthrow representationalist doctrines, an effort which embroiled him in endless controversies about objectivity, truth, and relativism, was undertaken because he thought that these doctrines had become impediments to human beings' sense of self-reliance. I think that he was right about this, and that his effort is worth continuing. The papers in this volume represent an attempt to contribute to it. The papers in the following volume are largely devoted to arguing, against Heidegger and others, that such a sense of self-reliance is a good thing to have.

---

30 Others have thought them greater – notably Sidney Hook, a man upon whose knees I was bounced as a baby and a philosopher who forgot more about Dewey than I shall ever learn. In the months just before his death, Hook and I engaged in a spirited correspondence about what Hook called my "irrationalized" and "Nietzscheanized" version of Dewey. I took the line that the scientistic, method-worshiping side of Dewey, his constant exaltation of something called "the scientific method," was an unfortunate legacy of Dewey's youth, a youth spent worrying about the warfare between science and theology. There would have been a lot to say on both sides, and I am sorry that Hook and I were unable to debate the matter further. For some preliminary skirmishes, see my "Pragmatism Without Method" in Part I of this volume and also my Introduction to *John Dewey: The Later Works, vol. 8: 1933,* Jo Ann Boydston, ed. (Carbondale, Ill.: Southern Illinois University Press, 1986), pp. ix–xviii.

PART I

Solidarity or objectivity?

There are two principal ways in which reflective human beings try, by placing their lives in a larger context, to give sense to those lives. The first is by telling the story of their contribution to a community. This community may be the actual historical one in which they live, or another actual one, distant in time or place, or a quite imaginary one, consisting perhaps of a dozen heroes and heroines selected from history or fiction or both. The second way is to describe themselves as standing in immediate relation to a nonhuman reality. This relation is immediate in the sense that it does not derive from a relation between such a reality and their tribe, or their nation, or their imagined band of comrades. I shall say that stories of the former kind exemplify the desire for solidarity, and that stories of the latter kind exemplify the desire for objectivity. Insofar as a person is seeking solidarity, she does not ask about the relation between the practices of the chosen community and something outside that community. Insofar as she seeks objectivity, she distances herself from the actual persons around her not by thinking of herself as a member of some other real or imaginary group, but rather by attaching herself to something which can be described without reference to any particular human beings.

The tradition in Western culture which centers around the notion of the search for Truth, a tradition which runs from the Greek philosophers through the Enlightenment, is the clearest example of the attempt to find a sense in one's existence by turning away from solidarity to objectivity. The idea of Truth as something to be pursued for its own sake, not because it will be good for oneself, or for one's real or imaginary community, is the central theme of this tradition. It was perhaps the growing awareness by the Greeks of the sheer diversity of human communities which stimulated the emergence of this ideal. A fear of parochialism, of being confined within the horizons of the group into which one happens to be born, a need to see it with the eyes of a stranger, helps produce the skeptical and ironic tone characteristic of Euripides and Socrates. Herodotus' willingness to take the barbarians seriously enough to describe their customs in detail may have been a necessary prelude to Plato's claim that the way to transcend skepticism is to envisage a common goal of humanity — a goal set by human nature rather than by Greek culture. The combination of Socratic alienation and Platonic hope gives rise to the idea of the intellectual as someone who is in touch with the nature of things, not by way of the opinions of his community, but in a more immediate way.

Plato developed the idea of such an intellectual by means of distinctions between knowledge and opinion, and between appearance and reality. Such distinctions conspire to produce the idea that rational inquiry should make visible a realm to which nonintellectuals have little access, and of whose very existence they may be doubtful. In the Enlightenment, this notion became concrete in the adoption of the Newtonian physical scientist as a model of the intellectual. To most thinkers of the eighteenth century, it seemed clear that the access to Nature which physical science had provided should now be followed by the establishment of social, political, and economic institutions which were in accordance with Nature. Ever since, liberal social thought has centered around social reform as made possible by objective knowledge of what human beings are like – not knowledge of what Greeks or Frenchmen or Chinese are like, but of humanity as such. We are the heirs of this objectivist tradition, which centers around the assumption that we must step outside our community long enough to examine it in the light of something which transcends it, namely, that which it has in common with every other actual and possible human community. This tradition dreams of an ultimate community which will have transcended the distinction between the natural and the social, which will exhibit a solidarity which is not parochial because it is the expression of an ahistorical human nature. Much of the rhetoric of contemporary intellectual life takes for granted that the goal of scientific inquiry into man is to understand "underlying structures," or "culturally invariant factors," or "biologically determined patterns."

Those who wish to ground solidarity in objectivity – call them "realists" – have to construe truth as correspondence to reality. So they must construct a metaphysics which has room for a special relation between beliefs and objects which will differentiate true from false beliefs. They also must argue that there are procedures of justification of belief which are natural and not merely local. So they must construct an epistemology which has room for a kind of justification which is not merely social but natural, springing from human nature itself, and made possible by a link between that part of nature and the rest of nature. On their view, the various procedures which are thought of as providing rational justification by one or another culture may or may not really *be* rational. For to be truly rational, procedures of justification *must* lead to the truth, to correspondence to reality, to the intrinsic nature of things.

By contrast, those who wish to reduce objectivity to solidarity – call them "pragmatists" – do not require either a metaphysics or an epistemology. They view truth as, in William James' phrase, what is good for *us* to believe. So they do not need an account of a relation between beliefs and objects called 'correspondence,' nor an account of human cognitive abilities which ensures that our species is capable of entering into that relation. They see the gap between truth and justification not as something to be bridged by isolating a natural and transcultural sort of rationality which can be used to criticize certain cultures and praise others, but simply as the gap between the actual good and the possible better. From a pragmatist point of view, to say that what is rational for us now to believe may not be *true*, is simply to say that somebody may come up with a better idea. It is to say that there is always room for improved belief, since new evidence, or new hypotheses, or a whole new vocabulary, may come along.[1] For pragmatists, the desire for objectivity is not the desire to escape the limitations of one's community, but simply the desire for as much intersubjective agreement as possible, the desire to extend the reference of "us" as far as we can. Insofar as pragmatists make a distinction between knowledge and opinion, it is simply the distinction between topics on which such agreement is relatively easy to get and topics on which agreement is relatively hard to get.

"Relativism" is the traditional epithet applied to pragmatism by realists. Three different views are commonly referred to by this name. The first is the view that every belief is as good as every other. The second is the view that "true" is an equivocal term, having as many meanings as there are procedures of justification. The third is the view that there is nothing to be said about either truth or rationality apart from descriptions of the familiar procedures of justification which a given society – *ours* – uses in one or another area of inquiry. The pragmatist holds the ethnocentric third view. But he does not hold the self-refuting first view, nor the eccentric second view. He thinks that his views are better than the realists', but he does not think that his views correspond to the nature of things. He thinks that the very flexibility of the word "true" – the fact that it is merely an expression of commendation – insures its univocity. The term "true," on his account, means the same in all cultures, just as equally flexible terms like "here," "there," "good," "bad," "you," and "me" mean the same in all cultures. But the identity of meaning is, of course, compatible with diversity of reference, and with diversity of procedures for assigning the terms. So he feels free to use the term "true" as a general term of commendation in the same way as his realist opponent does – and in particular to use it to commend his own view.

However, it is not clear why "relativist" should be thought an appropriate term for the ethnocentric third view, the one which the pragmatist *does* hold. For the pragmatist is not holding a positive theory which says that something is relative to something else. He is, instead, making the purely *negative* point that we should drop the traditional distinction between knowledge and opinion, construed as the

---

1 This attitude toward truth, in which the consensus of a community rather than a relation to a nonhuman reality is taken as central, is associated not only with the American pragmatic tradition but with the work of Popper and Habermas. Habermas' criticisms of lingering positivist elements in Popper parallel those made by Deweyan holists of the early logical empiricists. It is important to see, however, that the pragmatist notion of truth common to James and Dewey is not dependent upon either Peirce's notion of an "ideal end of inquiry" nor on Habermas' notion of an "ideally free community." For criticism of these notions, which in my view are insufficiently ethnocentric, see my "Pragmatism, Davidson and Truth" (below) and "Habermas and Lyotard on Postmodernity" in the second volume of these papers.

distinction between truth as correspondence to reality and truth as a commendatory term for well-justified beliefs. The reason that the realist calls this negative claim "relativistic" is that he cannot believe that anybody would seriously deny that truth has an intrinsic nature. So when the pragmatist says that there is nothing to be said about truth save that each of us will commend as true those beliefs which he or she finds good to believe, the realist is inclined to interpret this as one more positive theory about the nature of truth: a theory according to which truth is simply the contemporary opinion of a chosen individual or group. Such a theory would, of course, be self-refuting. But the pragmatist does not have a theory of truth, much less a relativistic one. As a partisan of solidarity, his account of the value of cooperative human inquiry has only an ethical base, not an epistemological or metaphysical one. Not having *any* epistemology, *a fortiori* he does not have a relativistic one.

The question of whether truth or rationality has an intrinsic nature, of whether we ought to have a positive theory about either topic, is just the question of whether our self-description ought to be constructed around a relation to human nature or around a relation to a particular collection of human beings, whether we should desire objectivity or solidarity. It is hard to see how one could choose between these alternatives by looking more deeply into the nature of knowledge, or of man, or of nature. Indeed, the proposal that this issue might be so settled begs the question in favor of the realist, for it presupposes that knowledge, man, and nature *have* real essences which are relevant to the problem at hand. For the pragmatist, by contrast, "knowledge" is, like "truth," simply a compliment paid to the beliefs which we think so well justified that, for the moment, further justification is not needed. An inquiry into the nature of knowledge can, on his view, only be a sociohistorical account of how various people have tried to reach agreement on what to believe.

The view which I am calling "pragmatism" is almost, but not quite, the same as what Hilary Putnam, in his recent *Reason, Truth, and History,* calls "the internalist conception of philosophy."[2] Putnam defines such a conception as one which gives up the attempt at a God's eye view of things, the attempt at contact with the nonhuman which I have been calling "the desire for objectivity." Unfortunately, he accompanies his defense of the antirealist views I am recommending with a polemic against a lot of the other people who hold these views – e.g., Kuhn, Feyerabend, Foucault, and myself. We are criticized as "relativists." Putnam presents "internalism" as a happy *via media* between realism and relativism. He speaks of "the plethora of relativistic doctrines being marketed today"[3] and in particular of "the French philosophers" as holding "some fancy mixture of cultural

2 Hilary Putnam, *Reason, Truth, and History* (Cambridge: Cambridge University Press, 1981), pp. 49–50.
3 Ibid., p. 119.

relativism and 'structuralism.' "⁴ But when it comes to criticizing these doctrines all that Putnam finds to attack is the so-called "incommensurability thesis": vis., "terms used in another culture cannot be equated in meaning or reference with any terms or expressions *we* possess."⁵ He sensibly agrees with Donald Davidson in remarking that this thesis is self-refuting. Criticism of this thesis, however, is destructive of, at most, some incautious passages in some early writings by Feyerabend. Once this thesis is brushed aside, it is hard to see how Putnam himself differs from most of those he criticizes.

Putnam accepts the Davidsonian point that, as he puts it, "the whole justification of an interpretative scheme . . . is that it renders the behavior of others at least minimally reasonable by *our* lights."⁶ It would seem natural to go on from this to say that we cannot get outside the range of those lights, that we cannot stand on neutral ground illuminated only by the natural light of reason. But Putnam draws back from this conclusion. He does so because he construes the claim that we cannot do so as the claim that the range of our thought is restricted by what he calls "institutionalized norms," publicly available criteria for settling all arguments, including philosophical arguments. He rightly says that there are no such criteria, arguing that the suggestion that there are is as self-refuting as the "incommensurability thesis." He is, I think, entirely right in saying that the notion that philosophy is or should become such an application of explicit criteria contradicts the very idea of philosophy.⁷ One can gloss Putnam's point by saying that "philosophy" is precisely what a culture becomes capable of when it ceases to define itself in terms of explicit rules, and becomes sufficiently leisured and civilized to rely on inarticulate know-how, to substitute *phronesis* for codification, and conversation with foreigners for conquest of them.

But to say that we cannot refer every question to explicit criteria institutionalized by our society does not speak to the point which the people whom Putnam calls "relativists" are making. One reason these people are pragmatists is precisely that they share Putnam's distrust of the positivistic idea that rationality is a matter of applying criteria.

Such a distrust is common, for example, to Kuhn, Mary Hesse, Wittgenstein, Michael Polanyi, and Michael Oakeshott. Only someone who did think of rationality in this way would dream of suggesting that "true" means something different in different societies. For only such a person could imagine that there was anything to pick out to which one might make "true" relative. Only if one shares the logical positivists' idea that we all carry around things called "rules of

4 Ibid., p. x.
5 Ibid., p. 114.
6 Ibid., p. 119. See Davidson's "On the very idea of a conceptual scheme," in his *Inquiries into Truth and Interpretation* (Oxford: Oxford University Press, 1984) for a more complete and systematic presentation of this point.
7 Putnam, p. 113.

language" which regulate what we say when, will one suggest that there is no way to break out of one's culture.

In the most original and powerful section of his book, Putnam argues that the notion that "rationality . . . is defined by the local cultural norms" is merely the demonic counterpart of positivism. It is, as he says, "a scientistic theory inspired by anthropology as positivism was a scientistic theory inspired by the exact sciences." By "scientism" Putnam means the notion that rationality consists in the application of criteria.[8] Suppose we drop this notion, and accept Putnam's own Quinean picture of inquiry as the continual reweaving of a web of beliefs rather than as the application of criteria to cases. Then the notion of "local cultural norms" will lose its offensively parochial overtones. For now to say that we must work by our own lights, that we must be ethnocentric, is merely to say that beliefs suggested by another culture must be tested by trying to weave them together with beliefs we already have. It is a consequence of this holistic view of knowledge, a view *shared* by Putnam and those he criticizes as "relativists," that alternative cultures are not to be thought of on the model of alternative geometries. Alternative geometries are irreconcilable because they have axiomatic structures, and contradictory axioms. They are *designed* to be irreconcilable. Cultures are not so designed, and do not have axiomatic structures. To say that they have "institutionalized norms" is only to say, with Foucault, that knowledge is never separable from power — that one is likely to suffer if one does not hold certain beliefs at certain times and places. But such institutional backups for beliefs take the form of bureaucrats and policemen, not of "rules of language" and "criteria of rationality." To think otherwise is the Cartesian fallacy of seeing axioms where there are only shared habits, of viewing statements which summarize such practices as if they reported constraints enforcing such practices. Part of the force of Quine's and Davidson's attack on the distinction between the conceptual and the empirical is that the distinction between different cultures does not differ in kind from the distinction between different theories held by members of a single culture. The Tasmanian aborigines and the the British colonists had trouble communicating, but this trouble was different only in extent from the difficulties in communication experienced by Gladstone and Disraeli. The trouble in all such cases is just the difficulty of explaining why other people disagree with us, of reweaving our beliefs so as to fit the fact of disagreement together with the other beliefs we hold. The same Quinean arguments which dispose of the positivists' distinction between analytic and synthetic truth dispose of the anthropologists' distinction between the intercultural and the intracultural.

On this holistic account of cultural norms, however, we do not need the notion of a universal transcultural rationality which Putnam invokes against those whom

8 Ibid., p. 126.

he calls "relativists." Just before the end of his book, Putnam says that once we drop the notion of a God's-eye point of view we realize that:

we can only hope to produce a more rational *conception* of rationality or a better *conception* of morality if we operate from *within* our tradition (with its echoes of the Greek agora, of Newton, and so on, in the case of rationality, and with its echoes of scripture, of the philosophers, of the democratic revolutions, and so on . . . in the case of morality.) We are invited to engage in a truly human dialogue.[9]

With this I entirely agree, and so, I take it, would Kuhn, Hesse, and most of the other so-called "relativists" – perhaps even Foucault. But Putnam then goes on to pose a further question:

Does this dialogue have an ideal terminus? Is there a *true* conception of rationality, an ideal morality, even if all we ever have are our conceptions of these?

I do not see the point of this question. Putnam suggests that a negative answer – the view that "there is only the dialogue" – is just another form of self-refuting relativism. But, once again, I do not see how a claim that something does not exist can be construed as a claim that something is relative to something else. In the final sentence of his book, Putnam says that "The very fact that we speak of our different conceptions as different conceptions of *rationality* posits a *Grenzbegriff,* a limit-concept of ideal truth." But what is such a posit supposed to do, except to say that from God's point of view the human race is heading in the right direction? Surely Putnam's "internalism" should forbid him to say anything like that. To say that *we* think we're heading in the right direction is just to say, with Kuhn, that we can, by hindsight, tell the story of the past as a story of progress. To say that we still have a long way to go, that our present views should not be cast in bronze, is too platitudinous to require support by positing limit-concepts. So it is hard to see what difference is made by the difference between saying "there is only the dialogue" and saying "there is also that to which the dialogue converges."

I would suggest that Putnam here, at the end of the day, slides back into the scientism he rightly condemns in others. For the root of scientism, defined as the view that rationality is a matter of applying criteria, is the desire for objectivity, the hope that what Putnam calls "human flourishing" has a transhistorical nature. I think that Feyerabend is right in suggesting that until we discard the metaphor of inquiry, and human activity generally, as converging rather than proliferating, as becoming more unified rather than more diverse, we shall never be free of the motives which once led us to posit gods. Positing *Grenzbegriffe* seems merely a way of telling ourselves that a nonexistent God would, if he did exist, be pleased with us. If we could ever be moved solely by the desire for solidarity, setting aside the desire for objectivity altogether, then we should think of human progress as

9   Ibid., p. 216.

making it possible for human beings to do more interesting things and be more interesting people, not as heading towards a place which has somehow been prepared for humanity in advance. Our self-image would employ images of making rather than finding, the images used by the Romantics to praise poets rather than the images used by the Greeks to praise mathematicians. Feyerabend seems to me right in trying to develop such a self-image for us, but his project seems misdescribed, by himself as well as by his critics, as "relativism."[10]

Those who follow Feyerabend in this direction are often thought of as necessarily enemies of the Enlightenment, as joining in the chorus which claims that the traditional self-descriptions of the Western democracies are bankrupt, that they somehow have been shown to be "inadequate" or "self-deceptive." Part of the instinctive resistance to attempts by Marxists, Sartreans, Oakeshottians, Gadamerians and Foucauldians to reduce objectivity to solidarity is the fear that our traditional liberal habits and hopes will not survive the reduction. Such feelings are evident, for example, in Habermas' criticism of Gadamer's position as relativistic and potentially repressive, in the suspicion that Heidegger's attacks on realism are somehow linked to his Nazism, in the hunch that Marxist attempts to interpret values as class interests are usually just apologies for Leninist takeovers, and in the suggestion that Oakeshott's skepticism about rationalism in politics is merely an apology for the status quo.

I think that putting the issue in such moral and political terms, rather than in epistemological or metaphilosophical terms, makes clearer what is at stake. For now the question is not about how to define words like "truth" or "rationality" or "knowledge" or "philosophy," but about what self-image our society should have of itself. The ritual invocation of the "need to avoid relativism" is most comprehensible as an expression of the need to preserve certain habits of contemporary European life. These are the habits nurtured by the Enlightenment, and justified by it in terms of an appeal of Reason, conceived as a transcultural human ability to correspond to reality, a faculty whose possession and use is demonstrated by obedience to explicit criteria. So the real question about relativism is whether these same habits of intellectual, social, and political life can be justified by a conception of rationality as criterionless muddling through, and by a pragmatist conception of truth.

I think that the answer to this question is that the pragmatist cannot justify

---

10 See, e.g., Paul Feyerabend, *Science in a Free Society* (London: New Left Books, 1978), p. 9, where Feyerabend identifies his own view with "relativism (in the old and simple sense of Protagoras)." This identification is accompanied by the claim that " 'Objectively' there is not much to choose between anti-semitism and humanitarianism." I think Feyerabend would have served himself better by saying that the scare-quoted word "objectively" should simply be dropped from use, together with the traditional philosophical distinctions which buttress the subjective-objective distinction, than by saying that we may keep the word and use it to say the sort of thing Protagoras said. What Feyerabend is really against is the correspondence theory of truth, not the idea that some views cohere better than others.

these habits without circularity, but then neither can the realist. The pragmatists' justification of toleration, free inquiry, and the quest for undistorted communication can only take the form of a comparison between societies which exemplify these habits and those which do not, leading up to the suggestion that nobody who has experienced both would prefer the latter. It is exemplified by Winston Churchill's defense of democracy as the worst form of government imaginable, except for all the others which have been tried so far. Such justification is not by reference to a criterion, but by reference to various detailed practical advantages. It is circular only in that the terms of praise used to describe liberal societies will be drawn from the vocabulary of the liberal societies themselves. Such praise has to be in *some* vocabulary, after all, and the terms of praise current in primitive or theocratic or totalitarian societies will not produce the desired result. So the pragmatist admits that he has no ahistorical standpoint from which to endorse the habits of modern democracies he wishes to praise. These consequences are just what partisans of solidarity expect. But among partisans of objectivity they give rise, once again, to fears of the dilemma formed by ethnocentrism on the one hand and relativism on the other. Either we attach a special privilege to our own community, or we pretend an impossible tolerance for every other group.

I have been arguing that we pragmatists should grasp the ethnocentric horn of this dilemma. We should say that we must, in practice, privilege our own group, even though there can be no noncircular justification for doing so. We must insist that the fact that nothing is immune from criticism does not mean that we have a duty to justify everything. We Western liberal intellectuals should accept the fact that we have to start from where we are, and that this means that there are lots of views which we simply cannot take seriously. To use Neurath's familiar analogy, we can *understand* the revolutionary's suggestion that a sailable boat can't be made out of the planks which make up ours, and that we must simply abandon ship. But we cannot take his suggestion seriously. We cannot take it as a rule for action, so it is not a live option. For some people, to be sure, the option *is* live. These are the people who have always hoped to become a New Being, who have hoped to be converted rather than persuaded. But we – the liberal Rawlsian searchers for consensus, the heirs of Socrates, the people who wish to link their days dialectically each to each – cannot do so. Our community – the community of the liberal intellectuals of the secular modern West – wants to be able to give a *post factum* account of any change of view. We want to be able, so to speak, to justify ourselves to our earlier selves. This preference is not built into us by human nature. It is just the way *we* live now.[11]

11 This quest for consensus is opposed to the sort of quest for authenticity which wishes to free itself from the opinion of our community. See, for example, Vincent Descombes' account of Deleuze in *Modern French Philosophy* (Cambridge: Cambridge University Press, 1980), p. 153: "Even if philosophy is essentially demystificatory, philosophers often fail to produce authentic critiques; they defend order, authority, institutions, 'decency,' everything in which the ordinary person

This lonely provincialism, this admission that we are just the historical moment that we are, not the representatives of something ahistorical, is what makes traditional Kantian liberals like Rawls draw back from pragmatism.[12] "Relativism," by contrast, is merely a red herring. The realist is, once again, projecting his own habits of thought upon the pragmatist when he charges him with relativism. For the realist thinks that the whole point of philosophical thought is to detach oneself from any particular community and look down at it from a more universal standpoint. When he hears the pragmatist repudiating the desire for such a standpoint he cannot quite believe it. He thinks that everyone, deep down inside, *must* want such detachment. So he attributes to the pragmatist a perverse form of his own attempted detachment, and sees him as an ironic, sneering aesthete who refuses to take the choice between communities seriously, a mere "relativist." But the pragmatist, dominated by the desire for solidarity, can only be criticized for taking his own community *too* seriously. He can only be criticized for ethnocentrism, not for relativism. To be ethnocentric is to divide the human race into the people to whom one must justify one's beliefs and the others. The first group — one's *ethnos* — comprises those who share enough of one's beliefs to make fruitful conversation possible. In this sense, everybody is ethnocentric when engaged in actual debate, no matter how much realist rhetoric about objectivity he produces in his study.[13]

believes." On the pragmatist or ethnocentric view I am suggesting, all that critique can or should do is play off elements in "what the ordinary person believes" against other elements. To attempt to do more than this is to fantasize rather than to converse. Fantasy may, to be sure, be an incentive to more fruitful conversation, but when it no longer fulfills this function it does not deserve the name of "critique."

12 In *A Theory of Justice* Rawls seemed to be trying to retain the authority of Kantian "practical reason" by imagining a social contract devised by choosers "behind a veil of ignorance" — using the "rational self-interest" of such choosers as a touchstone for the ahistorical validity of certain social institutions. Much of the criticism to which that book was subjected, e.g., by Michael Sandel in his *Liberalism and the Limits of Justice* (Cambridge: Cambridge University Press, 1982), has centered on the claim that one cannot escape history in this way. In the meantime, however, Rawls has put forward a meta-ethical view which drops the claim to ahistorical validity. Concurrently, T. M. Scanlon has urged that the essence of a "contractualist" account of moral motivation is better understood as the desire to justify one's action to others than in terms of "rational self-interest." See Scanlon, "Contractualism and Utilitarianism," in A. Sen and B. Williams, eds., *Utilitarianism and Beyond* (Cambridge: Cambridge University Press, 1982). Scanlon's emendation of Rawls leads in the same direction as Rawls' later work, since Scanlon's use of the notion of "justification to others on grounds they could not reasonably reject" chimes with the "constructivist" view that what counts for social philosophy is what can be justified to a particular historical community, not to "humanity in general." On my view, the frequent remark that Rawls' rational choosers look remarkably like twentieth-century American liberals is perfectly just, but not a criticism of Rawls. It is merely a frank recognition of the ethnocentrism which is essential to serious, nonfantastical, thought. I defend this view in "The Priority of Democracy to Philosophy" and "Postmodernist Bourgeois Liberalism" in Part III of this volume.

13 In an important paper called "The Truth in Relativism," included in his *Moral Luck* (Cambridge: Cambridge University Press, 1981), Bernard Williams makes a similar point in terms of a distinction between "genuine confrontation" and "notional confrontation." The latter is the sort of confrontation which occurs, asymmetrically, between us and primitive tribespeople. The belief-

What is disturbing about the pragmatist's picture is not that it is relativistic but that it takes away two sorts of metaphysical comfort to which our intellectual tradition has become accustomed. One is the thought that membership in our biological species carries with it certain "rights," a notion which does not seem to make sense unless the biological similarities entail the possession of something nonbiological, something which links our species to a nonhuman reality and thus gives the species moral dignity. This picture of rights as biologically transmitted is so basic to the political discourse of the Western democracies that we are troubled by any suggestion that "human nature" is not a useful moral concept. The second comfort is provided by the thought that our community cannot wholly die. The picture of a common human nature oriented towards correspondence to reality as it is in itself comforts us with the thought that even if our civilization is destroyed, even if all memory of our political or intellectual or artistic community is erased, the race is fated to recapture the virtues and the insights and the achievements which were the glory of that community. The notion of human nature as an inner structure which leads all members of the species to converge to the same point, to recognize the same theories, virtues, and works of art as worthy of honor, assures us that even if the Persians had won, the arts and sciences of the Greeks would sooner or later have appeared elsewhere. It assures us that even if the Orwellian bureaucrats of terror rule for a thousand years the achievements of the Western democracies will someday be duplicated by our remote descendants. It assures us that "man will prevail," that something reasonably like *our* world-view, *our* virtues, *our* art, will bob up again whenever human beings are left alone to cultivate their inner natures. The comfort of the realist picture is the comfort of saying not simply that there is a place prepared for our race in our advance, but also that we now know quite a bit about what that place looks like. The inevitable ethnocentrism to which we are all

systems of such people do not present, as Williams puts it, "real options" for us, for we cannot imagine going over to their view without "self-deception or paranoia." These are the people whose beliefs on certain topics overlap so little with ours that their inability to agree with us raises no doubt in our minds about the correctness of our own beliefs. Williams' use of "real option" and "notional confrontation" seems to me very enlightening, but I think he turns these notions to purposes they will not serve. Williams wants to defend ethical relativism, defined as the claim that when ethical confrontations are merely notional "questions of appraisal do not genuinely arise." He thinks they *do* arise in connection with notional confrontations between, e.g., Einsteinian and Amazonian cosmologies. (See Williams, p. 142.) This distinction between ethics and physics seems to me an awkward result to which Williams is driven by his unfortunate attempt to find *something* true in relativism, an attempt which is a corollary of his attempt to be "realistic" about physics. On my (Davidsonian) view, there is no point in distinguishing between true sentences which are "made true by reality" and true sentences which are "made by us," because the whole idea of "truth-makers" needs to be dropped. So I would hold that there is *no* truth in relativism, but this much truth in ethnocentrism: we cannot justify our beliefs (in physics, ethics, or any other area) to everybody, but only to those whose beliefs overlap ours to some appropriate extent. (This is not a theoretical problem about "untranslatability," but simply a practical problem about the limitations of argument; it is not that we live in different worlds than the Nazis or the Amazonians, but that conversion from or to their point of view, though possible, will not be a matter of inference from previously shared premises.)

condemned is thus as much a part of the realist's comfortable view as of the pragmatist's uncomfortable one.

The pragmatist gives up the first sort of comfort because he thinks that to say that certain people have certain rights is merely to say that we should treat them in certain ways. It is not to give a *reason* for treating them in those ways. As to the second sort of comfort, he suspects that the hope that something resembling *us* will inherit the earth is impossible to eradicate, as impossible as eradicating the hope of surviving our individual deaths through some satisfying transfiguration. But he does not want to turn this hope into a theory of the nature of man. He wants solidarity to be our *only* comfort, and to be seen not to require metaphysical support.

My suggestion that the desire for objectivity is in part a disguised form of the fear of the death of our community echoes Nietzsche's charge that the philosophical tradition which stems from Plato is an attempt to avoid facing up to contingency, to escape from time and chance. Nietzsche thought that realism was to be condemned not only by arguments from its theoretical incoherence, the sort of argument we find in Putnam and Davidson, but also on practical, pragmatic, grounds. Nietzsche thought that the test of human character was the ability to live with the thought that there was no convergence. He wanted us to be able to think of truth as:

a mobile army of metaphors, metonyms, and anthromorphisms – in short a sum of human relations, which have been enhanced, transposed, and embellished poetically and rhetorically and which after long use seem firm, canonical, and obligatory to a people.[14]

Nietzsche hoped that eventually there might be human beings who could and did think of truth in this way, but who still liked themselves, who saw themselves as *good* people for whom solidarity was *enough*.[15]

I think that pragmatism's attack on the various structure-content distinctions which buttress the realist's notion of objectivity can best be seen as an attempt to let us think of truth in this Nietzschean way, as entirely a matter of solidarity. That is why I think we need to say, despite Putnam, that "there is only the dialogue," only *us*, and to throw out the last residues of the notion of "transcultural rationality." But this should not lead us to repudiate, as Nietzsche sometimes did, the elements in our movable host which embody the ideas of Socratic conversation, Christian fellowship, and Enlightenment science. Nietz-

---

14 Nietzsche, "On Truth and Lie in an Extra-Moral Sense," in *The Viking Portable Nietzsche*, Walter Kaufmann, ed. and trans., pp. 46–47.

15 See Sabina Lovibond, *Realism and Imagination in Ethics* (Minneapolis: University of Minnesota Press, 1983), p. 158: "An adherent of Wittgenstein's view of language should equate that goal with the establishment of a language-game in which we could participate ingenuously, while retaining our awareness of it as a specific historical formation. A community in which such a language-game was played would be one . . . whose members understood their own form of life and yet were not embarrassed by it."

sche ran together his diagnosis of philosophical realism as an expression of fear and resentment with his own resentful idiosyncratic idealizations of silence, solitude, and violence. Post-Nietzschean thinkers like Adorno and Heidegger and Foucault have run together Nietzsche's criticisms of the metaphysical tradition on the one hand with his criticisms of bourgeois civility, of Christian love, and of the nineteenth century's hope that science would make the world a better place to live, on the other. I do not think that there is any interesting connection between these two sets of criticisms. Pragmatism seems to me, as I have said, a philosophy of solidarity rather than of despair. From this point of view, Socrates' turn away from the gods, Christianity's turn from an Omnipotent Creator to the man who suffered on the Cross, and the Baconian turn from science as contemplation of eternal truth to science as instrument of social progress, can be seen as so many preparations for the act of social faith which is suggested by a Nietzschean view of truth.[16]

The best argument we partisans of solidarity have against the realistic partisans of objectivity is Nietzsche's argument that the traditional Western metaphysico-epistemological way of firming up our habits simply isn't working anymore. It isn't doing its job. It has become as transparent a device as the postulation of deities who turn out, by a happy coincidence, to have chosen *us* as their people. So the pragmatist suggestion that we substitute a "merely" ethical foundation for our sense of community – or, better, that we think of our sense of community as having no foundation except shared hope and the trust created by such sharing – is put forward on practical grounds. It is *not* put forward as a corollary of a metaphysical claim that the objects in the world contain no intrinsically action-guiding properties, nor of an epistemological claim that we lack a faculty of moral sense, nor of a semantical claim that truth is reducible to justification. It is a suggestion about how we might think of ourselves in order to avoid the kind of resentful belatedness – characteristic of the bad side of Nietzsche – which now characterizes much of high culture. This resentment arises from the realization, which I referred to at the beginning of this chapter, that the Enlightenment's search for objectivity has often gone sour.

The rhetoric of scientific objectivity, pressed too hard and taken too seriously, has led us to people like B. F. Skinner on the one hand and people like Althusser on the other – two equally pointless fantasies, both produced by the attempt to be "scientific" about our moral and political lives. Reaction against scientism led

16 See Hans Blumenberg, *The Legitimation of Modernity* (Cambridge, Mass.: MIT Press, 1982), for a story about the history of European thought which, unlike the stories told by Nietzsche and Heidegger, sees the Enlightenment as a definitive step forward. For Blumenberg, the attitude of "self-assertion," the kind of attitude which stems from a Baconian view of the nature and purpose of science, needs to be distinguished from "self-foundation," the Cartesian project of grounding such inquiry upon ahistorical criteria of rationality. Blumenberg remarks, pregnantly, that the "historicist" criticism of the optimism of the Enlightenment, criticism which began with the Romantics' turn back to the Middle Ages, undermines self-foundation but not self-assertion.

to attacks on natural science as a sort of false god. But there is nothing wrong with science, there is only something wrong with the attempt to divinize it, the attempt characteristic of realistic philosophy. This reaction has also led to attacks on liberal social thought of the type common to Mill and Dewey and Rawls as a mere ideological superstructure, one which obscures the realities of our situation and represses attempts to change that situation. But there is nothing wrong with liberal democracy, nor with the philosophers who have tried to enlarge its scope. There is only something wrong with the attempt to see their efforts as failures to achieve something which they were not trying to achieve – a demonstration of the "objective" superiority of our way of life over all other alternatives. There is, in short, nothing wrong with the hopes of the Enlightenment, the hopes which created the Western democracies. The value of the ideals of the Enlightenment is, for us pragmatists, just the value of some of the institutions and practices which they have created. In this essay I have sought to distinguish these institutions and practices from the philosophical justifications for them provided by partisans of objectivity, and to suggest an alternative justification.

Science as solidarity

In our culture, the notions of "science," "rationality," "objectivity," and "truth" are bound up with one another. Science is thought of as offering "hard," "objective" truth: truth as correspondence to reality, the only sort of truth worthy of the name. Humanists – for example, philosophers, theologians, historians, and literary critics – have to worry about whether they are being "scientific," whether they are entitled to think of their conclusions, no matter how carefully argued, as worthy of the term "true." We tend to identify seeking "objective truth" with "using reason," and so we think of the natural sciences as paradigms of rationality. We also think of rationality as a matter of following procedures laid down in advance, of being "methodical." So we tend to use "methodical," "rational," "scientific," and "objective" as synonyms.

Worries about "cognitive status" and "objectivity" are characteristic of a secularized culture in which the scientist replaces the priest. The scientist is now seen as the person who keeps humanity in touch with something beyond itself. As the universe was depersonalized, beauty (and, in time, even moral goodness) came to be thought of as "subjective." So truth is now thought of as the only point at which human beings are responsible to something nonhuman. A commitment to "rationality" and to "method" is thought to be a recognition of this responsibility. The scientist becomes a moral exemplar, one who selflessly expresses himself again and again to the hardness of fact.

One result of this way of thinking is that any academic discipline which wants a place at the trough, but is unable to offer the predictions and the technology provided by the natural sciences, must either pretend to imitate science or find some way of obtaining "cognitive status" without the necessity of discovering facts. Practitioners of these disciplines must either affiliate themselves with this quasi-priestly order by using terms like "behavioral sciences" or else find something other than "fact" to be concerned with. People in the humanities typically choose the latter strategy. They either describe themselves as concerned with "value" as opposed to facts, or as developing and inculcating habits of "critical reflection."

Neither sort of rhetoric is very satisfactory. No matter how much humanists talk about "objective values," the phrase always sounds vaguely confused. It gives with one hand what it takes back with the other. The distinction between the objective and the subjective was designed to parallel that between fact and value, so an objective value sounds as vaguely mythological as a winged horse. Talk about the humanists' special skill at critical reflection fares no better. Nobody really believes that philosophers or literary critics are better at critical thinking, or at taking big broad views of things, than theoretical physicists or microbiologists. So society tends to ignore both these kinds of rhetoric. It treats the humanities as on a par with the arts, and thinks of both as providing pleasure rather than truth. Both are, to be sure, thought of as providing "high" rather than "low" pleasures. But an elevated and spiritual sort of pleasure is still a long way from the grasp of a truth.

These distinctions between hard facts and soft values, truth and pleasure, and objectivity and subjectivity are awkward and clumsy instruments. They are not suited to dividing up culture; they create more difficulties than they resolve. It would be best to find another vocabulary, to start afresh. But in order to do so, we first have to find a new way of describing the natural sciences. It is not a question of debunking or downgrading the natural scientist, but simply of ceasing to see him as a priest. We need to stop thinking of science as the place where the human mind confronts the world, and of the scientist as exhibiting proper humility in the face of superhuman forces. We need a way of explaining why scientists are, and deserve to be, moral exemplars which does not depend on a distinction between objective fact and something softer, squishier, and more dubious.

To get such a way of thinking, we can start by distinguishing two senses of the term "rationality." In one sense, the one I have already discussed, to be rational is to be methodical: that is, to have criteria for success laid down in advance. We think of poets and painters as using some faculty other than "reason" in their work because, by their own confession, they are not sure of what they want to do before they have done it. They make up new standards of achievements as they go along. By contrast, we think of judges as knowing in advance what criteria a brief will have to satisfy in order to invoke a favorable decision, and of business people as setting well-defined goals and being judged by their success in achieving them. Law and business are good examples of rationality, but the scientist, knowing in advance what would count as disconfirming his hypothesis and prepared to abandon that hypothesis as a result of the unfavorable outcome of a single experiment, seems a truly heroic example. Further, we seem to have a clear criterion for the success of a scientific theory – namely, its ability to predict, and thereby to enable us to control some portion of the world. If to be rational means to be able to lay down criteria in advance, then it is plausible to take natural science as the paradigm of rationality.

The trouble is that in this sense of "rational" the humanities are never going to qualify as rational activities. If the humanities are concerned with ends rather than means, then there is no way to evaluate their success in terms of antecedently specified criteria. If we already knew what criteria we wanted to satisfy, we would not worry about whether we were pursuing the right ends. If we thought we knew the goals of culture and society in advance, we would have no use for the humanities – as totalitarian societies in fact do not. It is characteristic of democratic and pluralistic societies to continually redefine their goals. But if to be rational means to satisfy criteria, then this process of redefinition is bound to be nonrational. So if the humanities are to be viewed as rational activities, rationality will have to be thought of as something other than the satisfaction of criteria which are statable in advance.

Another meaning for "rational" is, in fact, available. In this sense, the word means something like "sane" or "reasonable" rather than "methodical." It names a set of moral virtues: tolerance, respect for the opinions of those around one, willingness to listen, reliance on persuasion rather than force. These are the virtues which members of a civilized society must possess if the society is to endure. In this sense of "rational," the word means something more like "civilized" than like "methodical." When so construed, the distinction between the rational and the irrational has nothing in particular to do with the difference between the arts and the sciences. On this construction, to be rational is simply to discuss any topic – religious, literary, or scientific – in a way which eschews dogmatism, defensiveness, and righteous indignation.

There is no problem about whether, in this latter, weaker, sense, the humanities are "rational disciplines." Usually humanists display the moral virtues in question. Sometimes they don't, but then sometimes scientists don't either. Yet these moral virtues are felt to be not enough. Both humanists and the public hanker after rationality in the first, stronger sense of the term: a sense which is associated with objective truth, correspondence to reality, and method, and criteria.

We should not try to satisfy this hankering, but rather try to eradicate it. No matter what one's opinion of the secularization of culture, it was a mistake to try to make the natural scientist into a new sort of priest, a link between the human and the nonhuman. So was the idea that some sorts of truths are "objective" whereas others are merely "subjective" or "relative" – the attempt to divide up the set of true sentences into "genuine knowledge" and "mere opinion," or into the "factual" and "judgmental." So was the idea that the scientist has a special method which, if only the humanists would apply it to ultimate values, would give us the same kind of self-confidence about moral ends as we now have about technological means. I think that we should content ourselves with the second, "weaker" conception of rationality, and avoid the first, "stronger" conception. We should avoid the idea that there is some special virtue in knowing in advance what criteria you are going to satisfy, in having standards by which to measure progress.

One can make these issues somewhat more concrete by taking up the current controversy among philosophers about the "rationality of science." For some twenty years, ever since the publication of Thomas Kuhn's book *The Structure of Scientific Revolutions,* philosophers have been debating whether science is rational. Attacks on Kuhn for being an "irrationalist" have been as frequent and as urgent

37

as were, in the thirties and forties, attacks on the logical positivists for saying that moral judgments were "meaningless." We are constantly being warned of the danger of "relativism," which will beset us if we give up our attachment to objectivity, and to the idea of rationality as obedience to criteria.

Whereas Kuhn's enemies routinely accuse him of reducing science to "mob psychology," and pride themselves on having (by a new theory of meaning, or reference, or verisimilitude) vindicated the "rationality of science," his pragmatist friends (such as myself) routinely congratulate him on having softened the distinction between science and nonscience. It is fairly easy for Kuhn to show that the enemies are attacking a straw man. But it is harder for him to save himself from his friends. For he has said that "there is no theory-independent way to reconstruct phrases like 'really there.' "[1] He has asked whether it really helps "to imagine that there is some one full, objective, true account of nature and that the proper measure of scientific achievement is the extent to which it brings us closer to that ultimate goal."[2] We pragmatists quote these passages incessantly in the course of our effort to enlist Kuhn in our campaign to drop the objective-subjective distinction altogether.

What I am calling "pragmatism" might also be called "left-wing Kuhnianism." It has been also rather endearingly called (by one of its critics, Clark Glymour) the "new fuzziness," because it is an attempt to blur just those distinctions between the objective and the subjective and between fact and value which the critical conception of rationality has developed. We fuzzies would like to substitute the idea of "unforced agreement" for that of "objectivity."

To say that unforced agreement is enough raises the specter of relativism. For those who say that a pragmatic view of rationality is unwholesomely relativistic ask: "Unforced agreement among whom? Us? The Nazis? Any arbitrary culture or group?" The answer, of course, is "us." This necessarily ethnocentric answer simply says that we must work by our own lights. Beliefs suggested by another culture must be tested by trying to weave them together with beliefs we already have. On the other hand, we can always enlarge the scope of "us" by regarding other people, or cultures, as members of the same community of inquiry as ourselves – by treating them as part of the group among whom unforced agreement is to be sought. What we cannot do is to rise above all human communities, actual and possible. We cannot find a skyhook which lifts us out of mere coherence – mere agreement – to something like "correspondence with reality as it is in itself."

One reason why dropping this latter notion strikes many people as "relativistic" is that it denies the necessity that inquiry should someday converge to a single point – that Truth is "out there," up in front of us, waiting for us to reach it. This

1 Thomas S. Kuhn, *The Structure of Scientific Revolutions,* 2d ed. (Chicago: University of Chicago Press, 1970), p. 206.
2 Ibid., p. 171.

latter image seems to us pragmatists an unfortunate attempt to carry a religious view of the world over into an increasingly secular culture. All that is worth preserving of the claim that rational inquiry will converge to a single point is the claim that we must be able to explain why past false views were held in the past, and thus explain how to go about reeducating our benighted ancestors. To say that we think we are heading in the right direction is just to say, with Kuhn, that we can, by hindsight, tell the story of the past as a story of progress.

But the fact that we can trace such a direction and tell such a story does not mean that we have gotten closer to a goal which is out there waiting for us. We cannot, I think, imagine a moment at which the human race could settle back and say, "Well, now that we've finally arrived at the Truth we can relax." We should relish the thought that the sciences as well as the arts will *always* provide a spectacle of fierce competition between alternative theories, movements, and schools. The end of human activity is not rest, but rather richer and better human activity.

Another way of characterizing this line of thought is to say that pragmatists would like to drop the idea that human beings are responsible to a nonhuman power. We hope for a culture in which questions about the "objectivity of value" or the "rationality of science" would seem equally unintelligible. Pragmatists would like to replace the desire for objectivity – the desire to be in touch with a reality which is more than some community with which we identify ourselves – with the desire for solidarity with that community. They think that the habits of relying on persuasion rather than force, of respect for the opinions of colleagues, of curiosity and eagerness for new data and ideas, are the *only* virtues which scientists have. They do not think that there is an intellectual virtue called "rationality" over and above these moral virtues.

On this view there is no reason to praise scientists for being more "objective" or "logical" or "methodical" or "devoted to truth" than other people. But there is plenty of reason to praise the institutions they have developed and within which they work, and to use these as models for the rest of culture. For these institutions give concreteness and detail to the idea of "unforced agreement." Reference to such institutions fleshes out the idea of "a free and open encounter" – the sort of encounter in which truth cannot fail to win. On this view, to say that truth will win in such an encounter is not to make a metaphysical claim about the connection between human reason and the nature of things. It is merely to say that the best way to find out what to believe is to listen to as many suggestions and arguments as you can.

My rejection of traditional notions of rationality can be summed up by saying that the only sense in which science is exemplary is that it is a model of human solidarity. We should think of the institutions and practices which make up various scientific communities as providing suggestions about the way in which the rest of culture might organize itself. When we say that our legislatures are "unrepresentative" or "dominated by special interests," or that the art world is dominated by "fashion," we are contrasting these areas of culture with areas which seem to be in better order. The natural sciences strike us as being such areas. But, on this view, we shall not explain this better order by thinking of the scientists as having a "method" which the rest of us would do well to imitate, nor as benefiting from the desirable hardness of their subjects compared with the undesirable softness of other subjects. If we say that sociology or literary criticism "is not a science," we shall mean merely that the amount of agreement among sociologists or literary critics on what counts as significant work, work which needs following up, is less than among, say, microbiologists.

Pragmatists will not attempt to explain this latter phenomenon by saying that societies or literary texts are squishier than molecules, or that the human sciences cannot be as "value-free" as the natural sciences, or that the sociologists and critics have not yet found their paradigms. Nor will they assume that "a science" is necessarily something which we want sociology to be. One consequence of their view is the suggestion that perhaps "the human sciences" *should* look quite different from the natural sciences. This suggestion is not based on epistemological or metaphysical considerations which show that inquiry into societies must be different from inquiry into things. Instead, it is based on the observation that natural scientists are interested primarily in predicting and controlling the behavior of things, and that prediction and control may not be what we want from our sociologists and our literary critics.

Despite the encouragement he has given it, however, Kuhn draws back from this pragmatist position. He does so when he asks for an explanation of "why science works." The request for such an explanation binds him together with his opponents and separates him from his left-wing friends. Anti-Kuhnians tend to unite in support of the claim that "merely psychological or sociological reasons" will not explain why natural science is so good at predicting. Kuhn joins them when he says that he shares "Hume's itch" – the desire for "an explanation of the viability of the whole language game that involves 'induction' and underpins the form of life we live."[3]

Pragmatists think that one will suffer from Hume's itch only if one has been scratching oneself with what has sometimes been called "Hume's fork" – the distinction between "relations of ideas" and "matters of fact." This distinction survives in contemporary philosophy as the distinction between "questions of language" and "questions of fact." We pragmatists think that philosophers of language such as Wittgenstein, Quine, Goodman, Davidson, and others have shown us how to get along without these distinctions. Once one has lived without them for a while, one learns to live without those between knowledge and opinion, or between subjective and objective, as well. The purposes served by the

---

3 Thomas S. Kuhn, "Rationality and Theory Choice," *Journal of Philosophy* 80 (1983):570.

latter distinctions come to be served by the unproblematic sociological distinction between areas in which unforced agreement is relatively infrequent and areas in which it is relatively frequent. So we do not itch for an explanation of the success of recent Western science any more than for the success of recent Western politics. That is why we fuzzies applaud Kuhn when he says that "one does not know what a person who denies the rationality of learning from experience is trying to say," but are aghast when he goes on to ask *why* "we have no rational alternatives to learning from experience."[4]

On the pragmatist view, the contrast between "relations of ideas" and "matters of fact" is a special case of the bad seventeenth-century contrasts between being "in us" and being "out there," between subject and object, between our beliefs and what those beliefs (moral, scientific, theological, etc.) are trying to get right. Pragmatists avoid this latter contrast by instead contrasting our beliefs with proposed alternative beliefs. They recommend that we worry only about the choice between two hypotheses, rather than about whether there is something which "makes" either true. To take this stance would rid us of questions about the objectivity of value, the rationality of science, and the causes of the viability of our language games. All such theoretical questions would be replaced with practical questions about whether we ought to keep our present values, theories, and practices or try to replace them with others. Given such a replacement, there would be nothing to be responsible to except ourselves.

This may sound like solipsistic fantasy, but the pragmatist regards it as an alternative account of the nature of intellectual and moral responsibility. He is suggesting that instead of invoking anything like the idea-fact, or language-fact, or mind-world, or subject-object distinctions to explicate our intuition that there is something out there to be responsible to, we just drop that intuition. We should drop it in favor of the thought that we might be better than we presently are – in the sense of being better scientific theorists, or citizens, or friends. The backup for this intuition would be the actual or imagined existence of other human beings who were already better (utopian fantasies, or actual experience, of superior individuals or societies). On this account, to be responsible is a matter of what Peirce called "contrite fallibilism" rather than of respect for something beyond. The desire for "objectivity" boils down to a desire to acquire beliefs which will eventually receive unforced agreement in the course of a free and open encounter with people holding other beliefs.

Pragmatists interpret the goal of inquiry (in any sphere of culture) as the attainment of an appropriate mixture of unforced agreement with tolerant disagreement (where what counts as appropriate is determined, within that sphere, by trial and error). Such a reinterpretation of our sense of responsibility would, if carried through, gradually make unintelligible the subject-object model of in-

4 Ibid., pp. 569–70.

41

quiry, the child-parent model of moral obligation, and the correspondence theory of truth. A world in which those models, and that theory, no longer had any intuitive appeal would be a pragmatist's paradise.

When Dewey urged that we try to create such a paradise, he was said to be irresponsible. For, it was said, he left us bereft of weapons to use against our enemies; he gave us nothing with which to "answer the Nazis." When we new fuzzies try to revive Dewey's repudiation of criteriology, we are said to be "relativistic." We must, people say, believe that every coherent view is as good as every other, since we have no "outside" touchstone for choice among such views. We are said to leave the general public defenseless against the witch doctor, the defender of creationism, or anyone else who is clever and patient enough to deduce a consistent and wide-ranging set of theorems from his "alternative first principles."

Nobody is convinced when we fuzzies say that we can be just as morally indignant as the next philosopher. We are suspected of being contritely fallibilist when righteous fury is called for. Even when we actually display appropriate emotions we get nowhere, for we are told that we have no *right* to these emotions. When we suggest that one of the few things we know (or need to know) about truth is that it is what wins in a free and open encounter, we are told that we have defined "true" as "satisfies the standards of our community." But we pragmatists do not hold this relativist view. We do not infer from "there is no way to step outside communities to a neutral standpoint" that "there is no rational way to justify liberal communities over totalitarian communities." For that inference involves just the notion of "rationality" as a set of ahistorical principles which pragmatists abjure. What we in fact infer is that there is no way to beat totalitarians in argument by appealing to shared common premises, and no point in pretending that a common human nature makes the totalitarians unconsciously hold such premises.

The claim that we fuzzies have no right to be furious at moral evil, no right to commend our views as true unless we simultaneously refute ourselves by claiming that there are objects out there which *make* those views true, begs all the theoretical questions. But it gets to the practical and moral heart of the matter. This is the question of whether notions like "unforced agreement" and "free and open encounter" – descriptions of social situations – can take the place in our moral lives of notions like "the world," "the will of God," "the moral law," "what our beliefs are trying to represent accurately," and "what makes our beliefs true." All the philosophical presuppositions which make Hume's fork seem inevitable are ways of suggesting that human communities must justify their existence by striving to attain a nonhuman goal. To suggest that we can forget about Hume's fork, forget about being responsible to what is "out there," is to suggest that human communities can only justify their existence by comparisons with other actual and possible human communities.

I can make this contrast a bit more concrete by asking whether free and open encounters, and the kind of community which permits and encourages such encounters, are for the sake of truth and goodness, or whether "the quest for truth and goodness" is simply the quest for that kind of community. Is the sort of community which is exemplified by groups of scientific inquirers and by democratic political institutions a means to an end, or is the formation of such communities the only goal we need? Dewey thought that it was the only goal we needed, and I think he was right. But whether he was or not, this question is the one to which the debates about Kuhn's "irrationalism" and the new fuzzies' "relativism" must eventually boil down.

Dewey was accused of blowing up the optimism and flexibility of a parochial and jejune way of life (the American) into a philosophical system. So he did, but his reply was that *any* philosophical system is going to be an attempt to express the ideals of *some* community's way of life. He was quite ready to admit that the virtue of his philosophy was, indeed, nothing more than the virtue of the way of life which it commended. On his view, philosophy does not justify affiliation with a community in the light of something ahistorical called "reason" or "transcultural principles." It simply expatiates on the special advantages of that community over other communities.

What would it be like to be less fuzzy and parochial than this? I suggest that it would be to become less genial, tolerant, open-minded, and fallibilist than we are now. In the nontrivial, pejorative, sense of "ethnocentric," the sense in which we congratulate ourselves on being less ethnocentric now than our ancestors were three hundred years ago, the way to avoid ethnocentrism is precisely to abandon the sort of thing we fuzzies are blamed for abandoning. It is to have only the most tenuous and cursory formulations of criteria for changing our beliefs, only the loosest and most flexible standards. Suppose that for the last three hundred years we had been using an explicit algorithm for determining how just a society was, and how good a physical theory was. Would we have developed either parliamentary democracy or relativity physics? Suppose that we had the sort of "weapons" against the fascists of which Dewey was said to deprive us – firm, unrevisable, moral principles which were not merely "ours" but "universal" and "objective." How could we avoid having these weapons turn in our hands and bash all the genial tolerance out of our own heads?

Imagine, to use another example, that a few years from now you open your copy of the *New York Times* and read that the philosophers, in convention assembled, have unanimously agreed that values are objective, science rational, truth a matter of correspondence to reality, and so on. Recent breakthroughs in semantics and meta-ethics, the report goes on, have caused the last remaining noncognitivists in ethics to recant. Similar breakthroughs in philosophy of science have led Kuhn formally to abjure his claim that there is no theory-independent way to reconstruct statements about what is "really there." All the new fuzzies have repudiated all their former views. By way of making amends for the intellectual confusion which the philosophical profession has recently caused, the philoso-phers have adopted a short, crisp set of standards of rationality and morality. Next year the convention is expected to adopt the report of the committee charged with formulating a standard of aesthetic taste.

Surely the public reaction to this would not be "Saved!" but rather "Who on earth do these philosophers think they *are?*" It is one of the best things about the intellectual life we Western liberals lead that this *would* be our reaction. No matter how much we moan about the disorder and confusion of the current philosophical scene, about the treason of the clerks, we do not really want things any other way. What prevents us from relaxing and enjoying the new fuzziness is perhaps no more than cultural lag, the fact that the rhetoric of the Enlightenment praised the emerging natural sciences in a vocabulary which was left over from a less liberal and tolerant era. This rhetoric enshrined all the old philosophical oppositions between mind and world, appearance and reality, subject and object, truth and pleasure. Dewey thought that it was the continued prevalence of such oppositions which prevented us from seeing that modern science was a new and promising invention, a way of life which had not existed before and which ought to be encouraged and imitated, something which required a new rhetoric rather than justification by an old one.

Suppose that Dewey was right about this, and that eventually we learn to find the fuzziness which results from breaking down such oppositions spiritually comforting rather than morally offensive. What would the rhetoric of the culture, and in particular of the humanities, sound like? Presumably it would be more Kuhnian, in the sense that it would mention particular concrete achievements – paradigms – more, and "method" less. There would be less talk about rigor and more about originality. The image of the great scientist would not be of somebody who got it right but of somebody who made it new. The new rhetoric would draw more on the vocabulary of Romantic poetry and socialist politics, and less on that of Greek metaphysics, religious morality, or Enlightenment scientism. A scientist would rely on a sense of solidarity with the rest of her profession, rather than a picture of herself as battling through the veils of illusion, guided by the light of reason.

If all this happened, the term "science," and thus the oppositions between the humanities, the arts, and the sciences, might gradually fade away. Once "science" was deprived of an honorific sense, we might not need it for taxonomy. We might feel no more need for a term which groups together paleontology, physics, anthro-pology, and psychology than we do for one which groups together engineering, law, social work, and medicine. The people now called "scientists" would no longer think of themselves as a member of a quasi-priestly order, nor would the public think of themselves as in the care of such an order.

In this situation, "the humanities" would no longer think of themselves as such, nor would they share a common rhetoric. Each of the disciplines which now

44

fall under that rubric would worry as little about its method or cognitive status as do mathematics, civil engineering, and sculpture. It would worry as little about its philosophical foundations. For terms which denoted disciplines would not be thought to divide "subject-matters," chunks of the world which had "interfaces" with each other. Rather, they would be thought to denote communities whose boundaries were as fluid as the interests of their members. In this heyday of the fuzzy, there would be as little reason to be self-conscious about the nature and status of one's discipline as, in the ideal democratic community, about the nature and status of one's race or sex. For one's ultimate loyalty would be to the larger community which permitted and encouraged this kind of freedom and insouciance. This community would serve no higher end than its own preservation and self-improvement, the preservation and enhancement of civilization. It would identify rationality with that effort, rather than with the desire for objectivity. So it would feel no need for a foundation more solid than reciprocal loyalty.

Is natural science a natural kind?

1. Introduction

One of the principal reasons for the development of a subarea within philosophy called "philosophy of science" was the belief that 'science' (or, at least, 'natural science') named a natural kind, an area of culture which could be demarcated by one or both of two features: a special method, or a special relation to reality. The further suggestion, implicit in Carnap's work and made explicit by Quine, that "philosophy of science is philosophy enough," was a natural extension of this belief. For just as Plato was content to leave the world of appearances to the philodoxers, so many of the logical empiricists were, implicitly or explicitly, content to leave the rest of culture to itself. On their view, once the job of demarcation had been accomplished, once the distinctive nature of science had been accurately described, there was no need to say much about the other activities of human beings. For, since man was a rational animal and science the acme of rationality, science was the *paradigmatic* human activity. What little there was to say about other areas of culture amounted to a wistful hope that some of them (e.g., philosophy) might themselves become more "scientific."[1]

Hempel and others, however, showed that demarcation was not as easy as it had first appeared. The increasing plausibility of Neurathian holism, once it had been revivified by Quine's "Two Dogmas" and by Wittgenstein's *Philosophical Investigations,* further undermined attempts to isolate "the scientific method," because it undermined attempts to isolate piecemeal connections between scientific theories and the world. Some philosophers followed Hempel in dropping both the question "how do we demarcate science from metaphysics?" and metaphysics itself. These philosophers turned to attempts to construct a logic of confirmation, without worrying greatly about whether the use of such logic distinguished science from nonscience. But other philosophers followed Quine in falling back into dogmatic metaphysics, decreeing that the vocabulary of the physical sciences "limns the true and ultimate structure of reality." It is significant that Quine

---

1 Sometimes this meant simply that the rest of culture should exemplify the moral virtues characteristic of the empirical scientist – openness, curiosity, flexibility, an experimental attitude toward
everything. Sometimes it meant, alas, that the rest of culture should adopt something called "the
scientific method." The former suggestion was bracing and useful, but the latter led to ludicrous
and unprofitable self-criticism sessions, particularly among social scientists. I discuss the relation
between these two aspects of science-worship in "Pragmatism Without Method" (below).

concluded that "the unit of empirical inquiry is the whole of science," when one might have expected, given the drift of his argument, "the whole of culture." Quine, and many other holists, persisted in the belief that the science-nonscience distinction somehow cuts culture at a philosophically significant joint.

The cash value of the claim that it does so is a refusal to rest content with a merely Baconian criterion for separating science from nonscience. On the (familiar, if Whiggish) interpretation of Bacon common to Macaulay and Dewey, Baconians will call a cultural achievement "science" only if they can trace some technological advance, some increase in our ability to predict and control, back to that development. (That is why Baconians boggle at the phrase 'Aristotelian science'.)

This pragmatic view that science is whatever gives us this particular sort of power will be welcome if one has developed doubts about traditional philosophical inquiries into scientific method and into the relation of science to reality. For it lets us avoid conundrums like "what method is common to paleontology and particle physics?" or "what relation to reality is shared by topology and entomology?" while still explaining why we use the word 'science' to cover all four disciplines. The same view lets us treat questions like "is sociology a science?" (or, "can the social sciences be as scientific as the natural sciences?") as empirical (indeed, sociological) questions about the uses to which the work of social scientists has been or might be put. This Baconian way of defining 'science' is, of course, no less fuzzy than the notions of prediction and control. Despite this fuzziness, it is probably the one most frequently employed by deans, bureaucrats, philanthropoids, and the lay public.

Since the forties, the period when Hempel and Quine began questioning the logical empiricists' basic assumptions, there have been two further stages in the discussion of the question of whether science is a natural kind. The first stage concentrated on the notion of method and centered around the work of Kuhn and Feyerabend. The second, in the midst of which we now find ourselves, concentrates on the question of science's relation to reality, and revolves around the ambiguous term 'scientific realism'.

The fracas over Kuhn's and Feyerabend's claim that some scientific theories were incommensurable with predecessor theories was created by philosophers who were intent upon salvaging a nonpragmatic criterion for distinguishing science from nonscience. Most of Kuhn's readers were prepared to admit that there were areas of culture – e.g., art and politics – in which vocabularies, discourses, Foucaultian "*epistēmēs*" replaced one another, and to grant that, in these areas, there was no overarching metavocabulary into which every such vocabulary might be translated. But the suggestion that this was true of the natural sciences as well was found offensive. Critics of Kuhn such as Scheffler and Newton-Smith thought of Kuhn as casting doubt on "the rationality of science." They sympathized with Lakatos' description of Kuhn as having reduced science to "mob psychology."

But although these critics might have hesitated to say explicitly that politics and art were matters of "mob psychology," their position implied just that. Defenders of the idea that there is a methodological difference between artistic, political, and scientific revolutions typically adopt a strong, criterial notion of rationality, one in which rationality is a matter of abiding by explicit principles. They thus find themselves, willy-nilly, questioning the "rationality" of the rest of culture. Kuhn's defenders, by contrast, typically draw the line between the rational and the nonrational sociologically (in terms of a distinction between persuasion and force) rather than methodologically (in terms of the distinction between possession and lack of explicit criteria).

The strong point of Kuhn's critics was that incommensurability seemed to entail indiscussability. The strong point of his defenders was that, given Hempel's critique of verificationism and Quine's of the fact-language distinction, nobody could answer Kuhn's challenge by explaining how commensuration was possible. So the Kuhnian wars dragged on, with both sides talking past each other.

These wars now seem to be drawing to a close. For both sides are coming to agree that untranslatability does not entail unlearnability, and that learnability is all that is required to make discussability possible. Most of Kuhn's critics have conceded that there is no ahistorical metavocabulary in terms of which to formulate algorithms for theory-choice (algorithms which might actually be useful to practicing scientists, rather than being *post factum* constructs). Most of his defenders have conceded that the old and the new theories are all "about the same world." So there is little left for them to quarrel about. The effect of this reconciliation is that the attempt to avoid a merely pragmatic and Baconian definition of the term 'science' has swung away from the question of science's rationality toward that of its relation to the world – from method to metaphysics. The resulting shift of attention has caused discussion to center around three different topics, all of which are discussed under the heading of 'scientific realism'.

First, there is the topic of "different worlds." This topic is still on the table because there are still recalcitrant Kuhnians who take the claim that Aristotle and Galileo "lived in different worlds" literally. These diehards play into the hands of diehard adherents of Putnam's erstwhile view that only a causal theory of reference can save us from relativism. The two sets of diehards engage in what Arthur Fine has called "a fine metaphysical *pas de deux*." Second, there is the topic of instrumentalism – of whether electrons *really exist,* in some sense of "really" in which tables uncontroversially do so exist. The distinction between "belief in *x*" and "heuristic use of the concept of *x*," discarded as verbal and "making no difference" by Deweyans such as Ernest Nagel and Sidney Morgenbesser, has recently been given a new lease on life by Michael Dummett, Bas van Fraassen, and others. Third, there is the claim, spelled out boldly and clearly by Bernard Williams, that science is distinguished from nonscience by the fact that although

48

nonscience – e.g., art and politics – may, *pace* Plato, attain the status of "knowledge" and may converge to lasting agreement, nevertheless it differs from science in not being "guided" to such agreement by the way the world is in itself.

Let me dub the first topic – the one about many worlds – "realism versus relativism." I shall call the second issue, the one resurrected by van Fraassen, "realism versus instrumentalism," and the third, the one discussed by Williams, "realism versus pragmatism." As Ernan McMullin has noted, the term 'antirealism' covers too much ground. One has to be careful to keep distinct various positions which people who call themselves "realists" dislike. One must also note, with Fine, that Dummett's term 'antirealism' tends to beg the question which the pragmatist wants to raise: the question of whether notions like "made true by the world," "fact of the matter," and "ontological status" should be used at all, or rather discarded. Fine, for example, wants to find a position which is beyond realism and antirealism.[2]

Since I share this aim with Fine,[3] most of my paper will be devoted to the quarrel between realism and pragmatism, viewed as a quarrel about whether the notions in terms of which Williams states his brand of realism are useful ones. I see this as a reflection of the deeper quarrel about whether we should persist in trying to view science as a natural kind, instead of just falling back on the Baconian-Deweyan view of the matter. I want to defend the latter view by urging that three notions which are used to defend opposing views are very dubious. These are: (1) the notion of "the world making sentences true," a notion essential to the diehard Kuhnian's claim about "many worlds"; (2) the notion of "the abductive method," a notion essential to the quarrel between realism and instrumentalism; (3) Williams' notion of the world "guiding" the work of scientists and causing their opinions to converge. I shall treat the first two notions relatively briefly and dogmatically, and then concentrate on the third.

2. *Realism versus relativism*

In order to see the role of the first of these notions, that of the world making beliefs true, consider the following inference:

(1) There is no way to *translate* the relevant portions of Aristotle's vocabulary into the relevant portions of Galileo's, although each could *learn* the other's vocabulary.

(2) So there is no way to argue against Aristotle's views on the basis of beliefs phrased in Galileo's vocabulary, nor conversely.

2 See A. Fine, "The Natural Ontological Attitude," in *Scientific Realism*, ed. J. Leplin (Berkeley: University of California Press, 1984), pp. 83–107.

3 See my "Beyond Realism and Anti-Realism," in *Wo Steht die Sprachanalytische Philosophie Heute?*, ed. Herta Nagl-Dockerl et al. (Vienna, 1986).

(3) So both Aristotle's and Galileo's views must be held to be true, and therefore the application of the term 'true' must be relativized to vocabularies.

(4) The world makes beliefs true.

(5) But the same world cannot make both Aristotle and Galileo true, and so *different* worlds must do so.

One can attack the inference to (5) in two ways: by questioning the step from (2) to (3) or by denying (4). I should want to do both, on the basis of the Davidsonian doctrine that 'true' does not name a relation between discourse and the world, and more generally that the term 'true' should not be analyzed or defined.[4] I would like to combine this doctrine with what I have elsewhere called "ethnocentrism,"[5] the view that our own present beliefs are the ones we use to decide how to apply the term 'true', even though 'true' cannot be *defined* in terms of those beliefs. Then we can admit (2) but deny (3) by saying that the internal coherence of either Aristotle or Galileo does not entitle their views to the term 'true', since only coherence with *our* views could do that. We thus get a position which *trivializes* the term 'true' (by detaching it from what Putnam calls a "God's-eye view") but does not *relativize* it (by defining it in terms of some specific "conceptual scheme").[6]

One consequence of this position is that we should not think of the relation between inquiry and the world on what Davidson calls the "scheme-content" model. Another is that, as Davidson says:

all the evidence there is is just what it takes to make our sentences or theories true. Nothing, however, no thing, makes sentences or theories true: not experience, not surface irritations, not the world, can make a sentence true.[7]

In other words, the equivalences between the two sides of Tarskian T-sentences do not parallel causal relationships which link sentences to nonsentences. This denial of (4) is, for purposes of arguing against relativism, more important than the denial of (3). For it gets at the essential point that there is no way to divide up the true sentences into those which express "matter of fact" and those which do not, and *a fortiori* no way to divide them up into those which express facts about one world and those which express facts about another.

Trivializing 'true' in the way Davidson does – holding that the reason this term is not synonymous with "justified by our lights" is not that it is synonymous with "justified by the world's lights" but because it is not synonymous with *anything* – seems to me the best way to *aufheben* both the diehard Kuhnian "differ-

---

4 See Donald Davidson, "A Coherence Theory of Truth and Knowledge," in *Truth and Interpretation: Perspectives on the Philosophy of Donald Davidson,* ed. E. LePore (Oxford: Blackwell, 1986), p. 308.

5 See my "Solidarity or Objectivity?" (above).

6 For more on this point, see my "Pragmatism, Davidson and Truth" in Part II of this volume.

7 D. Davidson, *Inquiries into Truth and Interpretation* (Oxford: Oxford University Press, 1984), p. 194.

ent world" thesis and the diehard Putnamesque claim that only a nonintentional theory of reference can save us from relativism.[8] On this Davidsonian view, every sentence anybody has ever used will refer to the world *we* now believe to exist (e.g., the world of electrons and such). This claim, however, is not – as it once was for Putnam – the controversial result of a new, Kripkean, theory of reference. It is as trivial as the claim that Aristotle and Galileo both have to face the tribunal of our present beliefs before we shall call anything either said "true."

This is all that I want to say about realism versus relativism. As far as I can see, relativism (either in the form of "many truths" or "many worlds") could only enter the mind of somebody who, like Plato and Dummett, was antecedently convinced that some of our true beliefs are related to the world in a way in which others are not. So I am inclined to think that Kuhn himself was unconsciously attached to such a distinction, despite the fact that *The Structure of Scientific Revolutions* has done so much to undermine the Platonic distinction between *epistēmē* and *doxa*. If one drops that distinction and follows through on Quinean holism, one will not try to mark off "the whole of science" from "the whole of culture," but instead will see all our beliefs and desires as parts of the same Quinean web. The web will not, *pace* Quine, divide into the bit which limns the true structure of reality and the part which does not. For carrying through on Quine brings one to Davidson: to the refusal to see either mind or languages as standing to the rest of the world as scheme to content.

3. Realism versus instrumentalism

Let me try to be equally brief on the subject of realism versus instrumentalism. I do not want to take up the question of whether we can get an interesting distinction between the observable and the unobservable. Rather, I want to focus on some questions about the relations between pragmatism and instrumentalism which have been raised by McMullin. McMullin, commenting on the work of Putnam and myself, writes as follows:

Recall that the original motivation for the doctrine of scientific realism was not a perverse philosopher's desire to inquire into the unknowable or to show that only the scientist's entities are "really real." It was a response to the challenges of fictionalism and instrumentalism, which over and over again in the history of science asserted that the entities of the scientist are fictional, that they do not exist in the everyday sense in which chairs and goldfish do. Now, how does Rorty respond to this? Has he an argument to offer? If he has, it would be an argument for scientific realism. It would also (as far as I can see) be a return to philosophy in the "old style" that he thinks we ought to have outgrown.[9]

---

8 The latter claim is preserved in, for example, Richard Boyd's "The Current Status of Scientific Realism," in *Scientific Realism*, ed. J. Leplin, pp. 41–82; see p. 62.
9 Ernan McMullin, "A Case for Scientific Realism," in *Scientific Realism*, ed. J. Leplin, pp. 8–40; pp. 24–25.

My answer to McMullin's question is that we pragmatists try to distinguish ourselves from instrumentalists not by arguing against their answers but against their questions. Unless one were worried about the really real, unless one had already bought in on Plato's claim that degrees of certainty, or of centrality to our belief system, were correlated with different relations to reality, one would not know what was meant by "the everyday sense of existence." It takes, after all, a good deal of acculturation to get the point of questions like "Do numbers, or justice, or God, exist in the sense that goldfish do?" Before we can get our students to approach these questions with appropriate respect, we have to inculcate a specifically philosophical use of the term 'existence', one in which it is pretty well interchangeable with 'ontological status'. I do not think that this use can be taught unless the teacher at least hints at an invidious hierarchy – the divided line, the primary-versus-secondary quality distinction, the distinction between canonical and noncanonical notations, or something of the sort. We pragmatists think that once we stop taking such hierarchies seriously we shall see instrumentalism as just a quaint form of late Platonism.

So I think the only argument we pragmatists need against the instrumentalist is the one McMullin himself gives when he says, "The realist claim is that the scientist is discovering the structures of the world; it is not required that these structures be imaginable in the categories of the macroworld."[10] But this is not a return to philosophy in the old style, nor is it really an "argument." It is just an attempt to shift the burden of argument to the instrumentalist by asking him: why do you attach more importance to the features which goldfish have and electrons lack than to the features which goldfish have and tables lack?

One popular instrumentalist answer to this question is: "because I am an empiricist." But this just shoves the issue back a step. Why, we Davidsonians want to know, does the instrumentalist think that some beliefs (e.g., about goldfish) are made true by experience? This question can be broken down into: (1) Why does he think they are made true by anything? (2) Why does he think that experience – in the sense of "the product of the human sense-organs" – has a crucial role to play with respect to certain beliefs and not to others? I shall defer the former, more general, question until my discussion of Williams. But let me venture a quick and partial answer to the second, viz.: the instrumentalist thinks this because he thinks that there is a special method, peculiarly bound up with modern science, called 'abduction', whose results stand in contrast to "the evidence of the senses."

Many of the philosophers of science whom I most admire, including McMullin, Sellars, and Fine, are guilty of encouraging the instrumentalist in this belief. McMullin, for example, begins the article which I have been citing by saying that

10 Ibid., p. 14.

When Galileo argued that the familiar patterns of light and shade on the face of the full moon could best be accounted for by supposing the moon to possess mountains and seas like those of earth, he was employing a joint mode of inference and explanation that was by no means new to natural science but which since then has come to be recognized as central to scientific explanation.[11]

Here McMullin lends aid and comfort to the idea that "scientific explanation" is explanation of a distinctive sort – that science can be distinguished from nonscience by its use of a special sort of inference. One suspects that he might agree with Clark Glymour that the principal motive of philosophy of science is to provide what Glymour calls: "a plausible and precise theory of scientific reasoning and argument: a theory that will abstract general patterns from the concreta of debates over genes and spectra and fields and delinquency."[12]

Fine too sometimes writes as if we all knew what a certain sort of inference called "abductive" is. Boyd represents Fine's argument against scientific realism accurately, I think, when he says that Fine accuses the realist of using an abductive argument for the nature of reality when explaining the success of science. Boyd concludes that Fine thus begs the question against the instrumentalist. For the instrumentalist has doubts about whether, in Boyd's words, "abduction is an epistemologically justifiable inferential principle, especially when, as in the present case, the explanation postulated involves the operation of unobservable mechanisms."[13]

It seems safe to say that almost everybody who tries to resolve, rather than dissolve, the issue of realism versus instrumentalism takes for granted that we can find something like an "inferential principle" which can be called "abductive" and which is more prevalent in modern science than in, say, Homeric theology or transcendental philosophy. My own, strictly amateurish, guess would be that any "inferential principle" which is "central to scientific explanation" is going to turn out to be central to practically every other area of culture. In particular, postulating things you can't see to explain things you can see seems no more specific to those activities normally called "science" than is *modus ponens*. The last fifty years' worth of attempts to give Glymour what he wants suggests that we shall find nothing which both meets Glymour's requirements and is specific to what has traditionally been called "science."

4. Realism versus pragmatism

With this dogmatic claim, I pass on from the issue of realism versus instrumentalism to my principal topic – realism versus pragmatism. Not only does the

11 Ibid., p. 8.
12 Clark Glymour, "Explanation and Realism," in *Scientific Realism*, ed. J. Leplin, pp. 173–92; p. 173.
13 Boyd, "The Current Status of Scientific Realism," p. 66.

absence of an inferential principle specific to science make it hard for the instrumentalist to answer questions about why the observable-unobservable distinction matters, it also makes it hard for the realist who wants to claim that realism "explains the success of science." The reason is, once again, that the absence of a way of isolating a specifically scientific method makes the nature of the *explanandum* unclear. For realists badly need the idea that "science" is a natural kind.

It is not enough for them, e.g., to explain the success of technology based on belief in elementary particles by the existence of elementary particles. For they recognize that this sort of explanation is trivial. All it does is to say that we describe our successful actions as we do because we hold the theories we hold. Such an explanation of current success is as vacuous as our ancestors' explanations of past successes. (Why are we able to predict eclipses so well? Because Ptolemy's *Almagest* is an accurate representation of the heavens. Why is Islam so spectacularly successful? Because of the will of Allah. Why is a third of the world Communist? Because history really *is* the history of class struggle.)

To get beyond such vacuity, the realist must explain something called "science" on the basis of something called "the relation of scientific inquiry to reality" — a relation not possessed by all other human activities. So, to get his project off the ground, he must have in hand some independent criterion of scientificity other than this relation to reality. He wants to claim that "because there really *are* elementary particles" is part of the best explanation of the success of IBM, whereas "because history really *is* the history of class struggle" is no part of the best explanation of the success of the KGB. So he must find some feature of elementary particle theory which makes it an example of "science" and does not also make Marxist theory "science." It is hard to see how this feature could be other than a methodological one.

This point is made by Boyd — who seems to me not to realize how hot the water is into which he is prepared to plunge his fellow realists. Boyd says that:

When philosophers of whatever persuasion assert that the methods of science are instrumentally (or theoretically, for that matter) reliable, their claim is of very little interest if nothing can be said about which methods are the methods in question. . . . Moreover, it will not do to countenance as "methods of science" just any regularities that may be discerned in the practice of scientists. If the reliability thesis is to be correctly formulated, one must identify those features of scientific practice that contribute to its instrumental reliability.[14]

---

14 Ibid., p. 70. Boyd continues, "This is a nontrivial intellectual problem, as one may see by examining the various different attempts — behaviorist, reductionist and functionalist — to explain what a scientific foundation for psychology would look like." I quite agree that it is nontrivial, but I do not understand Boyd's example. This is because I do not see the connection of the debates between, e.g., Skinner and Chomsky, or Fodor and his opponents, to issues about scientificity.

This point complements a point made by Michael Levin, who notes that any realist who wants to explain the success of a scientific theory by reference to its truth had better answer the question "what kind of *mechanism* is truth?"[15] If realists are going to do any explaining that is not of the "dormitive power" sort they are going to have to describe two bits of mechanism and show how they interlock. They are going to have to isolate some reliability-inducing methods which are not shared with all the rest of culture and then isolate some features of the world which gear in with these methods. They need, so to speak, two independently describable sets of cogwheels, exhibited in sufficiently fine detail so that we can see just how they mesh.

To illustrate how far contemporary discussion of the realism versus pragmatism issue is from any attempt to offer such detailed descriptions, consider Bernard Williams' defense of his claim that: "in scientific [as opposed to ethical] inquiry there should ideally be convergence on an answer, where the best explanation of the convergence involves the idea that the answer represents how things are."[16]

Williams offers a reply to the Davidsonian objection that notions like "how things are" or "the world" (and, *a fortiori*, truth defined as "correspondence to the world") cannot explain anything because each of these is "an empty notion of something completely unspecified and unspecifiable."[17] His reply consists in the suggestion that we can form the idea of "an absolute conception of reality" as one which "might be arrived at by any investigators, even if they were very different from us."[18] Our present scientific theories, he thinks, tell us that "*green*, for certain, and probably *grass* are concepts that would not be available to every competent observer of the world and would not figure in the absolute conception." He continues:

The substance of the absolute conception (as opposed to those vacuous or vanishing ideas of "the world" that were offered before) lies in the idea that it could non-vacuously explain how it itself, and the various perspectival views of the world, are possible.[19]

To explain how a set of beliefs *is possible* is a high transcendental task, one which contrasts with simply explaining why these beliefs rather than others are actual. The latter sort of explanation is provided by intellectual history, including the history of science. That sort of explanation is not good enough for Williams. For he thinks it stays on a "perspectival" level, the level of beliefs and desires succeeding one another and interacting with one another over the course of time. Such an explanation of convergence of belief cannot, in Williams' view, be "the best

15 Michael Levin, "What Kind of Explanation is Truth?" in *Scientific Realism*, ed. J. Leplin, pp. 124–39; p. 126.
16 Bernard Williams, *Ethics and the Limits of Philosophy* (Cambridge, Mass.: Harvard University Press, 1985), p. 136.
17 Ibid., p. 138.
18 Ibid., p. 139.
19 Ibid.

explanation." The best explanation, presumably, would be one which gives us the sort of thing Levin wants, a mechanistic account as opposed to one phrased in intentional terms. It would be one which, in Williams' terms, shows how 'convergence has been guided by the way things actually are,"[20] – one which spells out the details of this "guiding" in a way in which, e.g., a theological explanation of the success of Islam cannot spell out the operation of the will of Allah.

Williams does not try to spell out these details, but instead relies on the claim that such a spelling out is in principle possible and that, when actual, it would constitute the "best explanation" of the success of science. His approach to the science-ethics distinction, and his depreciation of explanations by reference to belief and desire, parallels a line taken by Gilbert Harman and Thomas Nagel. Consider the following passage from Harman, quoted approvingly by Nagel:

Observation plays a role in science that it does not seem to play in ethics. The difference is that you need to make assumptions about certain physical facts to explain the occurrence of the observations that support a scientific theory, but you do not seem to need to make assumptions about any moral facts to explain the occurrence of . . . so-called moral observations. . . . In the moral case, it would seem that you need only make assumptions about the psychology or moral sensibility of the person making the moral observation.[21]

It seems to me that we can explain the observations made – that is, the beliefs acquired without inference – by *both* the moralist and the scientist by reference simply to their respective "psychologies and sensibilities." For both, we can explain propensities to react with certain sentences to certain stimuli – stimuli described in neutral psychologese – by reference to their upbringing. The scientists have been programmed so as to respond to certain retinal patterns with "there goes a neutrino," just as the moralists have been programmed to respond to others with "that's morally despicable." One would naturally assume that the explanation of how a given human organism got programmed to make non-inferential reports in a given vocabulary would contain about nine parts intellectual history to one part psycho-physiology. This would seem as true for scientists as for moralists.

But for Williams, Harman, and Nagel, such an explanation would not be the "best." The best explanation would be one which somehow replaced the intellectual history parts and used none but "nonperspectival" terms. Presumably one advantage these philosophers see in such a replacement, one criterion for "best" which they tacitly employ, is that such an explanation will tell us, as intellectual history does not, how the world causes us to acquire the vocabularies we employ. Further, it would provide what Mary Hesse has suggested (rightly, on my view)

---

20 Ibid., p. 136.
21 Gilbert Harman, *The Nature of Morality* (New York: Oxford University Press, 1977), p. 6. See Thomas Nagel's discussion of this passage in *The View from Nowhere* (Oxford: Oxford University Press, 1986), p. 145.

we are not going to get: a sense of "convergence" which covers convergence of concepts as well as of beliefs.[22] The history of science tells us only that one day Newton had a bright idea, namely *gravity*, but stays silent on how gravity caused Newton to acquire the concept of itself – or, more generally, how the world "guides" us to converge on "absolute" rather than merely "perspectival" terms. The best explanation will presumably fill this gap. It will do for *gravity, atom, quantum*, etc., what (supposedly) psycho-physiology does for *green* – explain how the universe, under a nonperspectival description, gets itself described both under that description and under perspectival ones.

But is it not clear that science can do this even for *green*, much less for *gravity*. Remember that what is in question is the first acquisition of a concept by a human being, not its transmission from the old to the young. Do we have the slightest idea of what happened when somebody first used some word roughly coextensive with 'green'? Do we even know what we are looking for when we ask for an explanation of the addition of a concept to a repertoire of concepts, or of a metaphor to a language? Once we give up the Myth of the Given, the Lockean idea that (as Geach put it) when we invent "green" we are just translating from Mental into English, there seems nowhere to turn.

The closest I can come to imagining what such an explanation would be like would be to describe what happens in the brain of the genius who suddenly uses new vocables, or old ones in new ways, thereby making possible what Mary Hesse calls "a metaphoric redescription of the domain of the explanandum."[23] Suppose that the psycho-physiology of the future tells us that the brains of linguistic innovators are hit by neutrinos at the right time in the right way. When the brains of certain language-using organisms are hit by neutrinos under certain conditions, these organisms blurt out sentences containing either neologisms like 'green' or metaphors like 'grace' or 'gravity'. Some of these neologisms and metaphors may then get picked up and bandied about by the organism's linguistic peers. Of these, those which "fit" either the world as it is in itself or our peculiarly human needs (the "nonperspectival" and the "perspectival" ones, respectively) will survive. They will be literalized and take their place in the language.

Given such an explanation, all we need is a way of telling which of these new concepts are perspectival and which absolute. We do so by reminding ourselves which we need to describe the acquisition of concepts. Sure enough: *neutrino* is on the list and *green* is not, just as Williams suspected. But this little fantasy takes us around a rather tiny circle. We had to know in advance in what sort of discourse an explanation of concept-formation might be formulated. Given our present scientific theories, the best we could think of was the discourse of neuro-

22 See Mary Hesse, *Revolutions and Reconstruction in the Philosophy of Science* (Bloomington: Indiana University Press, 1980), pp. x–xi.
23 Ibid., p. 111. See also my "Unfamiliar Noises" in Part II below.

physiology. So we knew in advance that neither greenness nor Divine Grace nor the class struggle would turn up in the explanation of our acquisition of the terms 'green' or 'grace' or 'class struggle'. This is not an empirical discovery about how the world guided us. It is just physicalism employed as a regulative idea, a consequence of our present guesses about how we might some day explain something which we actually have no idea how to explain. But why should we say that a terminology which might conceivably enable us to do something we presently have no idea how to do is the best candidate for the "absolute" conception of reality?

This last question raises a more basic one: what is so special about prediction and control? Why should we think that explanations offered for this purpose are the "best" explanations? Why should we think that the tools which make possible the attainment of these particular human purposes are less "merely" human than those which make possible the attainment of beauty or justice? What is the relation between facilitating prediction and control and being "nonperspectival" or "mind-independent"?

For us pragmatists, the trail of the human serpent is, as William James said, over all. Williams finds it "obvious" that the pragmatist is wrong, that there is a difference between practical deliberation and the search for truth[24] – precisely the distinction which James tried to collapse when he said that "the true is the good in the way of belief." Yet even if we grant this dubious distinction for the sake of argument, we shall still want to know what special connection exists between the search for "nonperspectival" truth and the quest for beliefs which enable us to predict and control. As far as I can see, Williams also takes it as "obvious" that there is such a connection.

The argumentative impasse between Williams' realism and pragmatism is evident in the penultimate paragraph of Williams' paper "The Truth in Relativism":

Phlogiston theory is, I take it, not now a real option; but I doubt that just means that to try to live the life of a convinced phlogiston theorist in the contemporary Royal Society is as incoherent an enterprise as to try to live the life of a Teutonic knight in 1930's Nuremberg. One reason that phlogiston theory is not a real option is that it cannot be squared with a lot of what we know to be true.[25]

But from the pragmatist's point of view, that is just what the claim that phlogiston theory is not now a real option *does* mean. The two enterprises are on a par. Nowadays the beliefs essential to living the life of a Teutonic knight cannot be squared with what we know to be true. To see the analogy, all one needs is the same

24 Williams, *Ethics and the Limits of Philosophy*, p. 135.
25 Williams, "The Truth in Relativism," *Proceedings of the Aristotelian Society* 75 (1974–75), 215–28; reprinted in Williams' *Moral Luck* (Cambridge: Cambridge University Press, 1981), and also in, e.g., *Relativism: Cognitive and Moral*, ed. Michael Krausz and Jack Meiland (Notre Dame, Ind.: University of Notre Dame Press, 1982).

self-confidence in one's moral knowledge as the Royal Society has in its chemical knowledge. To prevent moral dogmatism, all one needs is the same open-mindedness which – one trusts – would permit the Royal Society to reinvent phlogiston if that happened to be what the next scientific revolution demanded.

In *Ethics and the Limits of Philosophy*, Williams changes his position slightly. He is now prepared to apply the honorific term 'knowledge' to the ethical beliefs most of us share, and from which would-be Teutonic knights dissent. But he still wants to keep a sharp line between science and ethics by claiming that, in the terms he used in his earlier article, "questions of appraisal do not genuinely arise" in the extreme cases of ethical disagreement, i.e., clashes of cultures. In his later terminology, this appears as the claim that "the disquotation principle"[26] applies to the former but not to the latter. That is, he wants to relativize ethics, but not science, to membership in a culture. The pragmatist wants to derelativize both by affirming that in both we aim at what Williams thinks of as "absolute" truth, while denying that this latter notion can be explicated in terms of the notion of "how things really are." The pragmatist does not want to explicate 'true' at all, and sees no point either in the absolute-relative distinction, or in the question of whether questions of appraisal *genuinely* arise. Unlike Williams, the pragmatist sees *no* truth in relativism.

As far as I can see, all the apparent ways out of this impasse just lead to other impasses. One could, for example, go back to the question of the perspectival character of *green* and run through the usual arguments concerning Berkeley's claim that *mass* is equally perspectival.[27] But this would just wind up with an impasse at the question of whether or not all words of a human language are equally tainted with relativity to human interests. One might try to break that impasse by asking about the correctness of Wittgenstein's picture of the relation of language to the world (one which allows no room for Thomas Nagel's "subjective-objective" distinction or for Williams' "genuine appraisal–nongenu-ine appraisal" distinction). Nagel rightly says that Wittgenstein's view of how thought is possible "clearly implies that any thought we can have of a mind-independent reality must remain within the boundaries set by our human form of life."[28] He concludes, following Kripke, that realism "cannot be reconciled with Wittgenstein's picture of language."

26 That is: "*A* cannot correctly say that *B* speaks truly in uttering *S* unless *A* could also say something tantamount to *S*." The question of the applicability of this principle is the question of whether all sentences are on a par in respect to truth or whether in some cases we can make use of locutions like "true for Teutonic knights, but not for me," "true for phlogiston theorists but not for me," etc. I would reject all locutions of the latter sort, and fill their place with "consistent with the beliefs and desires of . . . , but not with mine."

27 It is worth noting, in this connection, that Peirce regarded pragmatism as a generalization of Berkeley's way of breaking down the primary-secondary quality distinction. See his review of A. C. Fraser's edition of Berkeley's works, reprinted in his *Collected Papers*, ed. Arthur W. Burks (Cambridge, Mass.: Harvard University Press, 1966), vol. 7, 9–38.

28 Nagel, *The View from Nowhere*, p. 106.

Wittgenstein's picture of the relation of language to the world is much the same as Davidson's. They both want us to see the relation as merely causal, rather than also representational. Both philosophers would like us to stop thinking that there is something called "language" which is a "scheme" which can organize, or fit, or stand in some other noncausal relation to, a "content" called "the world."[29] So to discuss whether to give up Wittgenstein or to give up realism would be to bring us back around to the question of whether notions like "best explanation" can be employed *sans phrase*.

From a Wittgensteinian or Davidsonian or Deweyan angle, there is no such thing as "the best explanation" of anything; there is just the explanation which best suits the purpose of some given explainer. Explanation is, as Davidson says, always under a description, and alternative descriptions of the same causal process are useful for different purposes. There is no description which is somehow "closer" to the causal transactions being explained than the others. But the only sort of person who would be willing to take this relaxed pragmatic attitude toward alternative explanations would be somebody who was content to demarcate science in a merely Baconian way. So there seems little point in pursuing the issue between realism and pragmatism by switching from philosophy of science to philosophy of language. The impasses one comes to in either area look pretty much the same.

5. Scientificity as moral virtue

There is another way of breaking this impasse, but it is one which looks much more attractive to pragmatists than to realists. It is to ask the intellectual historian for an account of why the science versus nonscience distinction ever attained the importance it did. Why was there a demarcation problem in the first place? How did we ever start going around these circles?

One familiar attempt to answer this question starts with a claim which Williams discusses and dislikes: the thesis, common to Nietzsche and Dewey, that the attempt to distinguish practical deliberation from an impersonal and nonperspectival search for truth (the sort of search of which natural science is thought to be paradigmatic) is an attempt at "metaphysical comfort," the sort of comfort which was once provided by religion. Williams thinks that any such answer in terms of social psychology is "not in the least interesting."[30] He thereby adds one more disagreement to the list of those which divide realists and pragma-

---

29 See Davidson's claim that "there is no such thing as a language, not if a language is anything like what philosophers, at least, have supposed," in his "A Nice Derangement of Epitaphs," in *Truth and Interpretation*, ed. E. LePore, p. 446. Compare Henry Staten, *Wittgenstein and Derrida* (Lincoln: University of Nebraska Press, 1984), p. 20: "The deconstructive critique of language could even be phrased as a *denial that there is a language*."

30 Williams, *Ethics and the Limits of Philosophy*, p. 199.

tists. We pragmatists, following up on Hegel and Dewey, are very much interested in finding psycho-historical accounts of philosophical impasses. We particularly enjoy reading and writing dramatic narratives which describe how philosophers have backed themselves into the sort of corner which we take contemporary realists to be in.[31] For we hope that such narratives will serve therapeutic purposes, that they will make people so discouraged with certain issues that they will gradually drop the vocabulary in which those issues are formulated. For realists like Williams, on the other hand, this strategy is a sneaky way of avoiding the real issues – namely, issues about which explanations are best, best *sans phrase*.

Though I disagree with Williams about whether these issues are worth discussing, I agree with him that we should not be content to dismiss the idealization of science, the attempt to demarcate and then sacralize it, as *merely* an attempt at metaphysical comfort. For a second, complementary, psycho-historical answer to the question about the origin of the demarcation problem is available – an answer which can be made considerably more concrete and detailed, and one with which Williams might have some sympathy. This is that natural scientists have frequently been conspicuous exemplars of certain moral virtues. Scientists are deservedly famous for sticking to persuasion rather than force, for (relative) incorruptibility, for patience and reasonableness. The Royal Society and the circle of *libertins érudits* brought together, in the seventeenth century, a morally better class of people than those who were at home in the Oxford or the Sorbonne of the time. Even today, more honest, reliable, fair-minded people get elected to the Royal Society than to, for example, the House of Commons. In America, the National Academy of Sciences is notably less corruptible than the House of Representatives.

It is tempting – though, on a pragmatist view, illusory – to think that the prevalence of such virtues among scientists has something to do with the nature of their subject or of their procedures. In particular, the rhetoric of nineteenth-century scientism – of a period in which a new clerisy (typified by T. H. Huxley, as its predecessor was typified by his episcopal opponent) was coming to self-consciousness and developing a vocabulary of self-congratulation – confused these moral virtues with an intellectual virtue called "rationality." The attempt to find a non-Baconian way of demarcating science thus gets part of its justification from the assumption that we need a metaphysical (or, better yet, a physicalist) account of the relation between human faculties and the rest of the world, an account in which "reason" is the name of the crucial link between humanity and the nonhuman, our access to an "absolute conception of reality," the means by which the world "guides" us to a correct description of itself.

But if, as I do, one views pragmatism as a successor movement to romanticism,

31 Examples of such narratives are Hegel's *Phenomenology of Spirit*, Nietzsche's *Twilight of the Idols*, Dewey's *The Quest for Certainty*, Heidegger's *The Question Concerning Technology*, and Blumenberg's *The Legitimacy of the Modern Age*.

one will see this notion of reason as one of its principal targets.[32] So we pragmatists are inclined to say that there is no *deep* explanation of why the same people who are good at providing us with technology also serve as good examples of certain moral virtues. That is just a historical accident, as is the fact that, in contemporary Russia and Poland, poets, playwrights, and novelists serve as the best examples of certain other moral virtues. On a pragmatist view, rationality is not the exercise of a faculty called "reason" – a faculty which stands in some determinate relation to reality. Nor is the use of a method. It is *simply* a matter of being open and curious, and of relying on persuasion rather than force.

"Scientific rationality" is, on this view, a pleonasm, not a specification of a particular, and paradigmatic, kind of rationality, one whose nature might be clarified by a discipline called "philosophy of science." We will not call it science if force is used to change belief, nor unless we can discern some connection with our ability to predict and control. But neither of these two criteria for the use of the term 'science' suggests that the demarcation of science from the rest of culture poses distinctively philosophical problems.[33]

32 I try to develop this connection between romanticism and pragmatism in the first two chapters of my *Contingency, Irony, and Solidarity* (Cambridge: Cambridge University Press, 1989). An opposing view, objecting to my attempt to "becloud the sober insights of pragmatism with the Nietzschean pathos of a *Lebensphilosophie* turned linguistic" is offered by Habermas. (For this passage, see his *The Philosophical Discourse of Modernity*, trans. F. Lawrence (Cambridge, Mass.: MIT Press, 1987), p. 206. Habermas believes that "a partiality for reason has a different status than any other commitment" (*Habermas: Autonomy and Solidarity: Interviews*, ed. Peter Dews [London: Verso, 1986], p 51.) I would like to substitute "a partiality for freedom," and in particular for freedom of thought and communication, for "a partiality for reason." The difference may seem merely verbal, but I think that it is more than that. It is the difference between saying "let us defend liberal democracy by politically neutral accounts of the nature of reason and science" and saying "let our philosophical accounts of reason and science be corollaries of our commitments to the customs and institutions of liberal democracy." The latter, "ethnocentric" approach seems to me more promising, since my holist view of inquiry suggests that there are no politically neutral instruments to use for defending political positions.

33 I am grateful to Paul Humphreys for helpful comments on an earlier version of this paper.

Pragmatism without method

American pragmatism has, in the course of a hundred years, swung back and forth between an attempt to raise the rest of culture to the epistemological level of the natural sciences and an attempt to level down the natural sciences to an epistemological par with art, religion, and politics.

C. S. Peirce sometimes thought of himself as carrying the methods of laboratory science into philosophy and sometimes (in the manner later made fashionable by Russell) claimed to deduce all his philosophical views from the results of mathematical logic. But at other times he subordinated logic to ethics (and ultimately to aesthetics) and raged against the positivism of his "nominalist" opponents.

William James sometimes comes on as tough-minded, empirical, in love with hard facts and concrete details. But at other times, notably in "The Will to Believe," it becomes clear that his principal motive is to place his father's belief in Society as the Redeemed Form of Man on a par with the theories of the "hard" sciences. By taking a true belief as a successful rule for action, he hoped to rub out the purported difference between scientific beliefs as "evidenced" and religious beliefs as adopted without evidence.

Dewey, in turn, was grateful to natural science, especially as represented by Darwin, for rescuing him from his early Hegelianism. But Hegel had taught him to (in a phrase I borrow from Marjorie Grene) "treat history as our basic phenomenon and draw the world of science, as a limiting case, out of historical reality." Dewey's insistence that *everything* could be made "scientific" often seemed to his positivist critics merely to make science itself look unscientific by softening the contrast between it and the rest of culture.

One can describe these two sides of pragmatism in another way: as the side turned toward the general public and the side turned toward competitors within the philosophical profession. On the public scene, the principal social and cultural function of this movement has been to break through the crust of convention, to favor receptivity to the new rather than attachment to the old, and in particular to shake a nation free from the religious culture in which it began and which still permeates its public life. On this side, it has tried to break down the influence of old moral codes and replace them with an "experimental" attitude, not afraid of seemingly revolutionary social legislation, nor of new forms of artistic and personal freedom. So this side of pragmatism has been scientistic. It has spent its time holding up the experimental scientist as a model to the rest of culture. Among their fellow philosophy professors, however, the pragmatists have differentiated themselves from other brands of scientism – utilitarianism, sense-data empiricism, and logical positivism. Within the philosophical community, they are best known as holists. Like the idealists, they are dubious about the suggestion that we can isolate little building-blocks called "meanings" or "sensations" or "pleasures and pains" and construct something interesting out of them. Notoriously, they share the idealists' doubts about the idea that "truth is correspondence to reality."

These various ambiguities have sometimes made pragmatism seem a very muddled movement indeed – neither hard enough for the positivists nor soft enough for the aesthetes, neither atheistical enough for descendants of Tom Paine nor transcendental enough for descendants of Emerson, a philosophy for trimmers. As David Hollinger has remarked, the cliché that pragmatism was *the* philosophy of American culture suddenly ceased to be heard around 1950, just before Dewey's death. It was as if pragmatism had been crushed between Tillich and Carnap, the upper and the nether millstones. Carnap, with his return to hard-edged empiricism, became the hero of the philosophy professors, but most American intellectuals turned their back on pragmatism and on analytic philosophy simultaneously. They began to look to Tillich, or Sartre, or Marcuse, or some other philosopher who sounded deeper and more intellectually ambitious than the Deweyan anti-ideological liberalism on which they had been reared. Liberalism had come to strike them as, at best, boringly platitudinous, or, at worst, a defensive apologia for the status quo.

This anti-ideological liberalism is, in my view, the most valuable tradition of American intellectual life. We owe a great debt to Sidney Hook for his sustained and courageous efforts to keep it alive, in a period in which it has become fashionable to despise it. In what follows, however, I shall be arguing against some of the tactics Hook has employed in doing so. In particular, I think he was wrong to opt for the "let's bring the scientific method to bear throughout culture" side of pragmatism, as opposed to the "let's recognize a pre-existent continuity between science, art, politics, and religion" side. Hook's adoption of this tactic – his identification of liberalism with "being scientific" or "the use of intelligence" – has led him into two positions that, I think, pragmatists ought to avoid. First, it has made him more positivistic than he needs to be. Post-positivistic philosophy of science (what Clark Glymour has called "the new fuzziness" – the common denominator of, say, Kuhn, Hesse, and Harré) has left his account of "scientific method" in the lurch. Second, it has led him to be more antagonistic to "Continental" (and, specifically, Heideggerian) philosophy than he needs to be. I think that by developing the other side of pragmatism – the holistic and syncretic side – one can make a better case for liberalism (a better "Defense of the Enlightenment," to use the title of Hook's essay on Polanyi) than by attempting to isolate the essence of "science."

64

Consider the following passage from Hook's 1955 essay "Naturalism and First Principles":

My contention is that what makes any reason in science a valid reason for believing an hypothesis is not historical, but invariant for all historical periods in the growth of science. But whether a reason is a strong reason for believing an hypothesis varies with the presence or absence of other leads and evidence for them. [1]

Hook is here making a distinction between "the logic of the scientific method" (which pronounces on "validity") and the various historical factors that influence theory-choice at a given stage of inquiry (and make for "strength"). This is just the distinction that, in the decades since Hook wrote, has come to seem more and more dubious thanks to (ironically enough) the "pragmatist" holism of Quine and Kuhn. These writers made clear the difficulties involved in holding language and world, theory and evidence, apart, as the positivists wanted to do. Whereas Hook attempted to enlist positivistic philosophy of science as an ally, and to interpret Dewey's talk about "scientific method" in those terms, most philosophers of science have been moving in the direction of Dewey's suspicion of attempts to contrast an objective "given" (e.g., "the evidence," "the facts") with human "takings."

Hook continues, shortly after the passage I just cited, by saying:

If the foregoing is sound then I think it constitutes some reason for believing that there is only one reliable method of reaching the truth about the nature of things anywhere and at any time, that this reliable method comes to full fruition in the methods of science, and that a man's normal behavior in adapting means to ends belies his words whenever he denies it. Naturalism as a philosophy not only accepts this method but also the broad generalizations which are established by the use of it; viz., that the occurrence of all qualities or events depends upon the organization of a material system in space-time, and that their emergence, development and disappearance are determined by changes in such organizations.

Let me call the claim that there is such a "reliable method" "scientism" and the the "broad generalizations" Hook offers "naturalism." By redefining "naturalism" in this way I can say that the other – holistic – side of pragmatism would like to be naturalistic without being scientistic. It wants to hold on to the materialistic world-view that typically forms the background of contemporary liberal self-consciousness, while refraining from the claim that this view has been "established" by a *method,* much less the "one reliable method for reaching the truth about the nature of things." If one takes the core of pragmatism to be its attempt to replace the notion of true beliefs as representations of "the nature of things" and instead to think of them as successful rules for action, then it becomes easy to

---

1 Sidney Hook, *The Quest for Being* (New York: Greenwood, 1963), p. 185.

recommend an experimental, fallibilist attitude, but hard to isolate a "method" that will embody this attitude.

Hard though it may be, there is an obvious temptation to do so. For pragmatists would like some stick with which to beat the people who refuse to share their naturalism, once they have deprived themselves of the ability to say that their antagonists are not "corresponding to the nature of things." The claim that anti-naturalists are being irrational, or not using "intelligence," seems the obvious alternative. For this suggests that there is some neutral ground upon which naturalists and anti-naturalists can meet, and naturalists conquer. Unless there is some such ground, the specter of "relativism" looms. So ever since "correspondence to reality" began to look dubious, "rationality" has been used as a substitute. Dewey's way of doing this was to emphasize the difference between the priests and the artisans, the contemplators and the doers. Hook reiterates this contrast when he says, for example,

Science and theology represent two different attitudes toward the mysterious: one tries to solve mysteries, the other worships them. The first believes that mysteries may be made less mysterious even though they are not cleared up, and admits that there will always be mysteries. The second believes that some specific mysteries are final.[2]

This distinction hooks up with that between the cognitive and the noncognitive, as when Hook says that "all knowledge that men have is scientific knowledge"[3] and quotes with approval the remark, "If scientific statements are to be called truth, then religious statements should be called something else – comforts, perhaps."[4] When "truth" is used in this contrastive way, we are clearly a long way from "The Will to Believe" and from the laissez-faire attitude that sees religion and science as alternative ways of solving life's problems, to be distinguished by success or failure, rather than rationality or irrationality.

The anti-scientific, holistic pragmatist who adopts the latter attitude wants us to adopt naturalism without thinking of ourselves as more rational than our theistic friends. He begins by granting the Quinean point that anything can, by suitably reweaving the web of belief, be fitted either into an anti-naturalistic world-view in which Divine Providence is a central element *or* into a naturalistic world-view in which people are on their own. This is to admit that James was right against Clifford: "evidence" is not a very useful notion when trying to decide what one thinks of the world as a whole. Such an admission only looks relativistic if one thinks that the lack of general, neutral, antecedently formulable criteria for choosing between alternative, equally coherent, webs of belief means that there can be no "rational" decision. Relativism seems a threat only to those who insist on quick fixes and knock-down arguments. To the holist, it is enough to debate

2 Ibid., p. 181.
3 Ibid., p. 214.
4 Ibid., p. 181.

naturalism and anti-naturalism in the old, familiar, inconclusive ways. If one drops the idea that there is a common ground called "the evidence," one is still far from saying that one person's web is as good as another. One can still debate the issue on all the old familiar grounds, bringing up once again all the hackneyed details, all the varied advantages and disadvantages of the two views. One will talk about the problem of evil, the stultifying effect of a religious culture upon intellectual life, the dangers of theocracy, the potentiality for anarchy in a secularist culture, the *Brave New World* consequences of a utilitarian, secular morality. One will contrast the lives of one's secularist and of one's religious friends and acquaintances. One will do, in short, just what the "new fuzzies" in philosophy of science say scientists do when some relatively large-scale proposal to change the way nature (or part of nature) is pictured is up for discussion. One will muddle through, hoping that some reweaving will happen on both sides, and that some consensus may thus emerge.

There is, in our culture, a sociological difference between the naturalists and the anti-naturalists. The former, on the average, have been in school longer and been exposed to more books. They are faster on their feet in developing the implications of views they like and in finding objections to views they don't. So it is tempting to think of the latter as having been insufficiently rational in adopting their views. The atypical anti-naturalists – those who fit nicely (e.g., as professors of physics or philosophy) into the modern *entzauberte* world of means-end rationality but for whose lives religious belief is still central – are accused by scientific naturalists like Hook of intellectual schizophrenia, or applying one method on weekdays and another on Sundays. But this accusation presupposes that one ought to formulate general methodological principles, that one has a duty to have a general view about the nature of rational inquiry and a universal method for fixing belief. It is not clear that we have any such duty. We do have a duty to talk to each other, to converse about our views of the world, to use persuasion rather than force, to be tolerant of diversity, to be contritely fallibilist. But this is not the same thing as a duty to have methodological principles.

It may be helpful – it sometimes has been helpful – to formulate such principles. It is often, however – as in the cases of Descartes' *Discourse* and Mill's "inductive methods" – a waste of time. The result is often just a string of platitudes, hoked up to look like an algorithm. The advice to profit by the example of some notably successful piece of inquiry makes sense if it means: look at the rest of your beliefs and see if the new beliefs you have acquired as a result of that success don't suggest some useful readjustments. This was one of the things that was said by admirers of the New Science to the orthodox of the seventeenth and eighteenth centuries. But unfortunately these admirers also thought that one could isolate the *method* used by the New Science. They made some good tries at describing such a method, but I take the history of epistemology to show that none of their attempts panned out (and the triumph of the new fuzziness to show that philosophy of science did not succeed where epistemology failed). The advice to see if it might not pay to reweave your web of belief in the interests of a better ability to solve your problems is not the advice to formulate epistemic principles. The one piece of advice would only entail the other if experience had shown that having a conscious epistemological view were always an efficient instrument for readjusting old beliefs to new.

But experience does not show this, any more than it shows the opposite. Having general epistemic principles is no more intrinsically good or bad than having moral principles – the larger genus of which epistemic ones are a species. The whole point of Dewey's experimentalism in moral theory is that you need to keep running back and forth between principles and the results of applying principles. You need to reformulate the principles to fit the cases, and to develop a sense for when to forget about principles and just rely on know-how. The new fuzzies in philosophy of science tell us that the apparatus of "the logic of confirmation" got in the way of understanding how science had been operating. This is a plausible, though not a self-evident claim. As such, it resembles the claim Dewey made in *Human Nature and Conduct* (a book that has been ably defended by Hook against those who found *it* fuzzy). Dewey there urged that the traditional attempt to describe moral problems in terms of clashes between Kantian and utilitarian principles was getting in the way of an understanding of moral deliberation. His central argument was that the use of new means changes ends, that you only know what you want after you've seen the results of your attempts to get what you once thought you wanted. Analogously, post-positivistic philosophy of science has been saying that we only know what counts as being "scientific" in a given area, what counts as a good reason for theory-change, by immersing ourselves in the details of the problematic situation. On this view, the wielder of an ahistorical scientific method – a method for judging "validity" rather than mere "strength" – is on a par with the ideal wielder of practical syllogisms, the person who knows in advance what results he or she desires and has no need to adjust his or her ends. Such idealizations may sometimes be heuristically useful, but we have no special duty to construct them.

This comparison of Dewey on morals with the new fuzzies on science brings me to a final formulation of my doubts about Hook's use of the notion of "scientific method." Hook wants this notion to stretch as far as morals and politics, but he does not want it to stretch as far as, e.g., Tillichian theology. I doubt that this can be done. If we stretch it as far as morals and politics, then we shall have to cover cases in which we are not choosing between alternative hypotheses about what will get us what we want, but between redescriptions of what we want, of what the problem is, of what the materials to hand are. We shall have to cover just the sorts of cases that Kuhnians emphasize in the history of science: cases in which the description of the problem to be solved changes, thus changing the "observation language" used to describe the "evidence." This is not to say that we cannot, retrospectively, describe the problems and the data of all earlier epochs in a single, up-to-date, commensurating vocabulary. But the ability to commensurate by hindsight – the ability to say that what Aristotle was looking for was what Newton found, or that what the Roman plebeians were trying for was what the United Automobile Workers later got – should not mislead us into trying to describe our favorite ancestors as using "the hypothetico-deductive observational method" (as Hook sometimes characterizes "scientific inquiry").[5] Dewey's description of moral and scientific progress is much more like somebody's description of how he or she managed to get from the age of twelve to the age of thirty (that paradigm case of muddling through) than like a series of choices between alternative theories on the basis of observational results.

Let me turn now to what I have described as a second disadvantage of Hook's scientific strategy. This is his treatment of the various figures currently lumped under the heading of "Continental philosophy." Tillich is a convenient example with which to begin, since he is the one whom Hook has discussed in most detail. But I have another, autobiographical reason for discussing Tillich in this connection. I was assigned years ago to teach a course in the philosophy of religion. Looking around for some interesting books on which to lecture, I picked, among others, Dewey's A Common Faith and Tillich's Dynamics of Faith. After making up a syllabus with neat little divisions ("analytic philosophy of religion," "pragmatist philosophy of religion," "existentialist philosophy of religion," "fideist philosophy of religion," etc.), I encountered a problem. When I actually got down to writing the lectures I couldn't see any difference between the pragmatist and the existentialist, between Dewey and Tillich. My syllabus suddenly appeared repetitive, for my lectures were making Tillich sound just like Dewey, and conversely. I could not seem to differentiate between Tillich's "ultimate concern" and Dewey's "moral faith," nor between Dewey's attempt to distinguish the religious from the supernatural and Tillich's to distinguish genuine from idolatrous faith. Tillich's "God beyond the God of theism" looked just like the God Dewey defined as "the active relation between ideal and actual."[6] Eventually I gave up and told my students that they should treat Dewey and Tillich as saying the same things to different audiences. When they asked why they should call this funny thing that both men were talking about "God," I could do no better than cite Dewey:

One reason why personally I think it fitting to use the word "God" to denote that uniting of the ideal and actual which had been spoken of, lies in the fact that aggressive atheism seems to me to have something in common with traditional supernaturalism. . . . What I have in mind especially is the exclusive preoccupation of both militant atheism and supernaturalism with man in isolation. . . . A religious attitude, however, needs the sense of a connection of man, in the way of both dependence and support, with the enveloping

5 Sidney Hook, *Pragmatism and the Tragic Sense of Life* (New York: Basic Books, 1974), p. xi.
6 John Dewey, *A Common Faith* (New Haven: Yale University Press, 1934), p. 51.

world that the imagination feels is a universe. Use of the words "God" or "divine" to convey the union of actual with ideal may protect man from a sense of isolation and from consequent despair or defiance.[7]

Dewey's seemed, and still seems, a good way to keep the term "God" in one's vocabulary, thus enabling one to keep some of the strands in one's web of belief which, at the time one became a naturalist, one had feared one might have to tease out. Hook disagrees. He tells us that the only thing he protested in the manuscript of *A Common Faith* was Dewey's "use of the term 'God' for faith in the validity of moral ideals." Part of Dewey's response, he says, was

. . . there are so many people who would feel bewildered if not hurt were they denied the intellectual right to use the term "God." They are not in the churches, they believe what I believe, they would feel a loss if they could not speak of God. Why then shouldn't I use the term?[8]

This parallels the response that Tillich used to make when people asked why he didn't stop pretending to be a Christian theologian and instead bill himself as a Heideggerian philosopher. He would say, in effect, that it was precisely the job of a Christian theologian these days to find a way of making it possible for Christians to continue using the term "Christ" even after they had given up supernaturalism (as he hoped they eventually would).

Some beliefs best expressed by using the word "God" were part of both Dewey's and Tillich's web at the points in their lives when they were converted to naturalism. They both asked themselves whether they could hang on to some of these old beliefs, and both experimented with various reweavings that might enable them to do so. Tillich also thought that he could hang on to some beliefs best expressed using the word "Christ," though Dewey did not. Both were, as far as I can see, doing the same thing – keeping as much of the old as they could in the face of the new. Their various reweavings do not seem different in "method" or "logic" from the tinkering that scientists engage in when trying to keep anomalous occurrences within the framework of old ways of picturing things or, conversely, trying to make a new way compatible with old observations. Dewey was, in writing *A Common Faith,* doing just the sort of creative problem-solving that he thought was illustrated by both scientific and moral progress. So, to repeat my previous point, I do not think that one can stretch "scientific method" as far as Dewey and Hook want to stretch it and still accuse Tillich of not using it.

This may, however, seem to be letting Tillich off the hook too easily. For what about his weird use of the term "Being-itself" – a habit for which he was frequently castigated by Hook? And, in any case, what about Heidegger's use of it? Heidegger is harder to make resemble Dewey than is Tillich. He would have been

7 Ibid., pp. 52–53.
8 *Pragmatism and the Tragic Sense of Life,* p. 114.

much less inclined, as Hook tells us Tillich was in debate, to "reply with manifest sincerity 'I agree with everything you have said' " and to embrace Hook "as a fellow religionist crusading for the Holy Grail of Being."[9] Even if Tillich, the conversable social democrat, can be excused for finding naturalism inadequate to express his ultimate concern, can Heidegger, the hermetic quasi-Nazi, also be seen as just another pragmatic reweaver?

To begin with what Hook calls "the quest for Being," Heidegger and Tillich would have agreed with Hook and Carnap that we are not going to find a property that distinguishes the existent from the nonexistent, that we should not treat the existential quantifier as referring to an activity (what Austin called "quietly ticking over, in a metaphysical sort of way"). I agree with Hook and Carnap, against Heidegger and Tillich, that the word "Being" is more trouble than it is worth. I would be happy if Heidegger had never employed it and if Tillich had never picked it up from Heidegger. But I do not think that the word "Being" was essential to the thought of either. My attitude toward its use in their work is the same as Hook's toward Dewey's use of "God" in *A Common Faith* – it is a rhetorical blemish, a misleading way of getting one's point across.

At best, its use is a technique for relating to an audience. The reason Heidegger used it, I think, was to tie himself into a tradition he admired, a tradition that he thought ran through Aristotle's *Metaphysics* and Hegel's *Logic*. He thought both philosophers had shared his goal of getting beyond the "ontic" to the "ontological," and that the distinction between Being and beings was a good starting point for telling the sort of story about Dasein he wanted to tell. As Hook wrote in 1930 about his student year in Germany, German philosophers of that period took German idealism "not as one of a number of possible logical alternatives but rather as a national possession, the blazing jewel in Germany's cultural crown."[10] Heidegger – nothing if not a "national" philosopher – was using "Being" to place himself in the context of this national tradition, thus differentiating himself from three movements he despised – the neo-Thomism of his youth, *Lebensphilosophie,* and the Haeckel-like naturalism that had been part of the nineteenth century's reaction to Hegelianism.

A few years after *Being and Time,* however, Heidegger dropped the notion of "ontology" altogether – though not, alas, before his admiring professional rival Tillich had become thoroughly imprinted with the earlier jargon. Ontological talk about "the Nothing" makes a brief appearance in the early thirties, just long enough to be satirized by Carnap, and then it too disappears. From then on Heidegger gradually got down to what, as it turned out, he was really good at – telling stories about the history of Western philosophy designed to show how a decisive turn of thought, already taken by Plato, had created the Western philo-

9 Ibid., p. 193.
10 Sidney Hook, "A Personal Impression of Contemporary German Philosophy," *The Journal of Philosophy,* 27 (1930), 145.

sophical tradition. Instead of doing "phenomenological ontology," Heidegger now tries to "overcome" the "onto-theological tradition," precisely the tradition that linked Aristotle to Hegel. As I have argued elsewhere, in this later period Heidegger's account of what is wrong with the presuppositions of the great European philosophers is not clearly distinguishable from Dewey's.

But still, why does Heidegger call what is wrong with the tradition "forgetfulness of Being"? Maybe ontology goes in the later Heidegger, but Being is still around – or rather, not around, but absent, concealing itself, *absconditus*. One can sympathize with Hook's 1930 remarks, referring to *Being and Time* and "On the Essence of Reasons," that "there is a mystical doctrine of creative emanation at the bottom of Heidegger's thought," and that "Heidegger is really asking theological questions."[11] These remarks are still in point for Heidegger's later work. But I would want to modify what Hook says by urging that, in his later work, it becomes clear that what Heidegger really wanted to do was to find a way of getting himself out from under theology while still keeping in touch with what theology (and the central books of the *Metaphysics,* and the *System of Logic*) had been about. Like Plato and Plotinus before him, he wanted to get away from the gods and the religion of the times to something "behind" them. So, although in one sense he is indeed still asking theological questions, in another sense he is trying to find some better questions that will replace theological (or, as he was later to say, "metaphysical") questions.

This is not a perverse or self-deceptive thing to do. I have suggested that it was just what Dewey was doing in *A Common Faith* (and elsewhere, as in parts of *Art as Experience*). Dewey was right, in responding to Hook's report of *Being and Time,* when he said, "It sounds like a description of 'the situation' in transcendental German."[12] That book's discussion of the priority of the "ready to hand" over the "present at hand" covers a lot of the same ground as Dewey's insistence on the "interactional" relationships between experience and nature. But, more important, this ground was covered in aid of a project Heidegger shared with Dewey – getting us out from under the metaphysical urge to find some ultimate, total, final context within which all our activities could be placed. Whatever motivated Heidegger's short-lived flirtation with the idea of "phenomenological ontology," it seems clear in retrospect that this discipline was intended as an anti-metaphysical enterprise. It was not just a joke when he later borrowed Carnap's title for his essay "Ueberwindung der Metaphysik." As it also did to Carnap, "metaphysics" means to Heidegger the objectionable idea of a superscience – something that would establish that what Dewey called "moral ideas" were pre-existent realities. If he can be imagined agreeing with anybody, Heidegger would agree with Dewey that

11 Ibid., p. 156.
12 *Pragmatism and the Tragic Sense of Life,* p. 103.

men have gone on to build up vast intellectual schemes, philosophies and theologies, to prove that ideas are real not as ideals but as antecedently existing actualities. They have failed to see that in converting moral realities into matters of intellectual assent they have evinced lack of moral faith. [13]

What Heidegger gives us that Dewey doesn't is a detailed treatment of the history of European philosophy showing how such "inauthentic" conversion of moral faith into superscience expressed itself at various periods. The role of the term "Being" in this treatment comes to be that of a name for what moved people to be metaphysical, but could not itself be an object of quasi-scientific inquiry. This is just the role of Dewey's "moral ideals," or, more exactly, the role of what Dewey calls "the sense of a connection of man, in the way of both dependence and support, with the enveloping world that the imagination feels is a universe." [14]

Heidegger would, of course, object to every word in this quotation from Dewey. For he thinks that just about *all* the words in currency nowadays are useless for what he calls "Thought" – the activity that replaces "phenomenological ontology" in his later work. He thinks that notions like "moral ideals," "imagination," "man," "support," and the like have been so cheapened by their use in ordinary *Gerede* that they are useless to the Thinker. That is why a lot of late Heidegger is in Greek, Greek which we are supposed to translate to Heidegger's own idiosyncratic specifications. Heidegger ended up not (alas!) as a reweaver of a web of beliefs, but as a thinker who tried to get away from beliefs, rules for action, altogether. He wanted a language that was not hammered out as an instrument for communicating, for helping us get what we want, but one that "is what it says" (a compliment he once paid to Greek). He wanted to discover a language that was as close to silence as possible, rather than to reweave the connections between the various things we want to say. *Being and Time* was (like *A Common Faith* and the first volume of *Systematic Theology*) a proposal to teach us a new way of talking – one that would let us ask about God or Being without thinking of ourselves as superscientists. The later work only hopes to show us how to be suitably still.

So, to answer the question I posed earlier, I do *not* think one can view Heidegger – the later, more important, Heidegger – as one more pragmatic reweaver. Here, if anywhere, one finds a figure who *cannot* be said to have used "the scientific method" (in the broad, fuzzy, un-Hookian sense of "muddling through"). He leans over so far backward to avoid being one more superscientist, one more metaphysician, one more theologian, that he ceases to reweave. He merely points and hints. But that means that we cannot criticize him for employing another method than the method of science. Heidegger doesn't employ *any* method. He is not, in *any* sense, competing with science. He would not dream of offering "knowl-

13 *A Common Faith*, p. 21.
14 Ibid., p. 53 (quoted above).

edge that is not scientific knowledge." He has nothing whatever to say against naturalism, for example, since he thinks that Thinking has nothing to say about the way things work, or about their causes, or even their "grounds" (if "ground" means what emanationists like Plotinus meant). Just as, in his early days, he redefined every important word he used so that it had an "ontological" rather than an "ontic" sense (thus making it impossible to converse with him about whether it was the right word for his purpose), so in his later work he takes care to assert only sentences that cannot be construed as "rules for action," as beliefs (thus making it impossible to converse with him at all).

The thing to criticize in Heidegger is not an attempt at a superscience that would use a different method (e.g., a "phenomenological" method) from that of the natural scientists. That attempt was, at most, an aberration of his early middle age. Rather, what needs criticism is his inhumanism – his attempt to find Dewey's "connection of man, in the way of both dependence and support, with the enveloping world that the imagination feels is a universe" by cutting himself off from connection with other men. Whereas Dewey saw European culture as moving in the direction of what he called "the aesthetic" by virtue of the leisure and freedom that technology had made possible, Heidegger saw nothing in technology save the punishment for our original Platonic sin. Dewey optimistically thought of Plato not as a disaster but as one of the important early steps in getting ourselves out from under religion, even though one of the prices paid was the invention of metaphysics. Pragmatically, he thought that you had to weigh the bad against the good consequences, and that on balance Plato came out ahead. To Heidegger, technological civilization was something so un-Thoughtful, so un-Greek, that only refusal to speak any of the words associated with it could help. But this could help only a very few. For Heidegger there is no community that plays the role that the Christians played for Tillich or the Americans for Dewey. So there is no attempt to help such a community find its way by helping it to reweave its beliefs, and thus its language.

To sum up what I have been saying: I take "Being" to be, in Heidegger and again, derivatively, in Tillich, merely "transcendental German" for a "connection of man with the enveloping world," which naturalism, construed as the generalization that "the occurrence of all qualities or events depends upon the organization of a material system in space-time," does *not* help us envisage. This is what certain forms of art (when not construed romantically and transcendentally as a peep into another world) and certain forms of religion (when not construed as an encounter with a pre-existent power that will rescue us) *do* help us envisage. But vision is not knowledge. If "knowledge" is to mean the sort of proposition that can be tested against explicitly formulated public criteria, then Hook is quite right in saying that "all knowledge which men have is scientific knowledge." But this use of "knowledge" merely forces us to find some new terminology for forms of discourse that are not subject to such criteria but which are nevertheless necessary for our lives. In *A Common Faith,* in some of his more Hegelian remarks about the social functions of philosophy, and in some of his equally Hegelian remarks about the function of art, Dewey tried to work out such a terminology. On my interpretation, this is also what Tillich and (sometimes) Heidegger were also doing.

Let me now try to bring together my doubts about scientific method with my attempt to make "the quest for Being" look respectable. As I see the matter, both pragmatism and "Continental" philosophy have a common interest in debunking a certain traditional conception of philosophy. This is the conception of a discipline that unites the argumentative rigor made possible by an appeal to commonly shared criteria with the ability to decide issues of ultimate significance for our lives. The traditional image of philosophy is of a discipline that will (any day now) produce noncontroversial results concerning matters of ultimate concern. The scientistic side of pragmatism – best represented by Hook – debunks this image of philosophy as a superscience, employing a privileged method and thus attaining a kind of knowledge not available to the mere natural scientist. The holistic side of pragmatism – best represented by James – debunks the suggestion that the results of the natural sciences suffice to give meaning to our lives (and the corollary that the unscientific attempt to do the latter is somehow a second-rate kind of intellectual activity, one which should be satisfied with painting pictures or writing lyrics, rather than attempting discursive prose). This side of pragmatism wants to avoid having the natural scientist step into the cultural role which the philosopher-as-superscientist vacated, as if the naturalistic world-picture were somehow enough to serve the purposes for which the gods, the Platonic Ideas, and the Hegelian Spirit were invented. It wants that cultural role to *remain* unfilled.

Heidegger's protest against the "metaphysics of presence" and Tillich's against "idolatry" share this aim of debunking the idea that either a superscience, or just plain science, are going to give us what we need. Both men see positivism and Hegelianism as two sides of the same coin – the attempt to be methodical about what will not allow of method, to transport techniques of relating various bits of the world to one another into the attempt to "imagine the enveloping world as a universe." The main theme of "Continental" philosophy in our century has been criticism of the presupposition common to Hegel and Carnap – that what matters is being "scientific" in the sense of rigorously carrying through some procedure (dialectical, inductive, hypothetico-deductive, analytical, or whatever). Just as Hook has debunked "Being" in the name of "method," Heidegger has debunked "method" in the name of "Being." I am suggesting that both Hook and Heidegger were right in debunking what they debunked, but that both sometimes found themselves using weapons that belonged to the tradition they were attacking. These weapons should now be thrown away.

If we do throw them away – if we try to have pragmatism without method and Heideggerian philosophy without ontology – then I think that Tillich, James, and the more holistic and syncretic side of Dewey suggest how intellectual life might be led. It would be pursued without much reference to the traditional distinctions between the cognitive and the noncognitive, between "truth" and "comfort," or between the propositional and the nonpropositional. In particular, it would not make much of the line between "philosophy" and something else, nor try to allot distinctive cultural roles to art, religion, science, and philosophy. It would get rid of the idea that there was a special sort of expert – the philosopher – who dealt with a certain range of topics (e.g., Being, reasoning, language, knowledge, mind). It would no longer think that "philosophy" was the name of a sacred precinct that must be kept out of the hands of the enemy. People in other disciplines would no longer come around to philosophy professors to get their concepts properly "clarified" (like the student of Mary McCarthy, who, after finishing her short story, needed help in putting in the symbols).

If we could get rid of the notion that there was a special *wissenschaftlich* way of dealing with general "philosophical" ideas (a notion Dewey did his best to discountenance), then we would have much less trouble thinking of the entire culture, from physics to poetry, as a single, continuous, seamless activity in which the divisions are merely institutional and pedagogical. This would prevent us from making a moral issue of where to draw the line between "truth" and "comfort." We would thus fulfill the mission of the syncretic and holistic side of pragmatism – the side that tries to see human beings doing much the same sort of problem-solving across the whole spectrum of their activities (*already* doing it and so not needing to be urged to start doing it).

I shall conclude, in suitably pragmatic style, by remarking on the relevance of what I have just been saying to a particular problem in contemporary American culture – the disdain for traditional American anti-ideological liberalism that I mentioned at the outset. Dewey and Hook fought, jointly and with great success, against the temptations that Marxism held out to American intellectuals in the thirties. Specifically, they battled the temptation to think, as we Americans so easily do, that our naive domestic forms of cultural life had been superseded by a more sophisticated import. The Stalinists and the Niebuhrians were at one in telling us American liberals that we were indeed naive. Dewey and Hook had a good time debunking both at once. Thanks to them most American intellectuals in the pre-war period were not buffaloed by German depth or French subtlety. But things are different nowadays. Some of our best students take Althusser seriously. The idea of "philosophical depth" is in the air once again, and this means, inevitably, a trip back to the Continent. This trip is by no means a bad thing in itself, but it has become associated with the idea that liberalism is both intellectually lightweight and in need of being "diagnosed." So we now have the dismal spectacle of what Hook used to call "knee-jerk liberalism" (i.e., trying to figure out how to blame anything bad that happens on American ruling circles) combining with specifically philosophical *Tiefsinnigkeit* in the claim that we need

76

"new philosophical foundations" for criticism of "contemporary bourgeois society" (i.e., the surviving parliamentary democracies).

It would be absurd to blame the post-war failure of American nerve on the presence or absence of various views about philosophy. It is a much more massive phenomenon – the loss of America's hope to lead the nations. The frustrations and dilemmas of the last four decades may have made this loss inevitable. But it does not seem inevitable that it should have been accompanied by the sense that we have been found *morally* unworthy of the role we once thought we might play. Such self-indulgent *Schadenfreude* is, I think, the origin of the idea that Deweyan experimentalism, the dominant intellectual movement of a more hopeful time, was not "real" philosophy, but merely a rationalizing apology for certain institutions.

This latter suggestion has, of course, its grain of truth. Dewey and his followers were, to be sure, betting that reformist politics (internally and internationally) could do what Marxists think only revolution can do. More generally, pragmatism is the sort of movement that is only conceivable within a certain kind of polity with a certain kind of history. But, having admitted all that, one should continue to resist the individuous distinction between expressing the spirit of a time and place (and thus of various institutions) in philosophical terms and "real philosophy." The latter notion means, if it means anything, a discipline that would produce *more* than such an expression – that would detach itself from a time and place and see reality plain.

Such notions embody the hope that some new jargon is about to do (any day now) what no old jargon has done – take us right down to the things themselves, stripping away opinion and convention and the contingencies of history. They represent the old Platonic dream. Dewey and Hook helped several generations of American intellectuals to avoid falling back into his dream, to avoid "philosophical depth" and thus to turn to the detailed, particular dangers of their times. My criticism of some of Hook's tactics – those he adopted when dealing with some of his fellow philosophy professors, as opposed to those he adopted on the wider, public scene – has been intended as an assist to his overall debunking strategy. If pragmatism (stripped of "method") and "Continental" philosophy (stripped of "depth") could come together, we might be in a better position to defend the liberalism that is exemplified by Hook's contributions to American political life.

Texts and lumps

Like most other disciplines, literary criticism swings back and forth between a desire to do small-scale jobs well and carefully and a desire to paint the great big picture. At the moment it is at the latter pole, and is trying to be abstract, general, and theoretical. This has resulted in literary critics taking more of an interest in philosophy, and philosophers returning the compliment. This exchange has been useful to both groups. I think, however, that there is a danger that literary critics seeking help from philosophy may take philosophy a bit too seriously. They will do this if they think of philosophers as supplying "theories of meaning" or "theories of the nature of interpretation," as if "philosophical research" into such topics had recently yielded interesting new "results."

Philosophy too swings back and forth between a self-image modeled on that of Kuhnian "normal science," in which small-scale problems get definitively solved one at a time, and a self-image modeled on that of Kuhnian "revolutionary science," in which all the old philosophical problems are swept away as pseudoproblems and philosophers busy themselves redescribing the phenomena in a new vocabulary. The field presently called "literary theory" has profited primarily from the latter sort of philosophy (which has lately been fashionable in France and Germany). Unfortunately, however, it has often tried to describe itself as if it were profiting from philosophy of the former sort. It has employed the scientistic rhetoric characteristic of the early period of analytic philosophy. One often finds critics using sentences beginning "Philosophy has shown . . ." to formulate a justification for taking a certain favored approach to a literary text, or to literary history, or to literary canon-formation.

I think critics would do better to realize that philosophy is no more likely to produce "definitive results" (in the sense in which microbiology can show how to create immunity to a certain disease, or nuclear physics how to build a better bomb) than is literary criticism itself. This should not be viewed as undesirable "softness" on the part of either discipline, but simply as an illustration of the fact that there are lots of areas in which desiderata are not as well agreed upon as they are in medicine or in the munitions industry. It would be better for critics to simply have favorite philosophers (and philosophers to have favorite literary critics) – favorites picked by consonance with their own desiderata. If a literary critic wants to see the great big picture, tell a great big story, then he or she is going to have to engage in the same sort of canon-formation in respect to philosophers as he or she does in respect to novelists or poets or fellow critics.[1] As Geoffrey Hartman sensibly puts it, "Theory itself is just another text; it does not enjoy a privileged status."[2]

The need to have a general theory (of something as grand as "interpretation" or "knowledge" or "truth" or "meaning") is the sort of need which James and Dewey tried to put in perspective by insisting, with Hegel, that theory follows after, rather than being presupposed by, concrete accomplishment. On this pragmatical view, a "theoretical" style – the "Aristotelian" style which depends heavily on definitions or the "Galilean" style which depends on generalizations – is useful principally for pedagogic purposes, to provide succinct formulations of past achievements. When applied to literary criticism, pragmatism offers reasons why critics need not worry about being "scientific," and why they should not be frightened of the appearance of "subjectivity" which results from the adoption of an untheoretical, narrative style. It suggests that we neither be afraid of subjectivity nor anxious for methodology, but simply proceed to praise our heroes and damn our villains by making invidious comparisons. It urges that we not try to show that our choice of heroes is imposed upon us by, or underwritten by, antecedently plausible principles. For pragmatists, telling stories about how one's favorite and least favorite literary texts hang together is not to be distinguished from – is simply a species of – the "philosophical" enterprise of telling stories about the nature of the universe which highlight all the things one likes best and least. The misguided attempt to be "scientific" is a confusion between a pedagogical device – the device of summarizing the upshot of one's narrative in pithy little formulae – and a method for discovering truth.

In what follows, I shall first offer a general account of pragmatism's view of the nature of truth and of science, in order to fill out the sketch I have just offered. Then I shall turn to the question of what the notion of "meaning" looks like when seen from a pragmatist point of view. In both sections, I shall be urging that we avoid Dilthey's suggestion that we set up distinct parallel metavocabularies, one for the *Geistes*- and one for the *Naturwissenschaften*. We should instead assume that if a philosophical doctrine is not plausible with respect to the analysis of lumps by chemists, it probably does not apply to the analysis of texts by literary critics either.

Pragmatists say that the traditional notion that "truth is correspondence to reality" is an uncashable and outworn metaphor. Some true statements – like "the cat is on the mat" – can be paired off with other chunks of reality so as to associate

---

1 See my "The Historiography of Philosophy: Four Genres," in *Philosophy in History: Essays in the Historiography of Philosophy*, ed. Richard Rorty, J. B. Schneewind, and Quentin Skinner (Cambridge, 1984), for a defense of the claim that *Geistesgeschichte*, because of its role in creating canons, has taken over in our culture the role that philosophical systems (of the sort exemplified by Leibniz and Kant) had played earlier.

2 Geoffrey Hartman, *Criticism in the Wilderness* (New Haven, 1980), p. 242.

parts of the statement with parts of the chosen chunk. Most true statements – like "the cat is *not* on the mat" and "there are transfinite numbers" and "pleasure is better than pain" – cannot. Furthermore, we will be no better off even if we construct a metaphysical scheme which pairs off something in the world with each part of *every* true statement, and some first-order relation with every relevant metalinguistic relation. For we should still be faced with the question of whether the first-order language we use *itself* "corresponds to reality." That is, we should still wonder whether talk of cats or numbers or goodness is the right way to break up the universe into chunks, whether our language cuts reality at the joints. The pragmatists conclude that the intuition that truth is correspondence should be extirpated rather than explicated.[3] On this view, the notion of reality as having a "nature" to which it is our duty to correspond is simply one more variant of the notion that the gods can be placated by chanting the right words. The notion that some one among the languages mankind has used to deal with the universe is the one the universe prefers – the one which cuts things at the joints – was a pretty conceit. But by now it has become too shopworn to serve any purpose.

This line of argument about truth is usually met by changing the subject from truth to factuality. Science, it is said, deals with hard facts, and other areas of culture should either imitate, or confess their inability to imitate, the scientists' respect for brute factuality. Here the pragmatist invokes his second line of argument. He offers an analysis of the nature of science which construes the reputed hardness of facts as an artifact produced by our choice of language game. We construct games in which a player loses or wins if something definite and uncontrollable happens. In some Mayan ball game, perhaps, the team associated with a lunar deity automatically loses, and is executed, if the moon is eclipsed during play. In poker, you know you've won if you're dealt an ace-high straight flush. In the laboratory, a hypothesis may be discredited if the litmus paper turns blue, or the mercury fails to come up to a certain level. A hypothesis is agreed to have been "verified by the real world" if a computer spits out a certain number. The hardness of fact in all these cases is simply the hardness of the previous agreements within a community about the consequences of a certain event. The same hardness prevails in morality or literary criticism if, and only if, the relevant community is equally firm about who loses and who wins. Some communities do not take cheating at cards, or intertribal marriage, too seriously; others may make one or the other decisive for their treatment of their fellow humans. Some of Stanley Fish's "interpretive communities" throw you out if you interpret "Lycidas" as "really" about intertextuality. Others will take you in only if you do so.

This pragmatist analysis of the hardness of data may seem to confuse the causal, physical force of the event with the merely social force of the consequences of the

---

3 See my "Pragmatism, Davidson and Truth" (below). I argue there that Davidson's holism in the theory of meaning coincides with the outcome of pragmatism, once pragmatism renounces the attempt to define *true* (by, for example, invoking the Peircean notion of the "ideal end of inquiry").

event. When Galileo saw the moons of Jupiter through his telescope, it might be said, the impact on his retina was "hard" in the relevant sense, even though its consequences were, to be sure, different for different communities. The astronomers of Padua took it as merely one more anomaly which had somehow to be worked into a more or less Aristotelian cosmology, whereas Galileo's admirers took it as shattering the crystalline spheres once and for all. But the datum *itself*, it might be argued, is utterly real quite apart from the interpretation it receives.

The pragmatist meets this point by differentiating himself from the idealist. He agrees that there is such a thing as brute physical resistance – the pressure of light waves on Galileo's eyeball, or of the stone on Dr. Johnson's boot. But he sees no way of transferring this nonlinguistic brutality to *facts,* to the truth of sentences. The way in which a blank takes on the form of the die which stamps it has no analogy to the relation between the truth of a sentence and the event which the sentence is about. When the die hits the blank something causal happens, but as many *facts* are brought into the world as there are languages for describing that causal transaction. As Donald Davidson says, causation is not under a description, but explanation is. Facts are hybrid entities; that is, the causes of the assertibility of sentences include both physical stimuli and our antecedent choice of response to such stimuli. To say that we must have respect for facts is just to say that we must, if we are to play a certain language game, play by the rules. To say that we must have respect for unmediated causal forces is pointless. It is like saying that the blank must have respect for the impressed die. The blank has no choice, nor do we.

The philosophical tradition has yearned for a way of approximating the total passivity of the blank. It has seen language as interposed, like a cushion, between us and the world. It has regretted that the diversity of language games, of interpretive communities, permits us so much variation in the way in which we respond to causal pressures. It would like us to be machines for cranking out true statements in "direct" response to the pressures of reality upon our organs. Pragmatists, by contrast, think the metaphor of language as cushioning the effect of causal forces is not one which can fruitfully be spun out any further. But if that metaphor goes, so does the traditional notion of an ideal language, or of the ideal empirical theory, as an ultrathin cushion which translates the brutal thrust of reality into statement and action as directly as possible.

The metaphors which the pragmatist suggests we put in the place of all this masochistic talk about hardness and directness are those of linguistic behavior as tool-using, of language as a way of grabbing hold of causal forces and making them do what we want, altering ourselves and our environment to suit our aspirations. The pragmatist thus exalts spontaneity at the cost of receptivity, as his realist opponent did the reverse. In doing so, he shows his indebtedness to Romanticism and Absolute Idealism. But the pragmatist does not try to justify his metaphors by philosophical argument – by claiming to have made some new discovery about the nature of the universe or of knowledge which shows that the nature of truth is quite different than had been thought. He abjures Aristotelian appeals to the nature of this and that. Instead, like Dewey, he tells stories about how the course of Western thought has been stultified by the metaphors he dislikes. His own technique in philosophy is that same Homeric, narrative style which he recommends to the literary critic. His recommendation to the critic is thus not grounded in a theory about literature or about criticism, but in a narrative whose details he hopes the literary critic will help him fill in. The pragmatist philosopher has a story to tell about his favorite, and least favored, books – the texts of, for example, Plato, Descartes, Hegel, Nietzsche, Dewey, and Russell. He would like other people to have stories to tell about other sequences of texts, other genres – stories which will fit together with his. His appeal is not to the latest philosophical discoveries about the nature of science or language, but to the existence of views on these matters which chime with certain views other people (for example, contemporary critics looking for the big picture) hold about other matters.

In what I have said so far I have been concurring with Walter Michaels, whose work links American pragmatism with a Fish-like account of the nature of interpretation. Michaels sums up this attitude by saying, "Our beliefs are not obstacles between us and meaning, they are what makes meaning possible in the first place."[4] My account of pragmatism is designed to show that this claim can best be seen as a corollary of the more general claim that our beliefs, our theories, our languages, our concepts – everything which Kant located on the side of "spontaneity" – are not to be seen as defenses against the hardness of data, much less veils between us and objects, but as ways of putting the causal forces of the universe to work for us. In the case of texts, these forces merely print little replicas on our retinas. From there on it is up to us to make something out of these replicas by telling a story about their relation to other texts, or the intentions of its author, or what makes life worth living, or the events of the century in which the poem was written, or the events of our own century, or the incidents of our own lives, or whatever else seems appropriate in a given situation. The question of whether any of these stories *really is* appropriate is like the question of whether Aristotelian hylomorphism or Galilean mathematization is *really* appropriate for describing planetary motion. From the point of view of a pragmatist philosophy of science, there is no point to such a question. The only issue is whether describing the planets in one language or the other lets us tell stories about them which will fit together with all the other stories we want to tell.

Anybody who argues from a pragmatist philosophy of science to a Fish-like philosophy of literary interpretation is, however, going to have to account for the

4 Walter Michaels, "Saving the Text," *Modern Language Notes*, 93 (1978), 780. See also Jeffrey Stout, "What Is the Meaning of a Text?" *New Literary History*, 14 (1982), 1–12.

apparent difference between chemistry and criticism. There *seems* to be a difference between the hard objects with which chemists deal and the soft ones with which literary critics deal. This apparent difference is the occasion for all the neo-Diltheyan theories which insist on a distinction between explanation and understanding, and all the neo-Saussurean theories which insist upon a distinction between lumps and texts. The pragmatist objects to both distinctions, but he has to admit that there is a prima facie difference to be accounted for. For when chemists say that gold is insoluble in nitric acid, there's an end on it. Yet when critics say that the problem of *The Turn of the Screw*, or *Hamlet*, or whatever, is insoluble with the apparatus of New, or psychoanalytic, or semiotic criticism, this is just an invitation to the respective critical schools to distill even more powerful brews.

Kant's idealist way of dealing with this difference has become canonical. He thought that hard objects were ones which we constituted according to *rules* – rules laid down by unavoidable concepts wired into our transcendental faculties – whereas soft objects were those which we constituted without being bound by any rules. This distinction – the transcendental underpinning of the traditional cognitive versus aesthetic distinction – is unsatisfactory for the dialectical reasons offered by Hegel and the evolutionary ones offered by Dewey. One cannot formulate a rule without saying what it would be like to break the rule. As soon as one does so, the question of whether to stick to the rule becomes of interest. When, with Hegel, we begin to view rules as historical stages or cultural products, we blur the Kantian distinction between rule-governed and playful behavior. But whereas Hegel has to see natural science as a rather early and primitive form of Spirit's self-consciousness, Dewey can see chemistry and literary criticism and paleontology and politics and philosophy all striding along together – equal comrades with diverse interests, distinguished *only* by these interests, not by cognitive status. James and Dewey appreciated Kant's point that you can't compare your beliefs with something that isn't a belief to see if they correspond. But they sensibly pointed out that that doesn't mean that there is nothing out there to have beliefs *about*. The *causal* independence of the gold or the text from the inquiring chemist or critic does not mean that she either can or should perform the impossible feat of stripping her chosen object bare of human concerns, seeing it as it is in itself, and then seeing how our beliefs measure up to it. So Kant's distinction between constituting gold by rule-governed synthesis and constituting texts by free and playful synthesis must be discarded.

The pragmatists replace this idealist formulation with a wholehearted acceptance of the brute, inhuman, causal stubbornness of the gold or the text. But they think this should not be confused with, so to speak, an *intentional* stubbornness, an insistence on being *described in a certain way,* its *own* way. The object can, given a prior agreement on a language game, cause us to hold beliefs, but it cannot suggest beliefs for us to hold. It can only do things which our practices will react to with preprogrammed changes in beliefs. So when he is asked to interpret the felt difference between hard objects and soft objects, the pragmatist says that the difference is between the rules of one institution (chemistry) and those of another (literary criticism). He thinks, with Stanley Fish, that "all facts are institutional, are facts only by virtue of the prior institution of some such [socially conceived dimensions of assessment]."[5] The only way to get a noninstitutional fact would be to find a language for describing an object which was as little ours, and as much the object's own, as the object's causal powers. If one gives up that fantasy, no object will appear softer than any other. Rather, some institutions will appear more internally diverse, more complicated, more quarrelsome about ultimate desiderata than others.

So much for the pragmatist's view of truth and of science. I turn now to a discussion of some issues raised by my colleague E. D. Hirsch, Jr. Hirsch has argued for the possibility of objective interpretation by making a distinction between isolating the meaning of a text (a task to which the normal tests of historical objectivity apply) and relating that meaning to something else. The latter activity Hirsch calls finding *significance* in the text, as opposed to finding its *meaning*. I agree with Hirsch that we need some such distinction as this. I also agree with him that, in his words, "the much-advertised cleavage between thinking in the sciences and the humanities does not exist."[6] I think he is right in suggesting that philosophy of science and literary theory ought to carry over into each other. But I think that his distinction between "meaning" and "significance" is misleading in certain respects. My holistic strategy, characteristic of pragmatism (and in particular of Dewey), is to reinterpret every such dualism as a momentarily convenient blocking-out of regions along a spectrum, rather than as recognition of an ontological, or methodological, or epistemological divide. So I shall construct such a spectrum and use it as a heuristic device for commenting on Hirsch's dualism.

In the table below there is a column for texts and one for lumps, a division which corresponds roughly to things made and things found. Think of a paradigmatic text as something puzzling which was said or written by a member of a primitive tribe, or by Aristotle, or by Blake. Nonlinguistic artifacts, such as pots, are borderline cases of texts. Think of a lump as something which you would

---

5 Stanley Fish, *Is There a Text in This Class?* (Cambridge, Mass., 1980), p. 198. Of course, neither the gold nor the text is institutional when considered as a locus of causal power – to resist the attacks of an acid, or to cause certain patterns to appear on the retina. Using a causal vocabulary we can say that the same object is the stimulus for manifold uses of language. But as soon as we ask for *facts* about the object, we are asking how the object should be described in a particular language, and that language is an institution. The fact that the same object is commented on by many different communities does not, *pace* Richard Wollheim's criticism of Fish, show that the object can help us decide which community to belong to.

6 E. D. Hirsch, Jr., *Validity in Interpretation* (New Haven, 1967), p. 264.

bring for analysis to a natural scientist rather than to somebody in the humanities or social sciences – something which might turn out to be, say, a piece of gold or the fossilized stomach of a stegosaurus. A wadded-up plastic bag is a borderline case of a lump. Most philosophical reflection about objectivity – most epistemology and philosophy of science – has concentrated on lumps. Most discussion of interpretation has concentrated on texts. A lot of controversies about the objectivity of interpretation can, I think, be smoothed out by insisting, as far as possible, on the text-lump parallelism. In particular, I think that if one starts from a Kuhnian philosophy of science, one can preserve most of what Hirsch wants to say about validity in interpretation. So I should like to convince Hirsch that his view can be reconciled with the Dewey-Wittgenstein-Davidson-Kuhn sort of pragmatism which I am advocating.

Texts	*Lumps*
I. The phonetic or graphic features of an inscription (philology is in point here).	I. The sensory appearance and spatio-temporal location of a lump (avoidance of perceptual illusion is in point here).
II. What the author would, under ideal conditions, reply to questions about his inscription which are phrased in terms which he can understand right off the bat.	II. The real essence of the lump which lurks behind its appearances – how God or Nature would describe the lump.
III. What the author would, under ideal conditions, reply to *our* questions about his inscription – questions he would have to be reeducated to understand (think of a Cambridge-educated primitive, an Aristotle who had assimilated Freud and Marx) but which are easily intelligible to a present-day interpretive community.	III. The lump as described by that sector of *our* "normal" science which specializes in lumps of that sort (for example, a routine analysis performed by a chemist, or routine identification performed by a biologist).
IV. The role of the text in somebody's revolutionary view of the sequence of inscriptions to which the text belongs (including revolutionary sugges-	IV. The lump as described by a scientific revolutionary, that is, somebody who wants to redo chemistry, or entomology, or whatever, so that the

tions about which sequence that is) – for example, the role of an Aristotle text in Heidegger or a Blake text in Bloom.

currently "normal" chemical analyses or biological taxonomies are revealed as "mere appearances."

V. The role of the text in somebody's view of something other than the "kind" to which the text belongs – for example, its relation to the nature of man, the purpose of my life, the politics of our day, and so forth.

V. The place of the lump, or of that *sort* of lump, in somebody's view of something other than the science to which the lump has been assigned (for example, the role of gold in the international economy, in sixteenth-century alchemy, in Alberich's fantasy life, my fantasy life, and so forth, as opposed to its role in chemistry).

Numbers II–V under "texts" can be thought of as four possible meanings of "meaning"; the same numbers under "lumps" can be thought of as so many meanings of "nature." One can think of the bottom four-fifths of the table as four definitions of each term, arranged in levels. The point which the pragmatist brings over from philosophy of science, the point that conditions his attitude toward questions in literary theory, is his claim that the definition under "lumps" at Level II is not a useful notion. The *anti*pragmatist in philosophy of science and philosophy of language (for example, Kripke, Boyd) is the philosopher who thinks that there are such things as "real natures" or "real essences." But for the pragmatist, we can only distinguish better and worse nominal essences – more and less useful descriptions of the lump. For him, there is no need for the notion of a convergence of scientific inquiry toward what the lump really, truly, is in itself. So the pragmatist philosopher of science may be tempted to interpret Hirsch's distinction between "meaning" and "significance" as a distinction between meaning *in se* and meaning *ad nos,* and to dismiss Hirsch as a belated Aristotelian who has not yet got the word that all essences are nominal.[7]

Such a dismissal would be overhasty. For there obviously *is* something called "the author's intention" which we can and do use to give sense to Level II in the case of texts, but which we cannot use to give sense to Level II in the case of

---

7 For discussion of the realism-pragmatism issue in the philosophy of science, see, e.g., W. H. Newton-Smith, *The Rationality of Science* (London, 1981), and a useful collection of essays on Kuhn, *Paradigms and Revolutions,* ed. Gary Gutting (Notre Dame, 1980). The best recent statement of the pragmatist case is Hilary Putnam's *Reason, Truth, and History* (Cambridge, 1981).

lumps. The *only* interesting difference between texts and lumps is that we know how to form and defend hypotheses about the author's intentions in the one case but not in the other. Reinterpreting Hirsch's reinterpretation of Vico, I would claim that the fact that Level II makes sense for texts but not for lumps is the kernel of truth in "Vico's insight that the human realm is genuinely knowable while the realm of nature is not."[8] I would also claim that the source of realist, antipragmatist philosophy of science is the attempt, characteristic of the Enlightenment, to make "Nature" do duty for God – the attempt to make natural science a way of conforming to the will of a power not ourselves, rather than simply facilitating our commerce with the things around us. On my account, our ideal of perfect knowledge is the sympathetic knowledge we occasionally have of the state of mind of another person. Realistic epistemologies have been ill-starred attempts to transfer this sort of knowledge to our knowledge of lumps. As Nietzsche said, "The concept of substance is a consequence of the concept of the subject; not the reverse."[9] Realistic interpretations of natural science are thus hopeless attempts to make physical science imitate the *Geisteswissenschaften*. But once we give up primitive animism, and the more sophisticated forms of anthropomorphization of nature essayed by Plato and Aristotle, we can admit that the lumps are just whatever it is presently convenient to describe them as – that they have no "inside" in the way that persons do. So whereas Hirsch wants to make realistic philosophy of science look good in order to make "meaning" at Level II look good for texts, I want to do the opposite. I want to admit everything Hirsch says about the objective validity of inquiry into meaning (in that sense) in order to make realistic philosophy of science look bad. I want to insist that we *can* have what Hirsch wants at Level II for texts, just in order to ram home the point that we *cannot* have anything of the sort for lumps.

But even though I agree with Hirsch that we can have the same sort of objectivity about the mind of the author as we can have about the chemical composition of a lump, I want to disagree with the way he draws a distinction between meaning and significance. Hirsch defines these terms in the following passage: " 'Meaning' refers to the whole verbal meaning of a text, and 'significance' to textual meaning in relation to another context, i.e., another mind, another era, a wider subject matter, an alien system of values, and so on. In other words, 'significance' is textual meaning as related to some context, indeed any context, beyond itself."[10] These definitions permit him to say that "from the standpoint of knowledge, valid criticism is dependent on valid interpretation,"[11] where "criticism" means the discovery of significance and "interpretation" the discovery of meaning. These intertwined distinctions are backed up by Hirsch's

---

8 Hirsch, *Validity in Interpretation,* p. 273.
9 Friedrich Nietzsche, *The Will to Power,* tr. Walter Kaufmann (New York, 1967), par. 485.
10 E. D. Hirsch, Jr., *Aims of Interpretation* (Chicago, 1976), p. 3.
11 Hirsch, *Validity in Interpretation,* p. 162.

claim that "if we could not distinguish a content of consciousness from its contexts, we could not know any object at all in the world."[12]

From my Wittgensteinian point of view, Hirsch's Husserlian talk of contents of consciousness and of intentional objects can be replaced by talk about our ability to agree on what we are thinking about – that is, to agree on what propositions using the same referring expressions we accept, even while disagreeing about the truth-value of others. With Wittgenstein, I regard talk of "intuition" (and of "consciousness" and "intentionally") as an unnecessary shuffle – incapable of explaining our use of language and unneeded if we take that use as primitive.[13] Pragmatism views knowledge not as a relation between mind and an object, but, roughly, as the ability to get agreement by using persuasion rather than force. From this point of view, the distinction between an object X and the context in which it is put is never more than a distinction between two batches of propositions – roughly, the ones using the word X which are currently presupposed and undoubted, and those which are currently being debated. There is no way to identify an object save by talking about it – putting it in the context of some other things you want to talk about. (This I take to be one of the morals of Wittgenstein's criticism of the idea of ostensive definition.) What we know of both texts and lumps is nothing more than the ways these are related to the other texts and lumps mentioned in or presupposed by the propositions which we use to describe them. At Level I a text of Aristotle is just the thing which is found on a certain page, has this visual form when printed in that font, and so on. At Level II the meaning of a text of Aristotle is whatever, for example, an un-reeducated Aristotle would say about it. At Level III it is what somebody like Werner Jaeger says about it; at Level IV it is what, for example, Heidegger says about it; at Level V it is, for example, what I am saying about it here.

It is a mistake to ask what it is that is the *same* at each level, as if we were in quest of an enduring substrate of changing descriptions. All that is needed to make communication and persuasion, and thus knowledge, possible is the linguistic know-how necessary to move from level to level. An account of the acquisition of that know-how does not require that we postulate an object – the very text itself, or the true meaning of the text, or the very lump itself, or the real essence of the lump – which is present to consciousness at each level. All that is required

---

12 Hirsch, *Aims of Interpretation*, p. 3.

13 Whether one can be so blithe about consciousness and intentionality is a matter of dispute between, for example, Daniel Dennett and John Searle. I defend Dennett against Searle in "Contemporary Philosophy of Mind" and "Comments on Dennett," and Dennett demurs from some parts of my defense in "Comments on Rorty," all in *Synthèse*, 53 (1982). A related dispute is how seriously to take the notion of "reference." Kripke is the best example of a philosopher who takes it very seriously. For the anti-Kripke case, see Donald Davidson, "Reality Without Reference," in his *Inquiries into Truth and Interpretation* (Oxford: Oxford University Press, 1984); Putnam, *Reason, Truth, and History;* and my "Is There a Problem about Fictional Discourse?" in *Consequences of Pragmatism* (Minneapolis, 1982).

is that agreement should be obtainable about what we are talking about – and this just means agreement on a reasonable number of propositions using the relevant term. Propositions at *any* level will do the job. The epistemological tradition common to Hirsch and to the "theory of semantic autonomy" (which Hirsch attributes to the New Critics and the deconstructionists) insists that one of these levels has to be picked out as "what we are *really* talking about" at each of the other levels. Both insist that knowledge of meaning at that level is the foundation of discussion at other levels. But this common doctrine is, it seems to me, the analogue of the doctrine common to phenomenalistic empiricism and to the current realistic reaction against phenomenalism – namely, the doctrine that either Level I (for phenomenalism) or Level II (for realism) is privileged (in the case of lumps) as that which "determines reference." From a pragmatist angle, this whole notion of privileging a level and putting it forward as a foundation of inquiry is one more unhappy attempt to save the notion of truth as correspondence. Hirsch and his opponents are both too preoccupied with the distinctive textuality of texts, just as both Kripke and his opponents are too preoccupied with the distinctive lumpishness of lumps. Rather than trying to locate sameness, we should dissolve both texts and lumps into nodes within transitory webs of relationships.

Criticism of attempts to privilege levels has, unfortunately, given rise to a kind of silly relativism which says that the views of idiosyncratic nature mystics about lumps are somehow "on a par with" the views of professors of chemistry (as in Feyerabend) or that free-association interpretations of texts are "on a par with" ordinary philological or historic ones. All that "on a par with" means in such contexts is "epistemologically on a par." So interpreted, the claim is true but trivial. Anybody, no matter how kooky he sounds, may, for all we know merely on *epistemological* grounds, be the originator of a brilliant new account of the meanings of some texts or the natures of some lumps. Time will tell, but epistemology won't – nor will philosophy of science, nor semiotics, nor any other theory which purports to give a taxonomy of all possible bright new ideas, all possible futures. We had, after all, to dream up a brand new philosophy of science to take care of Galileo and his friends, and a whole new aesthetics to take care of Duchamp and *his* friends. In the future we shall have to redo our narratives of how scientific theories or paintings or poems or literary essays fit together just as often as somebody does something so original and striking that it won't fit into the stories we have been accustomed to tell.

The recent prevalence of what I have called "silly relativism" – the bad inference from "no epistemological difference" to "no objective criterion of choice" – has led writers like Hirsch to try to form general theories of interpretation, theories which will help us retain the idea of "the right interpretation of the text" as opposed to that of a "good interpretation for certain purposes." I agree with Fish that the latter notion is all we need, and I do not see, *pace* Hirsch, that a meaning at Level II has to be assigned to a text before we can assign meanings at other levels. I think of objectivity as a matter of ability to achieve agreement on whether a particular set of desiderata has or has not been satisfied. So I think that we can have objective knowledge at any level without necessarily having it at any other.

In the preceding discussion of Hirsch I have tried to suggest that philosophy of language and epistemology not be taken as seriously as both he and his opponents take them. I do not think philosophers have discovered or will discover something about the nature of knowledge or language or intentionality or reference which is going to make life startlingly different for critics or historians or anthropologists. They do not have independent expertise, they just have stories which can be used to complement or buttress other stories. A discipline swinging toward atomism, for example, will want atomistic theories of meaning, and one swinging toward holism will want holistic theories. I agree with Geoffrey Hartman that we should not try very hard to separate philosophy from literary criticism, nor the figure of the philosopher from that of the critic. The way in which Derrida, Hartman, Bloom, and de Man weave together "literary" and "philosophical" texts and considerations, disregarding the frontiers between the traditional genres, seems to me just the right way to proceed. This is because I think the test of philosophical truth consists neither in "correct analyses" of individual concepts (for example, "meaning," "intentionality") nor in the internal coherence among hundreds of such analyses linked together in a philosophical system, but only in the coherence of such a system with the rest of culture, a culture which one hopes will continue to be as *ondoyant et divers* as is that of the Western democracies at the present time.

This means that the test of a philosophical theory of justice or meaning or truth (or, for that matter, of philosophy) is how well it coheres with the best work currently being done in, for example, both biochemistry and literary criticism. Precisely because philosophy deals with concepts which are used all over the place – places where people are analyzing texts as well as those where they are analyzing lumps – it is not in a position to lay down the law to any of them. The idea that philosophy is a matter of give and take with the "hard" sciences is familiar enough. The idea that the give-and-take extends to softer areas, combined with skepticism about the hard/soft distinction, begins with Hegel and is, to my mind, best developed in Dewey's naturalized Hegelianism. This idea is resisted by people on both sides of the artificial boundary drawn by Dilthey (a boundary penciled in, alas, by Hegel, in his own distinction between Nature and Spirit – the distinction which Dewey did his best to blur). On the "lump" side (a side where one finds many "analytic" philosophers), it is still widely believed, with Quine, that "philosophy of [fairly hard] science is philosophy enough." On the "text" side (where one finds a lot of "Continental" philosophers) it is still widely believed that it would be simplemindedly "positivist" – neglectful of the textuality of texts – to think that the same battery of concepts will work on both sides. But recently both "analytic" and "Continental" philosophers have been suggesting that, once the holism common to Quine and Gadamer is pushed along a few more steps, it cannot confine itself to one side of the text/lump distinction, but blurs that distinction. This seems to me the upshot of work by, for example, Donald Davidson and Mary Hesse on one side of the Channel and Lorenz Krüger and Wolf Lepenies on the other. If this work is followed up, then the French and the German philosophers might stop using "positivism" as a bogeyman to frighten their students, and the British and American philosophers might be able to stop giggling nervously at the mention of the word "hermeneutics."

In this essay I have been citing lots of debatable philosophical views – Davidson-like views of meaning, Kuhn-like views of science, Dennett-like views of intentionality – in order to support something like Fish's debatable view of literary interpretation. I think the degree of debatability is about the same on both sides of the philosophy/criticism divide, and that if literary theorists recognize this they may be able to make a freer and more flexible use of philosophical texts, rather than treating them as lumps to be swallowed or spit out. They could do so by getting in on the philosophical arguments rather than assuming that specialized, technical, philosophical research will produce something comparable to an assayer's report.

If this shift in attitude became general, it would help us to accept Hartman's view that literary criticism is as respectable and nonparasitic a genre as the lyric, or as the contributions to *Chemical Abstracts*. It might also help us see that critics are no more or less in need of a "general theory of interpretation" than poets are of aesthetics, or chemists of philosophy of science. The Deweyan pragmatism I am preaching develops this holistic way of seeing things by reclassifying culture in terms of genres, as opposed to "subject matters" and "methods." The tradition asked itself what joints the world wanted to be cut at and what methods were suitable for examining the various disjointed bits. Pragmatism treats every such division of the world into "subject matters" as an experiment, designed to see if we can get what we want at a certain historical moment by using a certain language.

Each new language creates or modifies a genre – that is, a sequence of texts, the later members of which take earlier members into account. These sequences may intertwine – as do, for example, poetry and criticism, or science and the history of science, or criticism and philosophy, or criticism and the history of criticism. But there are no rules for whether they should or shouldn't intertwine – no necessities lying in the nature of a subject or a method. There is nothing general and epistemological to be said about how the contributors to the various genres should conduct themselves. Nor is there any ranking of these disciplines according to degrees or kinds of truth. There is, in short, nothing to be said about the relation of these genres to "the world," only things to be said about their relations to each other. Further, there are no ahistorical things to be said about the latter sort of relations. There is no synoptic view of culture which is more than a narrative account of how various cultures managed to get to where they now are. All of us who want big broad pictures are contributing to such an account. If we could see ourselves *as* doing that, then we would worry less about having general principles which justify our procedures. Pragmatism declines to provide us with such principles. But it does tell a story about why we thought we needed such principles, and it offers some suggestions about what a culture might be like in which we did *not* think this.

Inquiry as recontextualization:
An anti-dualist account of interpretation

Think of human minds as webs of beliefs and desires, of sentential attitudes — webs which continually reweave themselves so as to accommodate new sentential attitudes. Do not ask where the new beliefs and desires come from. Forget, for the moment, about the external world, as well as about that dubious interface between self and world called "perceptual experience." Just assume that new ones keep popping up, and that some of them put strains on old beliefs and desires. We call some of these strains "contradictions" and others "tensions." We alleviate both by various techniques. For example, we may simply drop an old belief or desire. Or we may create a whole host of new beliefs and desires in order to encapsulate the disturbing intruder, reducing the strain which the old beliefs and desires put on it and which it puts on them. Or we may just unstitch, and thus erase, a whole range of beliefs and desires — we may stop *having* attitudes toward sentences which use a certain word (the word "God," or "phlogiston," for example).

By a familiar trick, you can treat desires as if they were beliefs. You do this by treating the imperative attitude toward the sentence S "Would that it were the case that S!" as the indicative attitude "It would be better that S should be the case than that not-S should be." So from here on I shall save space by leaving out "and desires," and just talk about beliefs. I can do this with an easier conscience because, as a good pragmatist, I follow Bain and Peirce in treating beliefs as habits of action. That is, I regard beliefs as states attributed to organisms of a certain complexity — attributions which enable the attributor to predict or retrodict (mostly retrodict) the behavior of that organism. So the web of belief should be regarded not just as a self-reweaving mechanism but as one which produces movements in the organism's muscles — movements which kick the organism itself into action. These actions, by shoving items in the environment around, produce new beliefs to be woven in, which in turn produce new actions, and so on for as long as the organism survives.

I say "mechanism" because I want to emphasize that there is no self distinct from this self-reweaving web. All there is to the human self is just that web. To view beliefs as habits of action is to view the self from the outside. From that angle, there is no distinction between mind and body other than the Rylean one between the organism's movements and the interior states of the organism which you need to posit in order to explain and predict those movements. Some of these states are states of muscles or heart or kidneys; others are states of mind. But to call them "mental" is just to say that they are intentional states, which is just to say that they are beliefs.

If one takes this Deweyan stance, one will naturally make a distinction between what Dewey called "habit" and what he called "inquiry." This is, like all of Dewey's distinctions, one of degree. At one end of a spectrum are situations where minimal reweaving is required – as when one moves one's left hand to pick up the fork, comes to believe that it is not there but rather on the other side of the plate, and so moves one's right hand. The reweaving involved in assimilating the novel belief "The fork is on the wrong side" is usually too minimal to deserve the name of "inquiry." But sometimes, in special situations, the acquisition of that belief will provoke the sort of large-scale, conscious, deliberate reweaving which does deserve that name. It might, for instance, lead one to realize that one's host is not who he claims to be, but a daring foreign imposter – a revelation which leads one to rethink one's long-term plans and, ultimately, the meaning of one's life. The same goes for the incursion of the belief that there are unexpected patterns of mold in a Petri dish, or unexpected flecks on a telescopic image. They may lead to "reflex" actions or they may initiate scientific breakthroughs. Which they do is a matter of what *other* beliefs happen to make up the mechanism which is reweaving itself.

As one moves along the spectrum from habit to inquiry – from instinctive revision of intentions through routine calculation toward revolutionary science or politics – the number of beliefs added to or subtracted from the web increases. At a certain point in this process it becomes useful to speak of "recontextualization." The more widespread the changes, the more use we have for the notion of "a new context." This new context can be a new explanatory theory, a new comparison class, a new descriptive vocabulary, a new private or political purpose, the latest book one has read, the last person one has talked to; the possibilities are endless.

One can, however, divide all contexts into two kinds: (a) a new set of attitudes toward some of the sentences previously in one's repertoire, and (b) the acquisition of attitudes toward new truth-value candidates, sentences toward which one had previously had no attitudes. This distinction between two senses of "context" is roughly coincident with the distinction between inference and imagination, and also with the distinction between translation and language-learning. We speak of inference when logical space remains fixed, when no new candidates for belief are introduced. Paradigms of inference are adding up a column of figures, or running through a sorites, or down a flow-chart. Paradigms of imagination are the new, metaphorical use of old words (e.g., *gravitas*), the invention of neologisms (e.g., "gene"), and the colligation of hitherto unrelated texts (e.g., Hegel and Genet [Derrida], Donne and Laforgue [Eliot], Aristotle and the Scriptures [the Schoolmen], Emerson and the Gnostics

94

[Bloom], Emerson and the skeptics [Cavell], cockfights and Northrop Frye [Geertz], Nietzsche and Proust [Nehamas]).[1]

Again, however, this is a distinction of degree, and it will be drawn differently by people with different concerns. Consider an accountant recontextualizing the figures on a corporate income tax return, provoked to do so by the thought that a certain depreciable item might plausibly be listed on Schedule H rather than on Schedule M. This belief will eventually lead him to infer to a different bottom line. We usually think of this process as clever rearrangement of antecedent material, clever inference from antecedent beliefs about the contents of the tax laws. But there is of course a touch of imagination in it (as is suggested by the term "creative accounting"). Again, admirers of Derrida like myself think of Derrida's recontextualization of Western metaphysics, his neologistic redescription of it as "phallogocentrism," as a paradigm of creative imagination. But hostile critics of Derrida think of this as merely rearranging old themes and slogans – just shoving the old pieces around the old board, to no good purpose.

The distinction between "rationality" and something else has traditionally been drawn so as to coincide roughly with this distinction between inference and imagination. We are being rational, so the story goes, insofar as we stick to the logical space given at the beginning of the inquiry and so long as we can offer an argument for the beliefs held at the end of the inquiry by referring back to the beliefs held at its beginning. Before the arrival of Kuhn, Toulmin, Feyerabend, and Hanson, it was often thought that the physical sciences were, in this sense, paradigmatically rational areas of culture. The scientists were thought of as going up or down flow-charts labeled "the logic of confirmation" or "the logic of explanation" and as operating within a logical space in which all possible descriptions of everything were already at hand. Insofar as this logical space was unavailable, or not clearly seen, it was the job of "conceptual analysis" to make it available and visible – to translate every unclear locution into a clear one, where "clear" meant something like "accessible to every rational inquirer."

On this view, proto-Kuhnian suggestions that we might have to learn a new language to do history of science, or anthropology, or that we might have to invent a new language to make scientific or political progress, were thought of as "irrationalist." In pre-Kuhnian philosophy of science, rational inquiry was a matter of putting everything into a single, widely available, familiar context – translating everything into the vocabulary provided by a set of sentences which any rational inquirer would agree to be truth-value candidates. The human sci-

---

1 Successful colligation of this sort is an example of rapid and unconscious reweaving: one lays one set of beliefs on top of another and finds that, magically, they have interpenetrated and become warp and woof of a new, vividly polychrome, fabric. I take this as analogous to what happens in dreams, and that analogy as the point of Davidson's remark that "Metaphor is the dreamwork of language."

ences were urged to get inside this context, while the arts were allowed to escape this requirement of "rationality." The idea was that there is a rough equivalence between being scientific and being rational. So being scientific is a matter of sticking within a logical space which forms an intrinsically privileged context.[2]

We enlightened post-Kuhnians are free from this idea, but we are not yet free from what I shall call "realism." This is the idea that inquiry is a matter of finding out the nature of something which lies outside the web of beliefs and desires. On this view, inquiry has a goal which is not simply the equilibrium state of the reweaving machine – a state which coincides with the satisfaction of the desires of the organism which contains that machine. For us pragmatists, by contrast, there is no such thing as an intrinsically privileged context. For realists there is some sense in which the object of inquiry – what lies outside the organism – has a context of its own, a context which is privileged by virtue of being the object's rather than the inquirer's. This realism is found in both the hard and the soft sciences – among anthropologists who dislike ethnocentrism,[3] literary critics who dislike deconstruction, Heideggerians who distrust Derrida,[4] as much as among those who prize the "absoluteness" of natural science's description of the world.[5]

For us pragmatists, by contrast, the object of inquiry is "constituted" by inquiry only in the following sense: we shall answer the questions "What are you talking about?" and "What is it that you want to find out about?" by listing some of the more important beliefs which we hold at the current stage of inquiry, and saying that we are talking about *whatever these beliefs are true of*. The model here is the familiar contextualist claim that a non-Euclidean space is whatever certain

2 This pre-Kuhnian notion of what it is to be scientific is criticized by Dewey at the end of his "The Influence of Darwin on Philosophy" (*The Middle Works of John Dewey*, vol. 4, Jo Ann Boydston, ed. [Carbondale, Ill.: Southern Illinois University Press, 1977], p. 14): ". . . conviction persists – though history shows it to be an hallucination – that all the questions that the human mind has asked are questions that can be answered in terms of the alternatives that the questions themselves present. But in fact intellectual progress usually occurs through sheer abandonment of questions together with both of the alternatives they assume – an abandonment that results from their decreasing vitality and a change of urgent interest. We do not solve them; we get over them."

3 See Clifford Geertz's "The Uses of Diversity," *Michigan Quarterly Review* 25 (1986), and my "On Ethnocentrism: A Reply to Clifford Geertz" (below).

4 Hubert Dreyfus and John Caputo are examples. See Dreyfus, "Holism and Hermeneutics," *Review of Metaphysics* XXXIV (1980), and Caputo, "The Thought of Being and the Conversation of Mankind: The Case of Heidegger and Rorty," *Review of Metaphysics* 36 (1983), pp. 661–83. Both articles are reprinted in Robert Hollinger, ed., *Hermeneutics and Praxis* (Notre Dame, Ind.: Notre Dame University Press, 1985).

5 See Charles Taylor's insistence on this absoluteness in his "Understanding in the Human Sciences," immediately following Dreyfus's "Holism and Hermeneutics" in the issue of *Review of Metaphysics* cited in n. 4. These two papers are followed by a paper of mine called "A Reply to Dreyfus and Taylor," and by debate between Dreyfus, Taylor, and myself. There I object to the notion of "absoluteness" which Taylor, like Bernard Williams, ascribes to the descriptions offered by natural science. For criticism of the positions which Dreyfus and I adopt in the aforementioned debate, see Mark Okrent, "Hermeneutics, Transcendental Philosophy and Social Science," *Inquiry* 27, pp. 23–49.

axioms are true of.[6] We pragmatists hear the question "But is there *really* any such thing?" as an awkward way of putting the question: "Are there other beliefs which we ought to have?" The latter question can only be answered by enumerating and recommending such other beliefs. So we do not countenance any *generalized* skepticism about other minds or cultures, or the external world, but only detailed skepticism about this or that belief or cluster of beliefs – detailed suggestions about how to reweave.[7]

One way of formulating the pragmatist position is to say that the pragmatist recognizes relations of *justification* holding between beliefs and desires, and relations of *causation* holding between these beliefs and desires and other items in the universe, but no relations of *representation*. Beliefs do not represent nonbeliefs. There are, to be sure, relations to *aboutness,* in the attentuated senses in which Riemann's axioms are about Riemannian space, Meinong talks about round squares, and Shakespeare's play is about Hamlet. But in this vegetarian sense of aboutness, there is no problem about how a belief can be about the unreal or the impossible. For aboutness is not a matter of pointing outside the web. Rather, we use the term "about" as a way of directing attention to the beliefs which are relevant to the justification of other beliefs, not as a way of directing attention to nonbeliefs.

We pragmatists must object to, or reinterpret, two traditional methodological questions: "What context is appropriate to this object?" and "What is it that we are putting in context?" For us, all objects are always already contextualized.[8]

6 On the importance of non-Euclidean geometry for the antiessentialist, increasingly playful, tone of twentieth-century philosophy, see my "From Logic to Language to Play," *Proceedings and Addresses of the American Philosophical Association* 59 (1986), pp. 747–53.

7 For criticism of the attitude toward generalized skepticism which I share with Davidson, see Colin McGinn, "Radical Interpretation and Epistemology," in *Truth and Interpretation: Perspectives on the Philosophy of Donald Davidson,* Ernest LePore, ed. (Oxford: Blackwell, 1986). McGinn shares Nagel's anti-Wittgensteinian and anti-Peircian view that there are aspects of experience which escape language, and thus escape contextualization. For a more general, very penetrating, discussion of generalized skepticism, and in particular of the attitude toward skepticism shared by Nagel, Barry Stroud, and McGinn, see Michael Williams, *Unnatural Doubts* (Oxford: Blackwell, forthcoming).

8 Contrast, e.g., Anthony Giddens's claim that "sociology, unlike natural science, deals with a pre-interpreted world where the creation and reproduction of meaning-frames is a very condition of that which it seeks to analyze, namely human social conduct: this is why there is a double hermeneutic in the social sciences" (*New Rules of Sociological Method,* p. 158). This passage is quoted approvingly by Habermas (*Theory of Communicative Action,* vol. 1, p. 110). Habermas glosses it by saying "Giddens speaks of a 'double' hermeneutic because in the social sciences problems of interpretive understanding do not come into play only through the theory-dependency of data description and the paradigm-dependency of theory-languages; there is already a problem of understanding below the threshold of theory construction, namely in *obtaining* data and not first in *theoretically describing* them; for the everyday experience that can be *transformed* into scientific operations is, for its part, already symbolically structured and inaccessible to mere observation."

My reaction to Habermas's gloss is that it is precisely "the theory-dependency of data description" which makes "mere observation" an *equally* useless notion in the *Natur-* and in the *Geisteswissenschaften*. I can no more see the point of Giddens's "double" hermeneutics than that of its near relative, Quine's "double" indeterminacy of translation. (The latter notion has been

They all come with contexts attached, just as Riemannian space comes with axioms attached. So there is no question of taking an object out of its old context and examining it, all by itself, to see what new context might suit it. There is only a question about which other regions of the web we might look to to find ways of eliminating the residual tensions in the region currently under strain. Nor is there an answer to the question of what it is that is being put in context except, boringly and trivially, "beliefs." All talk about doing things to objects must, in a pragmatic account of inquiry "into" objects, be paraphrasable as talk about reweaving beliefs. Nothing but efficiency will be lost in such translation, any more than anything else is lost if, with Peirce, we paraphrase talk about the object as talk about the practical effects which the object will have on our conduct.

Once one drops the traditional opposition between context and thing contextualized, there is no way to divide things up into those which are what they are independent of context and those which are context-dependent – no way to divide the world up into hard lumps and squishy texts, for example. Or, to put it another way, there is no way to divide the world up into internal and external relations, nor into intrinsic vs. extrinsic properties – nor, indeed, into things that are intrinsically relations and things that are intrinsically terms of relations. For once one sees inquiry as reweaving beliefs rather than discovering the natures of objects, there are no candidates for self-subsistent, independent entities save individual beliefs – individual sentential attitudes. But these are very bad candidates indeed. For a belief is what it is only by virtue of its position in a web. Once we view the "representation" and "aboutness" relations (which some philosophers have supposed to "fix the content" of belief) as fallout from a given contextualization of those beliefs, a belief becomes simply a position in a web. It is a disposition on the part of the web to react to certain additions or delections in certain ways. In this respect it is like a thing's value or its valence – it is just a disposition to respond in various ways to various stimuli.[9]

criticized in detail by Chomsky, Putnam, and others, and by me in "Indeterminacy of Translation and of Truth," *Synthèse* 23 [1972], pp. 443–62.)

9 I owe the analogy between doxastic content and value to Daniel Dennett. See his *The Intentional Stance* (Cambridge, Mass.: MIT Press, 1987), p. 208: "Propositions, as ways of 'measuring' semantic information by the topic-ful, *turn out to be more like dollars than like numbers.* Just as 'what is that worth in U.S. dollars?' asks a usefully unifying question in spite of the frequent occasions when the answer distorts the reality in which we are interested, so 'what proposition (in Standard Scheme P) does that store/transmit/express?' might exploit a valuable, somewhat systematic if often procrustean testbed. Only naive Americans confuse the former question with 'What is that worth in *real* money?', and it would be similarly naive to consider a proposition-fixing standard, however well established, to be even an approximation of the way semantic information is *really* parcelled out. *There are no real, natural, universal units of either economic value or semantic information.*"

Think of the question "What is that worth in *real* money?" as parallel to the equally naive questions "What sentence in the *real* language – the Language of Reason, or the Language of Nature, or the Language of Observation – is that behavioral disposition an attitude toward?" or "What piece of reality – reality as it *really* is – is that behavioral disposition directed toward?" or "What context does that disposition *really* belong in?"

If this dissolution of inquiry into a self-reweaving web of beliefs seems wacky to you, consider that such a dissolution is a natural and easy consequence of a generalized antiessentialism. Antiessentialism is, as Samuel Wheeler has noted,[10] the principal point of convergence between analytic philosophy and Continental philosophy. The same movement of thought which led Whitehead and Quine to sneer at Aristotle and to relativize the substance-property distinction led Heidegger to say that the West began to forget Being when the Greeks started distinguishing "that" from "what," and appearance from reality.[11] It leads Dennett and others to repudiate what Gareth Evans called "Russell's Principle" (viz.: "a subject cannot make a judgment about something unless he knows which object his judgment is about").[12]

The antiessentialist philosopher looks forward to the day when all the pseudo-problems created by the essentialist tradition – problems about the relation of appearance to reality, of mind to body, of language to fact – will be dissolved. She thinks that all these traditional dualisms collapse, like so many dominoes, once the distinction between essence and accident is collapsed. She sees the distinction between reality and appearance as a way of suggesting that some set of relations, some context, is intrinsically privileged. She sees the mind-body distinction as a way of suggesting that human beings have an inside which is beyond the reach of language (Nagel, McGinn), or possess an intrinsic intentionality (Searle), a kind which escapes recontextualization. She sees the distinction between language and fact as a way of intimating that some bits of language bear a special relation – that of accurate representation – to something which is what it is apart from language, apart from any description.

The essentialist philosopher, the one who wants to hold on to the notion of "intrinsic, context-independent, property," says that the "it" which inquiry puts in context *has* to be something precontextual. The antiessentialist rejoins by

---

10 See Samuel Wheeler, "The Extension of Deconstruction," *The Monist* 69 (1986), pp. 3–21, especially p. 10: "In a way, the most striking expression of the thought common to Quine and Derrida is that all thought can be at most brain-writing or spirit-writing, both of which modes of inscription yield texts with at least the hermeneutical problems of other texts." When this point is separated, by Davidson, from Quine's adventitious physicalism, the convergence between Derrida and Davidson becomes clear. See Wheeler, "Indeterminacy of French Translation: Derrida and Davidson," in *Truth and Interpretation: Perspectives on the Philosophy of Donald Davidson*, Ernest LePore, ed. (Oxford: Blackwell, 1986), pp. 477–94.

11 Martin Heidegger, *Nietzsche* II, pp. 14f. "The what (*das Was-sein, to ti estin*) and the that (*das Dass-sein, to estin*) reveal themselves in their difference along with the difference on which metaphysics everywhere reposes – the one which establishes itself firstly and in its finality (although capable of trasmutation to the point of unrecognizability) in the Platonic distinction between true being (*ontōs on*) and non-being (*mē on*)." At the bottom of p. 15 Heidegger says: "The what and the that volatilize themselves, with the growing unquestionability of the identification of Being with the beingness of beings (*die wachsende Fraglösigkeit der Seinendheit*), into empty 'concepts of reflection' and thus acquire ever greater strength, in proportion as metaphysics itself becomes more and more taken for granted."

12 Gareth Evans, *The Varieties of Reference* (Oxford: Clarendon Press, 1982), p. 89. See Dennett, *The Intentional Stance*, pp. 200, 210.

insisting that it is contexts all the way down. She does so by saying that we can only inquire after things under a description, that describing something is a matter of relating it to other things, and that "grasping the thing itself" is not something that precedes contextualization, but is at best a *focus imaginarius*. The latter is the idea of a simultaneous grasp of all the possible descriptions which the thing might be given, of all the possible contexts in which it might be placed. This is the impossible idea of comparing and contrasting all the infinitely many possible beliefs which, under some possible interpretation, might be viewed as beliefs about that thing.[13]

The essentialist rejoins by saying that although the descriptions may vary depending on the describer, the thing described does not. He accuses the antiessentialist of having confused the order of being with the order of knowing, of being a "verificationist." So he continues to press his question: what is it that is being related to what? Relativizing and contextualizing, he says, are all very well, but relations require terms. Sooner or later we have to be told what these terms are, what they *intrinsically* are. Once we are told *that*, we shall have to acknowledge the need for the traditional dualisms. For we shall have a clue to what is real rather than apparent, what it is that language attempts to represent accurately, what mind and body *intrinsically* are and how they are *really* related.

To evade this question about what the terms of all these relations are, about what sort of thing it is that gets endlessly recontextualized, the antiessentialist has to say that anything *can* be treated as a term of a relation *or* can be dissolved into a set of relations to other things, depending on one's current purposes. There will always be terms which are related, but which terms these are depends upon the purpose of the recontextualization currently being undertaken. You can dissolve macrostructure into microstructure – stars and tables into atoms – but you can also view microstructural entities as devices for predicting macrostructural behavior. You can dissolve a substance into a sequence of Whiteheadian events, but you can also treat events as relations between Aristotelian substances. You can dissolve persons into webs of beliefs and desires, but you can also dissolve a belief into the attitude a person has toward a sentence. You can dissolve a sentence into a pattern of words, but you can go on to remark that only in the context of a sentence does a word have meaning. The antiessentialist specializes in creating this hall-of-mirrors effect – in getting us to stop asking which is the real thing and which the image, and to settle for an ever-expanding choice of images, of Goodmanian "worlds."

This antiessentialist strategy thus seems to get rid of the *objects* of inquiry – of the things which get reflected in all those mirrors. But there is something dubious about the idea that it is mirrors all the way down. So the essentialist, at

13 See Hilary Putnam, *Representation and Reality* (Cambridge, Mass.: MIT Press, 1988), p. 89: "To ask a human being in a time-bound culture to survey all modes of human linguistic existence – including those that will transcend his own – is to ask for an impossible Archimedean point."

this stage of the argument, begins to call himself a "realist" and to call his opponent a "linguistic idealist." She is speaking, he says, as if there were nothing to do but rearrange our mental representations into pleasing or useful patterns – as if there were nothing for them to represent. The antiessentialist rejoins that her position has nothing in common with idealism save an acknowledgment that inquiry does not consist in confrontation between beliefs and objects, but rather in the quest for a coherent set of beliefs. She is a coherentist but not an idealist. For she believes, as strongly as does any realist, that there are objects which are *causally* independent of human beliefs and desires.

The realist rejoins that the antiessentialist must be saying that objects are unknowable as they are in themselves – that she must, therefore, be some newfangled kind of transcendental idealist. She replies that she can find no use for the notion "as they are in themselves," nor for the distinction between "as they are" and "as we describe them." We do in fact describe most objects as causally independent of us, and that is *all* that is required to satisfy our realistic intuitions. We are not also required to say that our descriptions *represent* objects. Representation is, on her view, a fifth wheel. If we have relations of justification between our beliefs and desires, and relations of causation between those and the rest of the universe, those are all the mind-world or language-world relations we need.

At this point one can imagine the realist saying: if you give up the notion of *representing* objects, then you had better give up the claim to be recontextualizing *objects*. You had better admit that all your conception of inquiry allows you to do is to recontextualize your beliefs and desires. You don't find out anything about objects at all – you just find out about how your web of beliefs and desires can be rewoven so as to accommodate new beliefs and desires. You never get outside your own head.

What I have been saying amounts to accepting this gambit. The antiessentialist should admit that what she calls "recontextualizing objects" could just as well be called "recontextualizing beliefs." Reweaving a web of beliefs is, if you like, all she does – all anybody can do. But, she will add, this is not as bad as the realist makes it sound. In the first place one of her more central, difficult-to-imagine-revising beliefs is that lots of objects she does not control are continually causing her to have new and surprising beliefs, beliefs which often require hasty and drastic reweaving on her part. She is no more free from pressure from outside, no more tempted to be "arbitrary," than anyone else. She is free from the questions "Are you representing accurately?" and "Are you getting at the way the object *really, intrinsically,* is?" but *not* from questions like "Can you fit in the belief that the litmus paper turned red (or that there are nonstellar sources of radiation, or that your lover has deceived you) with the rest of your beliefs?" In the second place, she is not stuck within her own head. At worst, the community of inquirers to which she belongs, the one which shares most of her beliefs, is stuck, for the time being, within its own vocabulary. But bemoaning this fact is like bemoaning the fact that we are, for the time being, stuck in our own solar system. Human finitude is not an objection to a philosophical view.

I turn now from this large debate between the essentialist and the antiessentialist to the topic of interpretation. Interpretation has become a theme for philosophers largely as a result of the attempt to split the difference between the essentialist and the antiessentialist. For "interpretation" is an exciting notion only as long as it contrasts with something harder, firmer, less controversial – something like "explanation" or "natural science."

Typically, those who take up the subject of interpretation divide culture into two areas – in one of which interpretations, recontextualizations, go all the way down and in another of which they do not. When we are told that a certain activity should be viewed as *interpretive,* we are usually being told that we should not, perhaps contrary to our earlier expectations, expect this activity to produce either knock-down arguments or a consensus among experts. We should not expect it to have a natural starting point, nor a method. Perhaps we should not even expect it to provide "objective truth." We should be prepared to settle for recontextualizing what lies to hand, and then playing various recontextualizations off against each other. But advising us to settle for this fuzziness is only interesting insofar as we have reason to think that other people, in other areas of culture, manage to be *less* fuzzy than this.

Suppose we are antiessentialist all the way. Then we shall say that *all* inquiry is interpretation, that *all* thought consists in recontextualization, that we have never done anything else and never will. We shall not grant that there is a useful contrast to be drawn between topics about which there is objective truth and topics about which there is not. We shall not grant that there is *any* area of culture in which the essentialist has a point. So, if we use it at all, we shall have to stretch the term "interpretation" to cover what stockbrokers, geologists, actuaries, and carpenters do. A notion stretched that thin, deprived of contrastive and polemical force, loses its pizzazz. If we had all been raised from our cradles to be antiessentialists, "interpretation" would never have been inscribed on the banners of a philosophical movement. Dilthey, Gadamer, and Charles Taylor would have had to find different topics.

The suggestion that one might be antiessentialist all the way is the suggestion that one might cease to see an interesting, Diltheyan, difference between the procedures of the physicist and the sociologist – or, more precisely, that one might find a context in which these differences became irrelevant, and then find advantages in staying within that context. It is a suggestion which Taylor once satirized by saying that Mary Hesse and I shared the "pleasing fancy" that "old-guard Diltheyans, their shoulders hunched from years-long resistance against the encroaching pressure of positivist natural science, suddenly pitch forward on their faces as all opposition ceases to the reign of universal hermeneutics."[14] I still share something like this fancy, but it is not exactly a fantasy of the reign of universal hermeneutics. It is rather the fantasy that the very idea of hermeneutics should disappear, in the way in which old general ideas do disappear when they lose polemical and contrastive force – when they begin to have universal applicability. My fantasy is of a culture so deeply antiessentialist that it makes only a sociological distinction between sociologists and physicists, not a methodological or philosophical one.

In order to spell out my fantasy in detail, I shall use strategies suggested by my favorite contemporary antiessentialist, Donald Davidson. Davidson seems to me to be doing the same job within the vocabulary of analytic philosophy (roughly, the vocabulary which has replaced "thoughts" by "sentences" and "ideas" by "words") which Dewey did within an earlier philosophical vocabulary. Both spend most of their time breaking down the Greek dualisms which, like Heidegger, they see essentialism as having built into the philosophical problematic. Davidson is particularly good at breaking down a distinction which his teacher, Quine, unfortunately left intact: that between the areas of culture in which there are "facts of the matter" (roughly, the physical sciences) and those in which there are not.

I begin with a Davidsonian topic about which Taylor is dubious – radical interpretation, the process by which Quine and Davidson think the anthropologist learns the native's hitherto unstudied language. Taylor says that Davidson's paper "Radical Interpretation" is inadequate for the same reason as are Quine's fables about occasions on which the native makes the sound "gavagai." "Like all naturalistic theories," Taylor says, those of Quine and Davidson are "framed as theories elaborated by an observer about an object observed but not participated in."[15] He admits that their theories may work for "the domain of middle-size dry goods, the ordinary material objects that surround us." But, he says, "when we come to our emotions, aspirations, goals, our social relations and practices, this cannot be. The reason is that these are already partly constituted by language, and you have to understand this language to understand them."[16]

I take the appropriate Davidsonian response to go as follows: the middle-sized dry goods are already as much or as little "constituted by language" as the emotions and the goals. For this notion that some things are "constituted by language" is just a way of saying that two groups are not talking about the same things if they talk about them very differently – if wildly different beliefs and desires are aroused in them by these things. It is not that nonlanguage constitutes

14 Taylor, "Understanding in Human Science," *Review of Metaphysics* XXXIV (1980), p. 26.
15 Charles Taylor, "Theories of Meaning," *Philosophical Papers* I, p. 255.
16 Ibid., p. 275.

some things and language others. It is rather that when the natives' and our behavior in response to certain situations is pretty much the same, we think of both of us as recognizing the plain facts of how things are – the noncontroversial objects of common sense. But when these patterns of behavior differ wildly, we shall say that we have different *Weltanschauungen,* or cultures, or theories, or that "we carve up the world differently." But it would create fewer philosophical problems just to say that when these patterns differ, communication becomes harder and translation less helpful. Translation may become so awkwardly periphrastic, indeed, that it will save time simply to go bilingual.

Examples may help make this point. Davidson thinks that you should not translate "gavagai" as "rabbit" nor "Unheimlichkeit" as "homelessness" unless you are prepared to say that most of what you translate the natives as saying about rabbits, and most of what you translate the Germans as saying about homelessness is true. You should also be prepared to say that most of their desires concerning these objects are reasonable ones. More simply, you should not make these translations unless you find the natives behaving toward gavagais pretty much as we behave toward rabbits, and the Germans toward Unheimlichkeit pretty much as we behave toward homelessness.

You will be led to revise your tentative translation of "Unheimlichkeit" by realizing that the Germans would have to be crazy to say *that* about *homelessness,* and to react in *that* way to the threat of it. You may be led to revise your translation of "gavagai" once you recognize the crucial role played by gavagais in the spiritual life of the tribe, and once you recall the occurrence of the root "gav" in various words which you have provisionally translated as specifically theological terms. It may turn out that Taylor will have to view gavagais, though not rabbits, as "constituted by language."

Conversely, it might turn out that the native word "boing," though the name of an emotion, is easily and elegantly translated by "nostalgia," and indeed that all known languages have a word equally easily so translated. The temptation to say that nostalgia is constituted by language would then become as slight as the temptation to say that toothache was. This suggests that the interesting line is not between the human and the nonhuman, nor between material objects and emotions, but between the behavioral patterns which you and the natives share and the patterns which you do not. If all humans regret the passing of all and only the sorts of things we regret the passing of, it is likely that all mankind will have a terse and unambiguous expression which English-speakers can translate as "nostalgia." So we may complacently view "boing" as just a label for something as banally intercultural as toothache. But if the natives take gavagais as central to the structure of the universe, then it is reasonable that they should have no terse and unambiguous expression which we can translate as "rabbit." Under these circumstances, we conclude that rabbits are less banally intercultural than we had thought. We turn out to have made, initially, the same sort of mistake as was made by certain natives who rearranged, for ease of carrying, the baggage of the first Christian missionaries to arrive on their shores. These natives thought that objects consisting of short pieces of wood perpendicularly fastened a third of the way down the length of long pieces of wood – a sort of middle-sized dry good for which, as it happened, they had a terse term in their own tongue – were banally intercultural objects.

The claim I made a little way back – that we are not talking about the same thing if we say very different things about it – is both central to Davidson's view and a good illustration of antiessentialism at work. This claim amounts, once again, to an implicit denial of Russell's Principle. This principle says, you recall, that *it is not possible to make a judgment about an object without knowing what object you are making a judgment about.*

Two ideas lie behind this principle: (a) the idea that you can only be wrong about what you are largely right about, and (b) the idea that you might be right only about *what something is* and wrong in everything else you believe about it. Davidson thinks that (a) is a good idea and (b) a bad one. For him, there is no such thing as "knowing what something is" as distinct from knowing that it stands in certain relations to certain other things.[17] His antiessentialism here amounts to the claim that we cannot divide things up into what they are and what properties they have, nor (*pace* Russell and C.I. Lewis) knowledge up into knowledge *of what* and knowledge *that.* To say that you can only be wrong about what you get mostly right is not to say that you can only misdescribe what you have previously identified. It is rather to say that you can only misdescribe what you are *also* able to describe quite well. If you accept the Russellian distinction between identifying and describing, you are likely to think of the world as presenting itself to the mind as divided up into objects, divisions detectable by some means which is prior to, and independent of, the process of forming beliefs. Or, at least, you may think this about the world of banally intercultural middle-sized dry goods. However, if you start reading the history of science, or ethnography, you may begin to wonder whether this Principle applies to the strange things mentioned in these books. Then you may find yourself saying that Aristotle was talking about something that didn't exist – something initially identifiable only as "what Aristotle called *kinesis*" – and that Polynesians talk about something else that doesn't exist ("whatever it is they call *mana*").

But the same essentialist instincts which led you to accept Russell's Principle may lead you to accept Parmenides' Principle: you cannot talk about what does not exist. If so, you will look for some special kind of existence for the putatively nonexistent to have: subsistence, or notional existence, or representational exis-

---

17 This is, of course, Wittgenstein's point when he says that it takes a lot of stage-setting in the language to get the point of an ostensive definition.

tence, or mental existence. Or, perhaps, "linguistic existence" – the sort of existence which things "constituted by language" have. Cheered by this notion, you become a Diltheyan, and divide the world up into the non–language-constituted domain of natural science and the linguistically-constituted domain of the sciences of man.[18]

But we antiessentialists who believe neither Russell nor Parmenides, and who do not distinguish between objects found prior to the process of belief-formation and objects made in the course of this process, can still cut culture at pretty much the same joints as does Taylor's Diltheyan distinction. We can draw a line between objects which cause you to have beliefs about them by fairly direct causal means and other objects. In the case of the latter sort of objects, the relevant causal relations are either terribly indirect or simply nonexistent. Most middle-sized pieces of dry goods are of the former sort. These will be the objects whose names come up fairly quickly in the course of a causal explanation of how you acquired certain beliefs and desires – namely, the ones which you express in sentences which contain those same names. Tracing the causes which have led us all to have beliefs and desires about Gorbachev, for example, leads us back fairly quickly to Gorbachev himself. By contrast, the explanation of how we have been caused to have beliefs and desires about happiness, chastity, and the will of God will not lead you back to these objects. (Or rather, they will do so only on the basis of theories of immaterial causality such as Plato's or Augustine's.) The same goes for beliefs and desires about neutrinos, the number pi, the round square, *mana*, and *kinesis*. Causal explanations of how we acquired the beliefs and desires which we express by sentences containing names of *such* things will *not* normally mention those things themselves.

We antiessentialists do not think that this shows that the number pi and the virtue of chastity have another kind of ontological status than that possessed by Gorbachev and the rabbits. Once we dump the idea that the aim of inquiry is to represent objects and substitute the view that inquiry aims at making beliefs and desires coherent, then the Parmenidean question of how we can represent accurately what does not exist is irrelevant, and the notion that there is truth only about what is *real* gets set aside. So the only notion of "object" we need is that of "intentional object." An intentional object is what a word or description refers to. You find out what it refers to by attaching a meaning to the linguistic expressions to that word or description. That, in turn, you do by either translat-

---

18 The same Parmenidean considerations may move you to become a van Fraassen–style instrumentalist in the philosophy of natural science–letting atoms be "constituted" and "accepted," whereas tables are "found" and "believed in." Or they may lead you to postulate as many worlds *tout court* as there are *notional* worlds, and thus to say, with Kuhn, that Aristotle and Galileo lived in different worlds. I discuss both van Fraassen's and Kuhn's suggestions in "Is Natural Science a Natural Kind?" (above).

ing or, if necessary, becoming bilingual in, the language in which the word or description occurs. Whether that is a useful language for your purposes is as irrelevant to objecthood as the question of whether the object has any causal powers.

Antiessentialists think of objects as what we find it useful to talk about in order to cope with the stimulations to which our bodies are subjected. *All* objects, including Quine's "stimulations," are what Quine calls "posits." If you are willing to give up the idea that you can identify some *non*-posits, and to agree that what precedes positing is just stimulation and not knowledge (not, e.g., "knowledge by acquaintance" or "perceptual knowledge" or "knowledge of your own experience"), then you can avoid the idea that some objects are constituted by language and others not. The difference between banally intercultural and controversial objects will be the difference between the objects you have to talk about to deal with the routine stimulations provided by your familiars, and the objects required to deal with the novel stimulations provided by new acquaintances (e.g., Aristotelians, Polynesians, avant-garde poets and painters, imaginative colligators of texts, etc.).

So far I have been making suggestions about how to capture some of Taylor's distinctions without talking about anything being "constituted by language." What about his distinction between observing the native culture and participating in it? More specifically, what about his claim that Davidson's truth-conditional account of radical interpretation will not work because "we cannot adequately grasp what some of the truth-conditions are without some grasp of the language"[19] – that is, without previously participating in the use of that language? This is a challenge which Davidson meets fairly directly. He poses to himself the question "Can a theory of truth be verified by appeal to evidence available before interpretation has begun?"[20] and answers it by saying: Yes, if we (a) can identify certain native behavior as the holding-true of a sentence, and (b) apply the Principle of Charity. The latter condition amounts to saying that our form of life and the natives' already overlap to so great an extent that we are already, automatically, for free, participant-observers, not *mere* observers. Davidson thinks that this overlap in effect reduces the intercultural case to an intracultural one – it means that we learn to handle the weirder bits of native behavior (linguistic and other) in the same way that we learn about the weird behavior of atypical members of our own culture. Such members include quantum physicists, metaphysicians, religious fanatics, psychotics, Oscar Wilde, Mrs.

---

19 Taylor, "Theories of Meaning," p. 275.
20. Donald Davidson, "Radical Interpretation," in his *Inquiries into Truth and Interpretation* (Oxford: Oxford University Press, 1984) p. 133.

Malaprop, and so on – all the people who express paradoxical beliefs and desires in (mostly) familiar words of our mother tongue.[21]

One can imagine Davidson asking Taylor: if you grant that we can learn to talk quantum mechanics, or learn how to understand Mrs. Malaprop, on the basis of the very considerable overlap between our linguistic behavior and Planck's or Malaprop's (plus a bit of curiosity and imagination), why should you think things are any harder or any different in, for example, your imagined case of the barbarian in ancient Athens?[22] In the case of Planck, we figure out what he's going on about by asking him questions and listening to the answers, including questions about what he means by a given expression. We are satisfied that we understand him once we find ourselves bickering about quanta with him like a brother. In the case of Malaprop, as in that of someone with a weird foreign accent, we guess what she might be saying, check our guesses by responding to what we think she *ought* to have said, and so gradually pick up the knack of understanding her without conscious puzzlement or inference. Surely the Persians did the same sorts of thing when trying to cope with the Athenians? If doing this sort of thing counts as "participating" rather than "observing," then the idea of a "mere observer" is a straw man. Quine and Davidson never imagined that the radical interpreter could do his job without stimulating responsive native behavior, any more than the marine biologist could do hers without stimulating her squids. But both might deny that he need have any more empathy with his subjects than she does.

It seems to me that Taylor interprets Davidson as a kind of atomist, someone who not only, as he says, "sees meaning entirely in terms of representation,"[23] but

21 On the analogies between malapropisms and metaphors, see Davidson, "What Metaphors Mean," in his *Inquiries into Truth and Interpretation;* Davidson, "A Nice Derangement of Epitaphs," in the LePore collection cited above; and my "Unfamiliar Noises" in Part II below.

22 Taylor writes, immediately after the passage about truth-conditions which I quoted above: "observers from some totally despotic culture, dropped into classical Athens, we keep hearing this word 'equal', and its companion 'like' (*isos, homoios*). We know how to apply these words to sticks, stones, perhaps also houses and ships; for there is a tolerably exact translation in our home language (Persian). And we also know *a* way of applying them to human beings, for instance physical likeness or equality of height. But there is a peculiar way these Hellenes have of using the words which baffles us. . . ."

Taylor continues: "Now our problem is not just that we have to grasp that this is a metaphorical use. Presumably this kind of thing is not unfamiliar to us. . . . But what we have not yet got is the positive value of this mode of life. We do not grasp the ideal of a people of free agents. . . . We do not see, in other words, the nobility of this kind of life. . . . Hence, to understand what these terms represent to grasp them in their representative function, we have to understand them in their articulating-constitutive function. We have to see how they can bring a horizon of concern to a certain articulation." ("Theories of meaning," pp. 275–7; my dots sometimes indicate omissions of a paragraph or more.)

23 Taylor, "Theories of Meaning," p. 279. See also p. 255: "Seeing theory as observer's theory is another way of allowing the primacy of representation; for a theory also, on this view, should be representation of an independent reality." Davidson's subsequent writings have made his antirepresentationalism clearer than it was in the articles which Taylor was discussing.

who assumes that one can represent a little hunk of reality without simultaneously representing lots and lots of reality. But this ignores the holism which Taylor and Davidson share, and the fact that both have equally little use for Russell's Principle. Davidson thinks that you can only have one belief if you have lots, and only interpret one bit of behavior if you can interpret lots.[24] Nor is it the case that Davidson sees meaning in terms of representation, if this means that, as Taylor puts it, he "maps what is said on what is the case in such a way that along with plausible hypotheses about people's desires and intentions it issues in plausible ascriptions of propositional attitudes to speakers."[25] He does not map what is said on what is the case. Rather, he correlates what is the case with what is said (e.g., that Kurt usually utters "Es regnet" only when it is raining, "Ich bin ein Esel" only when he looks sheepish, etc.), and uses these correlations as evidence for hypotheses about truth-conditions. This is no more a process of mapping, or of representing, than is the physical scientist's use of macrostructural correlations to inspire or confirm hypotheses about microstructure.

What I have been urging is that *holism takes the curse off naturalism,* and that one can be as naturalistic as Davidson as long as one is careful to be as holist as Taylor. To be a naturalist, in this sense, is to be the kind of antiessentialist who, like Dewey, sees no breaks in the hierarchy of increasingly complex adjustments to novel stimulation – the hierarchy which has amoebae adjusting themselves to changed water temperature at the bottom, bees dancing and chess players checkmating in the middle, and people fomenting scientific, artistic, and political revolutions at the top.

What is lost at this quasi-Skinnerian level of abstraction – this level where we view all inquiry as a matter of responding to the incoherence among beliefs produced by novel stimuli? What is lost is everything that makes it possible to draw a philosophically interesting distinction between explanation and understanding, or between explanation and interpretation. That is, of course, just the sort of thing we antiessentialists *want* to lose.

What do we hope to gain? Oddly enough, it is pretty much the same thing Taylor wants to gain from deploying his Diltheyan dualisms: a safeguard against reductionism, against the idea that human beings are "nothing but" something subhuman. For notice that one consequence of giving up notions of truth as accuracy of representation, or as correspondence to how things are in themselves, is that we pragmatists cannot divide up culture into the bits which do this job well and those which do not. So we are deaf to Skinnerian attacks on notions like

---

24 For a good statement of this holism, see the closing paragraphs of Davidson's "Reality without Reference," in his *Inquiries into Truth and Interpretation.* There (p. 225) he rejects what he calls "building-block theories" for "trying to give a rich content to each sentence directly on the basis of non-semantic evidence," and ends by saying "Reference, however, drops out. It plays no essential role in explaining the relation between language and reality." Neither, Davidson has subsequently argued, does "representation."

25 Taylor, "Theories of Meaning," p. 253.

"freedom" and "dignity," deaf to the appeal of "scientism." A Skinnerlike, but holistic, naturalization of the theory of inquiry brings with it an inability to take seriously a Skinnerlike reductionism. Viewing inquiry as recontextualization makes it impossible to take seriously the notion of some contexts being intrinsically privileged, as opposed to being useful for some particular purpose.

By getting rid of the idea of "different methods appropriate to the natures of different objects" (e.g., one for language-constituted and another for non–language-constituted objects), one switches attention from "the demands of the object" to the demands of the purpose which a particular inquiry is supposed to serve. The effect is to modulate philosophical debate from a methodologico-ontological key into an ethico-political key. For now one is debating what purposes are worth bothering to fulfill, which are more worthwhile than others, rather than which purposes the nature of humanity or of reality obliges us to have. For antiessentialists, all possible purposes compete with one another on equal terms, since none are more "essentially human" than any others.

One might insist that the "desire to know the truth," construed as the desire to recontextualize rather than (with Aristotle) as the desire to know essence, remains characteristically human. But this would be like saying that the desire to use an opposable thumb remains characteristically human. We have little choice but to use that thumb, and little choice but to employ our ability to recontextualize. We are going to find ourselves doing both, whatever happens. From an ethico-political angle, however, one can say that what is characteristic, not of the human species but merely of its most advanced, sophisticated subspecies – the well-read, tolerant, conversable inhabitant of a free society – is the desire to dream up as many new contexts as possible. This is the desire to be as polymorphous in our adjustments as possible, to recontextualize for the hell of it. This desire is manifested in art and literature more than in the natural sciences, and so I find it tempting to think of our culture as an increasingly poeticized one, and to say that we are gradually emerging from the scientism which Taylor dislikes into something else, something better.[26] But, as a good antiessentialist, I have no *deep* premises to draw on from which to infer that it is, in fact, better – nor to demonstrate our own superiority over the past, or the non-Western present. All I can do is recontextualize various developments in philosophy and elsewhere so as to make them look like stages in a story of poeticizing and progress.[27]

26 I read Taylor's "The Diversity of Goods" (included in his *Philosophical Papers*, vol. 2) as a splendid contribution to this poeticization. But there is a strain in Taylor's writing – one which I think of as unfortunately Aristotelian and as opposed to the laudable, dominant Hegelian strain – which leads him to want a theory of the self as *more* than a self-reweaving mechanism. It leads him to want something like metaphysical, as well as democratic, freedom.
27 I try to spell out this notion of "the poeticization of culture" in more detail in chapter 3 of *Contingency, Irony, and Solidarity* (Cambridge: Cambridge University Press, 1989).

PART II

Non-reductive physicalism

One of the obstacles which hinders communication between German and American philosophy is that, within German philosophy, materialism and physicalism are associated with reductionism and with scientism. Conversely, within American philosophy, German philosophy is associated with contempt for natural science. But, as I see it, American philosophy has now reached a position which, though still plausibly described as "materialist" or "physicalist", is no longer in any way scientistic. Contemporary American philosophers such as Putnam and Davidson represent a strain of philosophical thought which makes philosophy no more the ally of science than of any other area of culture, and which frees analytic philosophy from the familiar charge of "reductionism".

In this paper, I shall try to show how Davidson's views, in particular, help us work out a picture of the relations between the human self and the world which, though "naturalized" through and through, excludes nothing. Davidson's work seems to me the culmination of a line of thought in American philosophy which aims at being naturalistic without being reductionist. Just as Dewey prided himself equally on his naturalism and on his aestheticism – his view of culture as the transformation of experience into art – so Davidsonian philosophy of mind and language enables us to treat both physics and poetry evenhandedly. If, as I do, one views German idealism as an overreaction to the scientism of the Enlightenment, a reaction which had the fortunate side-effect of making the intellectual world a bit safer for the Romantic Movement, then one will see both Dewey and Davidson as accomplishing an up-dated version of the latter task while correcting the anti-scientism to which the Idealists succumbed (their attempt to make natural science the study of "the merely phenomenal").

Since Davidson's work has been almost entirely in the form of essays, and since he eschews large programmatic statements, it falls to his admirers to attempt a synoptic view of his work. I shall be suggesting a perspective from which three of the theses for which he is best known can be seen as interlinked. These are the thesis that reasons can be causes, the thesis that there is no relation between non-sentences and sentences (or between non-beliefs and beliefs) called "making true", and the thesis that metaphors do not have meanings.[1]

---

[1] The first of these theses is presented and in various articles reprinted in Davidson's *Essays on actions and events* (Oxford, Oxford University Press, 1980). The second can be found on p. 194 of his

Taken together these theses lay the foundations for a non-reductive physicalism.

Before offering a definition of this sort of physicalism, let me try to illustrate it by the example of Davidson's first thesis: that reasons can (*pace* various anti-reductionist philosophers such as Anthony Kenny, G. E. M. Anscombe, and Charles Taylor) be causes. This thesis amounts to the claim that a given event can be described equally well in physiological and psychological, non-intentional and intentional, terms. When something happens inside my head just after I have opened a door – if a constellation of a few million neurons takes on a certain configuration of electrical charges – something also happens in my mind. I may, if it is a house door, acquire the belief that it is raining. If it is a cupboard door, I may acquire the belief that there is no bread left. In either case I may act. I might, for example, say something which expresses disgust and indignation. That act of speech involves movements of parts of my body.

We hope that physiology may sometime trace a pathway from the distribution of electrical charges in my brain to nerve-muscle interfaces in my throat, and thereby enable us to predict utterances on the basis of brain-states. But we already have, in what has been called "folk psychology", an explanation which predicts my action on the basis of my newly-acquired belief, taken together with the rest of my beliefs and desires. Davidson suggests that we see these two explanations as two descriptions of the same process, and the "mental" and the "physical" events as the same events under two descriptions. The difference between mind and body – between reasons and causes – is thus no more mysterious than, e.g., the relation between a macro-structural and a micro-structural description of a table.

The point of this suggestion is that the inability to translate from movement-language into action-language, or to pair off brain-states with sentences which are believed to be true by the possessor of the brain, should be no impediment to a materialist outlook. These evident inabilities do not cast doubt on a physicalism which remains uncontaminated by reductionism. The failure to hook up words or sentences in one language to words or sentences in another language by relations of synonymy or equivalence does not, on Davidson's view, tell us anything about the "irreducibility" of, e.g., minds to brains or actions to movements. So it is irrelevant to the truth of physicalism.

Generalizing this point, I shall define a "physicalist" as someone who is prepared to say that every event can be described in micro-structural terms, a description which mentions only elementary particles, and can be explained by reference to other events so described. This applies, e.g., to the events which are Mozart composing a melody or Euclid seeing how to prove a theorem. Then to say that Davidson is an *anti-reductionist* physicalist is to say that he combines this

Inquiries into truth and interpretation (Oxford, Oxford University Press, 1984) and the third at p. 247 of the same volume. I have tried to develop some implications of Davidson's second thesis in "Pragmatism, Davidson and truth" (below).

claim with the doctrine that "reduction" is a relation merely between linguistic items, not among ontological categories. To reduce the language of X's to the language of Y's one must show either (a) that if you can talk about Y's you do not need to talk about X's, or (b) that any given description in terms of X's applies to all and only the things to which a given description in terms of Y's applies. But neither sort of reduction would show that "X's are *nothing but* Y's", any more than it shows the converse.

Nothing could show that. An X is what it is and no other thing. For to be an X is, roughly, to be signified by the set of true sentences which contain the term 'X' essentially. For most interesting examples of X and Y (e.g., minds and bodies, tables and particles) there are lots of true sentences about X's in which "Y" cannot be substituted for "X" while preserving truth. The only way to show that "there are no X's" would be to show that there are no such sentences. That would amount to showing that "X" and "Y" were merely, so to speak, stylistic variations of one another. It is unlikely that any philosophically interesting cases of putative ontological reduction would be of this sort.

Further, it is very rarely the case that we can accomplish either (a) or (b) — that we can show that a given language-game which has been played for some time is, in fact, dispensable. This is because any tool which has been used for some time is likely to continue to have a use. The cases in which a tool *can* be discarded will be recognized as such only after a new tool has been devised and has been employed for some time. E.g., after a hundred years of experience with Newtonian language we may all come to agree that we no longer need Aristotelian language. After five hundred years of experience with the language of a secular culture we may find ourselves no longer bothering to use religious terminology. In such cases, X-talk just fades away, not because someone has made a philosophical or scientific discovery that there are no X's, but because nobody any longer has a use for this sort of talk. Ontological parsimony is not to be attained (as the positivists thought) by armchair "linguistic analysis", but, if at all, in everyday practice.

So to be a physicalist is, on this non-reductionist account, perfectly compatible with saying that we shall probably continue to talk about mental entities — beliefs, desires, and the like — forever. Such talk is not metaphorical, does not need to be bracketed, does not need to be made more precise or scientific, does not need philosophical clarification. Further, it would be wrong to suggest that talk about minds is necessary for convenience but is not to be taken as "the truth about the way the world is". To say that we shall always be talking about beliefs and desires is to say that folk psychology will probably remain the best way of predicting what our friends and acquaintances will do next. That is all that one could possibly mean by saying "There really are mental entities". Similarly, the best way to predict the behavior of tables will probably remain to talk about them *qua* tables rather than as collections of particles or as fuzzy replicas of the Platonic archetypal Table. That is all that one could possibly mean by saying "There really are tables".

To explain the vague flavor of paradox in this anti-reductionist view we need to turn to the second of the theses I listed above: things in the world do not make sentences (nor, a fortiori, beliefs) true. This doctrine may seem clearly paradoxical. We are inclined to say, for example, that the rain or the bread is what makes the belief which I acquired on opening the door true. It also seems paradoxical not to make a distinction between "the way the world really is" and "convenient, but metaphorical, ways of talking about the world". Yet Davidson is willing to accept both paradoxes in order to escape from the traditional Western philosophical picture, the picture dominated by what he calls, "the dualism of scheme and content". This picture is the one which suggests that certain sentences in our language "correspond to reality" whereas others are true only, so to speak, by courtesy. Sentences about elementary particles are, among reductionist physicalists, the favorite candidates for the first status. Sentences about ethical or aesthetic value are their favorite candidates for the second status. Philosophers – following along the lines of Plato's claim that the objects of opinion must be different from the objects of knowledge – often suggest that the latter are not "made true by the world" but "by us". On this reductionist view, sentences which offer evaluations, if they have any sort of truth-value at all, have it as a matter of convenience, taste, convention, or something equally "subjective".

Davidson suggests that we just drop this distinction between first- and second-class truth – between sentences which express "matter of fact" and those which do not. We can replace it by a distinction between sentences which serve a certain purpose and those which serve other purposes. For example, one purpose which a language might fulfill is the ability to describe any portion of space-time, no matter how small or large. That purpose will be served by the vocabulary of contemporary particle physics. No other vocabulary will do *that* job so well. All other purposes – e.g., predicting what tables or people will do, praising God, curing mental and physical diseases, writing witty verse, etc. – will be better achieved by using other vocabularies. But these purposes are, for Davidson, on a par. Unlike Quine, he is not about to praise the language of physics on metaphysical grounds, as "limning the true and ultimate structure of reality".

We can now see how the first two Davidsonian theses tie together. To adopt Davidson's view toward the notions of "correspondence with reality" and "matter of fact" is to eschew the impulse which leads to reductionism, and a fortiori to a materialist reductionism. To adopt Davidson's view of the relation between reasons and causes, or more broadly, between the mental and the physical, is to grant the materialist everything he should want – to gratify all his legitimate needs, to permit him to pay all the compliments to the physical sciences which they deserve. But it will not permit him to gratify his metaphysical, reductionist

FIGURE 1

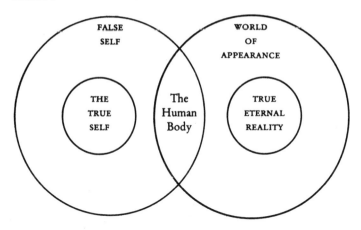

needs. It will not permit him to claim that he has finally grasped the "essence" of the world or of human beings.

As I have said, I see Davidson as the culmination of the holist and pragmatist strains in contemporary analytic philosophy. These motifs, in turn, are the culmination of a long struggle (which extends far outside the boundaries of "analytic" philosophy) against Platonic and religious conceptions of the world. So I shall try to exhibit the importance of this struggle by sketching three models of the relation between the human self and the world. I think these three models sum up – rather crudely, to be sure – the history of Western metaphysics.

The first model of the relation between the self and the world which I want to consider is a rather simple one. It is intended to represent the least common denominator of Platonism and Christianity. Figure 1 shows two intersecting spheres representing, respectively, the False Self and the World of Appearance. The intersection between the two spheres constitutes the Human Body, everything which we share with the beasts. The two larger spheres contain two smaller spheres, representing, respectively, the True Self and True Eternal Reality. The basic idea of Platonism and of Christianity is that insofar as we can clear away the outer spheres, the inner spheres will turn out to be connate, and perhaps even identical.

This model thus expresses a simple and uncomplicated hope to be reunited with something larger and better than oneself by "seeing through" veils of illusion, or by freeing oneself from the impurities caused by Sin. It culminates in the ascent to the highest level of Plato's "divided line", or in the Christian Beatific Vision, or, generally, in a sense of one's own identity with the larger and better being one has, unwittingly, been all the time. On this model, inquiry into contingent empirical facts is useful, at best, for the purpose of constructing a ladder which takes one up and away from such facts. It is a ladder which, we hope, can eventually be thrown away.

Once it is conceded (as the West conceded in the 17th and 18th centuries) that "True Reality" is as Democritus conceived it rather than as Plato conceived it, the moral and religious impulses common to Platonism and Christianity have to find their object in the True Self. God is now "within", in the sense that the attempt to escape from the world of time and chance is now pictured according to some variant of the model depicted in Figure 2.

In this diagram, the world (which now includes the human body) is thought of as "atoms and the void", devoid of moral or religious import. The Self, on the other hand, has grown more complex and interesting, just as the World has become simpler and less interesting. The Self is now conceived of as having three layers: an outermost layer consisting of empirical, contingent, beliefs and desires, a middle layer which contains necessary, a priori, beliefs and desires and which "structures" or "constitutes" the outer layer, and an ineffable inner core which is, roughly, the True Self of the Platonic-Christian model. The last is the realm of Fichtean noumenal agency, Schopenhauerian Will, Diltheyan *Erlebnisse*, Bergsonian intuition, the voice of conscience, intimations of immortality, etc. This ineffable core – the Inner Self – is what "has" the beliefs and desires which form the Middle and Outer Selves. It is not identical with that system of beliefs and desires, and its nature cannot be captured by reference to beliefs and desires.

I shall call this the "post-Kantian" model in order to suggest that some version of this model has been taken for granted by most Western philosophers during the last two centuries. After the world was turned over to physical science, only the Self remained as the preserve of philosophy. So most philosophy in this period has consisted in attempts to specify the relation between the three parts of this self, as well as the relation of each part to physical reality.

In Figure 2, the line labeled "causation" goes both ways between the Outer Self and the World, but there are other lines which go only one way. The line labeled "making true" goes from the World to the Outer Self, and that labeled "representation" goes from the Outer Self to the World. There is also a relation of "constitution" which goes from the Middle Self (the realm of necessary truths and a priori structures) to the World. The transformation of this second, post-Kantian, model into the third – the "non-reductive physicalist" model – is accomplished by erasing all these lines except the one labled "causation". This process of erasure can be thought of as having the following steps:

(a) We erase the line labeled "representation" by construing a belief as Peirce did: as rule for action rather than as a kind of picture made out of mind-stuff. That is, we think of beliefs as tools for handling reality, determinations of how to act in response to certain contingencies, rather than as representations of reality. On this view, we no longer have to worry about, e.g., the question "Does physics

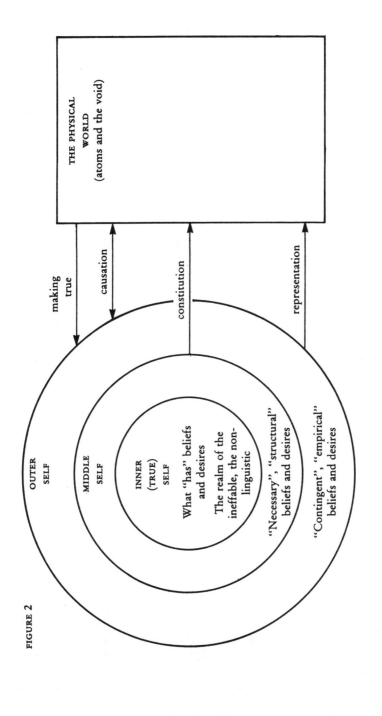

FIGURE 2

THE PHYSICAL
WORLD
(atoms and the void)

making
true

causation

constitution

representation

OUTER
SELF

MIDDLE
SELF

INNER
(TRUE)
SELF

What "has" beliefs
and desires

The realm of the
ineffable, the non-
linguistic

"Necessary", "structural"
beliefs and desires

"Contingent", "empirical"
beliefs and desires

correspond to the structure of the world as it is, or merely to the structure of the world as it appears to us?" because we cease to think of physics as *corresponding* to anything. The question of whether the heavens are actually laid out with the sun at the middle becomes equivalent to the question of whether Ptolemy or Copernicus gives us better tools for coping with the world.

(b) We erase the line labeled "constitution", having first erased the boundary between the Outer and Middle Selves. This latter erasure is the result of following Quine's lead: blurring the distinction between necessary and contingent truths. This latter distinction is blurred by adopting an "externalist" rather than an "internalist" approach to a person's utterances. Instead of asking the person to distinguish between the beliefs and desires he or she cannot imagine giving up (the so-called "a priori" ones) and the rest, one abandons introspection. Instead, one asks whether an observer of the person's linguistic behavior would be able to distinguish the expression of a "contingent" empirical platitude (Quine's example is "there have been some black dogs") from that of a "necessary truth" (e.g., "2 plus 2 is 4"). So posed, the answer which Quine gives to the question seems inevitable: all one is going to get by observation of behavior is a measure of the degree of stubbornness which the person exhibits toward giving up the belief. When this softening of a difference of kind into a difference of degree is internalized, all that introspection can do is to estimate the degree of "centrality" which a belief has in one's system of beliefs; the introspector can no longer spot an absolute property called "unimaginability of the opposite" but only one called "degree of difficulty in imagining how to fit the opposite in with the rest of one's beliefs". This means that there is no longer a distinction between constituting "structure" and constituted "empirical truth", nor between transcendental "categories" and mere "empirical concepts". Davidson generalizes this point as the claim that we should abandon the distinction between scheme and content.[2]

(c) Just as Peirce erased the line labeled "representation", and Quine the one labeled "constitution", so Davidson erases the one labeled "making true". This erasure amounts to saying that if we have causal relations (like that between the opening of the door and the acquisition of a belief) holding between the World and the Self, as well as relations of justification ("being a reason for") internal to the Self's network of beliefs and desires, we do not need any further relations to explain how the Self gets in touch with World, and conversely. We can tell an adequate story about the progress of human inquiry (in all spheres – logic and ethics as well as physics) by describing the continual reweaving of systems of belief and desire. This reweaving is made necessary by the acquisition of new beliefs and desires – e.g., the sort which are caused to occur in human beings by such events in the World as the opening of doors. (And, as I explain below, by the invention of "successful" metaphors.) We do not need to raise the question (cen-

---

2 See "On the very idea of a conceptual scheme" in Davidson's *Inquiries into truth and interpretation.*

tral to Michael Dummett's contrast between "realism" and "anti-realism") of whether there are things in the world which make algebraic and moral truths, or aesthetic judgments, true. For, although there are causes of the acquisition of beliefs, and reasons for the retention or change of beliefs, there are no causes for the *truth* of beliefs.

The result of these successive erasures is to leave us with the non-reductive materialist model, which may be diagrammed in Figure 3.

In this model, the distinction between Self and World has been replaced with the distinction between an individual human being (describable in both mental and physical terms) and the rest of the universe. The former is delimited by the contours of the body, and the task of explaining the relations between events occurring within that boundary and all other events is a matter of postulating, or observing, entities within these contours: inner causes of the human being's behavior. These causes include both micro-structural and macro-structural, and both mental and physical, items: among them are hormones, positrons, neural synapses, beliefs, desires, moods, diseases, and multiple personalities.

The way in which I have diagrammed this third model may suggest that something has been left out – namely, how things look from the inside. This, indeed, is one of the standard objections to materialism – that it leaves out "consciousness", how things look from within the individual human being.[3] I think that the answer to this is that the "inside view" discloses some, but not all, of the internal causes of the human being's behavior, and discloses them under "mental" descriptions. That is, what the individual human being identifies as "himself" or "herself" is, for the most part, his or her beliefs and desires, rather than the organs, cells, and particles which compose his or her body. Those beliefs and desires are, to be sure, physiological states under another description (though in order to preserve the ontological neutrality characteristic of a non-reductionist view, we must add that certain "neural" descriptions are of psychological states under a "physical" description).

The fact that human beings can be aware of certain of their psychological states is not, on this view, any more mysterious than that they can be trained to report on the presence of adrenalin in their bloodstreams, or on their body temperature, or on a lack of blood flow in their extremities. Ability to report is not a matter of "presence to consciousness" but simply of teaching the use of words. The use of sentences like "I believe that p" is taught in the same way as that of sentences like "I have a fever". So there is no special reason to cut off "mental" states from "physical states" as having a metaphysically intimate relation to an entity called "consciousness". To take this view is, at one stroke, to eliminate most of the problematic of post-Kantian philosophy.

---

3 See Thomas Nagel: *The view from nowhere* (New York, Oxford University Press, 1985) for arguments along these lines.

But once we drop the notion of "consciousness" there is no harm in continuing to speak of a distinct entity called "the self" which consists of the mental states of the human being: her beliefs, desires, moods, etc. The important thing is to think of the collection of those things as *being* the self rather than as something which the self *has*. The latter notion is a leftover of the traditional Western temptation to model thinking on vision, and to postulate an "inner eye" which inspects inner states. For this traditional metaphor, a non-reductive physicalist model substitutes the picture of a network of beliefs and desires which is continually in process of being rewoven (with some old items dropped as new ones are added). This network is not one which is rewoven by an agent distinct from the network — a master weaver, so to speak. Rather, it reweaves itself, in response to stimuli such as the new beliefs acquired when, e.g., doors are opened.

This picture is hard to reconcile with common speech, according to which the "I" is distinct from its beliefs and desires, picks and chooses among them, etc. But we must think with the learned while continuing to speak with the vulgar. The important thing is to avoid taking common speech as committing one to the view that there is, after all, such a thing as the "True Self", the inner core of one's being which remains what it is independent of changes in one's beliefs and desires. There is no more of a center to the self than there is to the brain. Just as the neural synapses are in continual interaction with one another, constantly weaving a different configuration of electrical charges, so our beliefs and desires are in continual interaction, redistributing truth-values among statements. Just as the brain is not something that "has" such synapses, but is simply the agglomeration of them, so the self is not something which "has" the beliefs and desires, but is simply the network of such beliefs and desires. Kant's argument that the "I think" must accompany all my representations can, on this view, be construed not as an argument for a quasi-substantial background for beliefs and desires (of the sort condemned in the "Paralogisms") but simply as a way of pointing out that to have one belief or desire is automatically to have many — that to have a belief or a desire is to have one strand in a large web. The "I" which is presupposed by any given representation is just the rest of the representations which are associated with the first — associated not by being "synthesized" but by being parts of the same network, the network of beliefs and desires which must be postulated as inner causes of the linguistic behavior of a single organism.

I hope that this brief and inadequate sketch gives at least the flavor of the philosophical view to which Davidson's work has, in my opinion, added the finishing touches. In what precedes, I have attempted to show how certain lines of thought in recent American philosophy (those which originate with Peirce, James, and Dewey, and are continued by Quine, Sellars, and Putnam, as well as by Davidson) have produced a view of human beings which is "naturalistic" (in Dewey's sense) while being at the same non-reductionist. In conclusion, I shall add a few words about how this version of physicalism is able to accommodate everything worth preserving of what the "transcendentalist" philosophical tradition has identified as "the realm of spirit".

It is often thought that a proper acknowledgment of the cultural role of imaginative literature (and, more generally, of art, myth, and religion – all the "higher" things) is incompatible with a naturalistic philosophy. But this is because naturalism has been identified with reductionism, with the attempt to find a single language sufficient to state all the truths there are to state. Such an attempt is associated with the attempt to identify "literal truth" with "scientific truth" and to treat literature as offering merely "metaphorical truth", something which is not really *truth* at all. The usual conception, since Plato, has been that at most one among the various vocabularies we use mirrors reality, and that the others are at best "heuristic" or "suggestive".

On a Davidsonian view of language, metaphors do not have meanings. That is to say that they have no place in the language-game which has been played prior to their production. But they may, and indeed do, have a crucial role in the language-games which are played afterwards. For, by being literalized, becoming "dead" metaphors, they enlarge logical space. So metaphor is an essential instrument in the process of reweaving our beliefs and desires; without it, there would be no such thing as a scientific revolution or cultural breakthrough, but merely the process of altering the truth-values of statements formulated in a forever unchanging vocabulary. Davidson's treatment of metaphor chimes with Mary Hesse's description of a scientific theory as "a metaphorical redescription of the domain of the explanandum". In science, in morality and politics, as well as in the arts, we sometimes find ourselves moved to utter a sentence which, despite being prima facie false, seems illuminating and fruitful. Such sentences are, at the beginning of their careers, "mere metaphors". But some metaphors are "successful", in the sense that we find them so compelling that we try to make them candidates for belief, for literal truth.

We do this by redescribing a portion of reality in the terms suggested by the new, surprising, metaphorical sentence. For example, when the Christians began saying "Love is the only law", and when Copernicus began saying "The earth goes round the sun", these sentences must have seemed merely "ways of speaking". Similarly, the sentences "history is the history of class struggle" or "matter can be changed into energy" were, at the first utterance, prima facie false. These were sentences which a simple-minded analytic philosopher might have diagnosed as "conceptually confused", as false by virtue of the meanings of such words as "law", "sun", "history", or "matter". But when the Christians, the Copernicans, the Marxists, or the physicists had finished redescribing portions of reality in the light of these sentences, we started speaking of these sentences as hypotheses which might quite possibly be true. In time, each of these sentences became accepted, at least within certain communities of inquiry, as *obviously* true.

This phenomenon of the production and "literalizaton" of metaphors is the phenomenon which the Western philosophical tradition has felt it necessary to account for by an opposition between "matter" and "spirit". That tradition has thought of artistic creativity, and of moral or religious "inspiration", as incapable of being explained in the terms used to explain the behavior of "merely physical reality". Hence the oppositions between "freedom" and "mechanism" which have dominated the post-Kantian period in Western philosophy. But on a Davidsonian view "creativity" and "inspiration" are merely special cases of the ability of the human organism to utter meaningless sentences – that is, sentences which do not fit into old language-games, and serve as occasions for modifying those language-games and creating new ones. This ability is exercised constantly, in every area of culture and of daily life. In daily life it appears as wit. In the arts and the sciences it appears, retrospectively, as genius. But in all these cases it simply demonstrates the fact that an (individual or collective) web of beliefs and desires has been rewoven to fit an "internal" rather than an "external" stimulus – a stimulus which is a new (unfamiliar, unparaphrasable, meaningless) use of words.

As philosophers like Jacques Derrida have noted, the Western philosophical tradition has treated metaphor as a dangerous enemy. It has made much of the contrast between "literal truth" conceived of as "correspondence to reality" and "*mere* metaphor", where the latter is thought of as an alluring, seductive, danger-ous temptation – a temptation to "escape from reality". This literal-metaphorical contrast lies in the background of the opposition, characteristic of the post-Kantian period in philosophy between science and art. Traditionally, science has been associated with responsibility, morality, social virtue, and universal human interest. Art has been associated with privacy, idiosyncrasy, selfish pleasure, extreme individualism, and irresponsibility. Both Derrida and Davidson offer us help in freeing ourselves from this artificial opposition.[4]

If the West were ever to break free from this opposition, one which goes back to the "quarrel between philosophy and poetry" described by Plato, then its culture might, in an important sense, cease to be distinctively Western. It might be able to overcome the temptations to scientism which its own scientific and technologi-cal success has engendered. Davidson's non-reductive physicalism gives us, I think, all the respect for science we need, combined with more respect for poetry than the Western philosophical tradition has usually allowed itself.

4 For parallels between Derrida and Davidson, see Samuel Wheeler: "The Extension of Deconstruc-tion," *The Monist* (Sept., 1985); and his "Indeterminacy of French Interpretation: Derrida and Davidson," in *Truth and Interpretation: Perspectives on the Philosophy of Donald Davidson,* ed. E. LePore (Oxford: Blackwell, 1986), pp. 477–494.

Pragmatism, Davidson and truth

1. *Less is more*

Davidson has said that his theory of truth 'provides no entities with which to compare sentences', and thus is a 'correspondence' theory only in 'an unassuming sense'.[1] His paper 'A Coherence Theory of Truth and Knowledge' takes as its slogan 'correspondence without confrontation'.[2] This slogan chimes with his repudiation of what he calls the 'dualism of scheme and content' – the idea that something like 'mind' or 'language' can bear some relation such as 'fitting' or 'organizing' to the world. Such doctrines are reminiscent of pragmatism, a movement which has specialized in debunking dualisms and in dissolving traditional problems created by those dualisms. The close affiliations of Davidson's work to Quine's and of Quine's to Dewey's make it tempting to see Davidson as belonging to the American pragmatist tradition.

Davidson, however, has explicitly denied that his break with the empiricist tradition makes him a pragmatist.[3] He thinks of pragmatism as an identification of truth with assertibility, or with assertibility under ideal conditions. If such an identification is essential to pragmatism, then indeed Davidson is as anti-pragmatist as he is anti-empiricist. For such an identification would merely be an emphasis on the 'scheme' side of an unacceptable dualism, replacing the emphasis on the 'content' side represented by traditional empiricism. Davidson does not want to see truth identified with anything. He also does not want to view sentences as 'made true' by anything – neither knowers or speakers on the one hand nor 'the world' on the other. For him, any 'theory of truth' which analyses a relation between bits of language and bits of non-language is already on the wrong track.

On this last, negative, point, Davidson agrees with William James. James thought that no traditional theory of truth had come close to explaining 'the particular go'[4] of such a special relation, and that it was a hopeless quest. On his

---

1 Donald Davidson, *Inquiries into Truth and Interpretation* (Oxford University Press, Oxford, 1984), p. xviii.
2 This article appears in the same volume in which the present paper first appeared: *Truth and Interpretation: Perspectives on the Philosophy of Donald Davidson* (Blackwell, Oxford, 1986), pp. 307–319. The quoted slogan is at p. 307.
3 *Inquiries*, p. xviii.
4 William James, *Pragmatism* (Hackett, Indianapolis, 1981), p. 92.

view, there was no point in trying to give sense to a notion of 'correspondence' which was neutral between, e.g., perceptual, theoretical, moral and mathematical truths. He suggested that we settle for 'the true' as being 'only the expedient in our way of thinking.'⁵ When his critics chorused that 'truths aren't true because they work; they work because they are true', James thought they had missed his point, viz., that 'true' was a term of praise used for endorsing, rather than one referring to a state of affairs the existence of which explained, e.g., the success of those who held true beliefs. He thought that the moral of philosophers' failures to discover, as it were, the micro-structure of the correspondence relation was that there was nothing there to find, that one could not use truth as an *explanatory* notion.

James, unfortunately, did not confine himself to making this negative point. He also had moments in which he inferred from the false premise that

If we have the notion of 'justified', we don't need that of 'truth'

to

'True' must mean something like 'justifiable'.

This was a form of the idealist error of inferring from

We can make no sense of the notion of truth as correspondence

to

Truth must consist in ideal coherence.

The error is to assume that 'true' needs a definition, and then to infer from the fact that it cannot be defined in terms of a relation between beliefs and non-beliefs to the view that it must be defined in terms of a relation among beliefs. But, as Hilary Putnam has pointed out in his 'naturalistic fallacy' argument, 'it might be true but not X' is always sensible, no matter what one substitutes for X (the same point G. E. Moore made about 'good').⁶

Suppose that we prescind from the moments in which James fell into this error, as well as from Peirce's unfortunate attempt (of which more later) to define truth in terms of 'the end of inquiry'. Suppose that we follow up James's negative point – his polemic against the notion of 'correspondence' – and forget his occasional attempts to say something constructive about truth. We can then, I think, isolate a sense for the term 'pragmatism' which will consist *simply* in the dissolution of the traditional problematic about truth, as opposed to a constructive 'pragmatist theory of truth'. This dissolution would start from the claim that 'true' has no explanatory use, but merely the following uses:

5   Ibid., p. 100.
6   Hilary Putnam, *Meaning and the Moral Sciences* (Cambridge University Press, Cambridge, 1978), p. 108.

(a) an endorsing use

(b) a cautionary use, in such remarks as 'Your belief that S is perfectly justified, but perhaps not true' – reminding ourselves that justification is relative to, and no better than, the beliefs cited as grounds for S, and that such justification is no guarantee that things will go well if we take S as a 'rule for action' (Peirce's definition of belief)

(c) A disquotational use: to say metalinguistic things of the form 'S' is true iff
_____.'[7]

The cautionary use of the term was neglected by James, as was the disquotational use. The neglect of the former led to the association of pragmatism with relativism. The misleading association of the latter (by Tarski) with the notion of 'correspondence' has led people to think that there must have been more to this notion than James realized. Davidson, on my view, has given us an account of truth which has a place for each of these uses while eschewing the idea that the expediency of a belief can be explained by its truth.

In the sense of 'pragmatism' in which Davidson and James are both pragmatists, the term signifies adherence to the following theses:

(1) 'True' has no explanatory uses.

(2) We understand all there is to know about the relation of beliefs to the world when we understand their causal relations with the world; our knowledge of how to apply terms such as 'about' and 'true of' is fallout from a 'naturalistic' account of linguistic behavior.[8]

(3) There are no relations of 'being made true' which hold between beliefs and the world.

(4) There is no point to debates between realism and anti-realism, for such debates presuppose the empty and misleading idea of beliefs 'being made true'.[9]

Notice that, so defined, pragmatism offers no 'theory of truth'. All it gives us is an explanation of why, in this area, less is more – of why therapy is better than system-building.

Both James and Davidson would urge that the only reason philosophers

---

7 There is much to be said about the relations between these three uses, but I shall not try to say it here. The best attempt to do so which I have seen is Robert Brandom's "Pragmatism, Phenomenalism and Truth Talk," *Midwest Studies in Philosophy* XII, pp. 75–94.

8 This thesis does not, of course, entail that you can define intentional terms in non-intentional terms, nor that a semantic metalanguage can somehow be 'reduced' to Behaviorese.

9 Jamesian pragmatists heartily agree with Dummett's claim that lots and lots of the traditional 'problems of philosophy' (including the problems which Peirce thought to solve with his "Scotistic realism") are best seen as issues between realists and anti-realists over whether there are "matters of fact" in, e.g., physics, ethics, or logic. But whereas Dummett sees himself as having rehabilitated these fine old problems by semanticizing them, the pragmatist sees him as having conveniently bagged them for disposal.

thought they needed an 'explanation of what truth consists in' was that they were held captive by a certain picture – the picture which Davidson calls 'the dualism of scheme and content' and which Dewey thought of as 'the dualism of Subject and Object'. Both pictures are of disparate ontological realms, one containing beliefs and the other non-beliefs. The picture of two such realms permits us to imagine truth as a relation between particular beliefs and particular non-beliefs which (a) is non-causal in nature, and (b) must be 'correctly analysed' before one can rebut (or concede victory to) the epistemological skeptic. To adopt (1)–(4) above is to erase this picture, and thereby to erase most of the traditional philosophical dualisms which Dewey thought ought to be erased. It is also to drop the picture which the epistemological skeptic needs to make his skepticism interesting and arguable – to make it more than the philosopher's pursuit of *Unheimlichkeit*, of a sense of the strangeness of the world.

2. Peirce's half-way measure

Before turning to the question of whether Davidson in fact adheres to (1)–(4), it may be helpful to say something about Peirce's 'end of inquiry' pragmatism. This is the version of the so-called 'pragmatist theory of truth' (a misleading textbook label for a farrago of inconsistent doctrines) which has received most attention in recent years. It represents, on my view, a half-way house between idealist and physicalist theories of truth on the one hand, and (1)–(4) on the other.

Idealism and physicalism have in common the hope that

(A) 'There are rocks' is true

is true if and only if

(B) At the ideal end of inquiry, we shall be justified in asserting that there are rocks

This suggestion requires them, however, to say that

(C) There are rocks

is implied by (B) as well as by (A). This seems paradoxical, since they also wish to assert

(D) 'There are rocks' is linked by a relation of correspondence – accurate representation – to the way the world is

and there seems no obvious reason why the progress of the language-game we are playing should have anything in particular to do with the way the rest of the world is.

Idealism and physicalism are attempts to supply such a reason. The idealists suggest that

(E) The world consists of representations arranged in an ideally coherent system

thus permitting them to analyse (C) as

(F) 'There are rocks' is a member of the ideally coherent system of representations

Idealists support this move by saying that the correspondence relation of (D) cannot be a relation whose existence could be established by confronting an assertion with an object to see if a relation called 'corresponding' holds. Nobody knows what such a confrontation would look like. (The relation of 'customary response to' which holds between tables and assertions of the presence of tables is clearly not what is wanted.) Since the only criterion of truth is coherence among representations, they say, the only way of saving (D) while avoiding skepticism is (E).

The physicalists, on the other hand, analyse (A) as (D) and then argue that playing the language-games we play will eventually lead us to correspond with reality. It will do so because, so to speak, the world takes a hand in the game. This is the view of philosophers like Friedrich Engels, Jerry Fodor, Michael Devitt, Jay Rosenberg and Hartry Field. They reject the possibility of a priori discovery of the nature of reality, illustrated by the idealists' (E), but they think that one or another empirical science (or the 'unified' ensemble of them all) will provide an answer to the skeptic. These philosophers think that, although there are no entailments, there are deeply buried connections between the conditions of the truth of (B) and (C). These connections will not be discovered by an analysis of meanings but by empirical scientific work which will pry out the causal connections between, e.g., rocks and representations of rocks.

Peirce, in his earlier period, wanted to avoid both the revisionary metaphysics of idealism and the promissory notes of physicalism. He tried for a quick fix by analysing (D) as (B). He shared with the idealist and the physicalist the motive of refuting the skeptic, but he thought it enough to say that 'reality' means something like 'whatever we shall still be asserting the existence of at the end of inquiry'. This definition of reality bridges the gap the skeptic sees between coherence and correspondence. It reduces coherence to correspondence without the necessity either for metaphysical system-building or for further empirical inquiry. A simple reanalysis of the term 'reality' does the trick.

I do not think (though I once did)[10] that Peircian pragmatism is defensible, but

10 As, for instance, when I said, falsely, that 'we can make no sense of the notion that the view which can survive all objections might be false' (*Consequences of Pragmatism* [University of Minnesota Press, Minneapolis, 1982], p. 165 – passage written in 1979). I started retracting this Peircianism in the Introduction to that book (e.g., p. xlv, written in 1981) and am still at it. I was persuaded of the untenability of Peircian view by Michael Williams' 'Coherence, Justification and Truth' (*Review of Metaphysics* XXXIV (1980), pp. 243–72), in particular by his claim (p. 269) that 'we have no idea what it would be for a theory to be ideally complete and comprehensive . . . or of what it would be for inquiry to have an end'.

before transcending it I want to remark that Peirce was moving in the right direction. The Peircian pragmatist is right in thinking that the idealist and the physicalist share a common fallacy – namely that 'correspondence' is the name of a relation between pieces of thought (or language) and pieces of the world, a relation such that the relata must be ontologically homogenous. The idealist generalizes Berkeley's point by saying: nothing can correspond to a representation except a representation. So he saves us from skepticism by redescribing reality as consisting of representations. The physicalist thinks that nothing can correspond to a bit of spatio-temporal reality except by being another bit linked to the first by appropriate causal relationships. So he saves us from skepticism by offering a physicalistic account of the nature of our representations – one which shows that, as Fodor once said, the correspondence theory of truth corresponds to reality. The Peircian rises above this debate by saying that the 'about' and 'true of' relations can link utterly disparate relata, and that problems of ontological homogeneity need not arise.[11] All that is necessary is to redefine 'reality' as what the winners of the game talk about, thus insuring that the conditions laid down by (B) and (D) coincide.

The Peircian redefinition, however, uses a term – 'ideal' – which is just as fishy as 'corresponds'. To make it less fishy Peirce would have to answer the question 'How would we know that we were at the end of inquiry, as opposed to merely having gotten tired or unimaginative?' This is as awkward as 'How do we know we are corresponding to reality, rather than merely making conventionally correct responses to stimuli?' Peirce's idea of 'the end of inquiry' might make sense if we could detect an asymptotic convergence in inquiry, but such convergence seems a local and short-term phenomenon.[12] Without such a clarification of 'ideal' or 'end', the Peircian is merely telling that the conditions laid down by (B) and (D) coincide without giving us any reason for thinking they do. Nor is it clear what such a reason could consist in.

Peirce went half-way towards destroying the epistemological problematic

---

11 Peircian pragmatism is often criticized on the ground that, like idealism, it raises problems about ontological homogeneity and heterogeneity through a counter-intuitive Kantian claim that 'objects in the world owe their fundamental structure – and, if they couldn't exist without displaying that structure, their existence – to our creative activity' (Alvin Plantinga, 'How To Be An Anti-Realist', *Proceedings of the American Philosophical Association*, 56 [1982], p. 52). But this confuses a criterial claim with a causal one: the Peircian claim that 'If there are rocks, they will display their structure at the end of inquiry' and the idealist claim that 'If there were no inquiry, there would be no rocks.'

12 See Mary Hesse's distinction between 'instrumental progress' – increase in predictive ability – and 'convergence of concepts' (*Revolutions and Reconstructions in the Philosophy of Science* [Indiana University Press, Bloomington, 1980], pp. x–xi). The possibility of scientific revolutions endangers conceptual convergence, which is the only sort of convergence which will do the Peircian any good. To insure against the indefinite proliferation of such revolutions in the future one would need something like Peirce's 'metaphysics of evolutionary love', or Putnam's attempt to certify contemporary physics as 'mature'.

which motivated the metaphysical quarrels between idealists and physicalists. He did so by leaving out 'mind' and sticking to 'signs'. But he went *only* half-way because he still thought that (D) was an intuition which any philosophy had to assimilate. James went the rest of the way by saying that not only was 'true of' not a relation between ontologically homogenous relata, but was not an analyzable relation at all, not a relation which could be clarified by a scientific or metaphysical description of the relation between beliefs and non-beliefs. Deciding that no reason could be given for saying that the constraints laid down by (B) and (D) would coincide, he simply dropped (D), and with it the problematic of epistemological skepticism. He thereby set the stage for Dewey's argument that it is only the attempt to supplement a naturalist account of our interaction with our environment with a non-naturalist account (involving some third thing, intermediate between the organism and its environment – such as 'mind' or 'language') which makes that problematic seem interesting.

3. Davidson and the field linguist

What justification is there for attributing (1)–(4) to Davidson? He has asserted (3) on various occasions. But it may seem odd to attribute (4) to him, since he has often been treated as a prototypical 'realist'. (2) may also sound unDavidsonian, since he has had no truck with recent 'causal theories' in semantics. Further, his association with Tarski, and Tarski's with the notion of 'correspondence', may seem to make him an unlikely recruit for the pragmatist ranks – for pragmatism, as I have defined it, consists very largely in the claim that only if we drop the whole idea of 'correspondence with reality' can we avoid pseudo-problems.

Nevertheless, I propose to argue that all four pragmatist theses should be ascribed to Davidson. To defend this claim, I shall begin by offering an account of what I shall call 'the philosophy of language of the field linguist'. I shall claim that this is all the philosophy of language (and, in particular, all the doctrine about truth) which Davidson has, and all that he thinks anybody needs.

Davidson, like the traditional philosopher who wants an answer to the epistemological skeptic, wants us to step out of our language-game and look at it from a distance. But his outside standpoint is not the metaphysical standpoint of the idealist, looking for an unsuspected ontological homogeneity between beliefs and non-beliefs invisible to science, nor the hopeful standpoint of the physicalist, looking to future science to discover such a homogeneity. Rather, it is the mundane standpoint of the field linguist trying to make sense of our linguistic behavior. Whereas traditional theories of truth asked 'what feature of the world is referred to by "true"?', Davidson asks 'how is "true" used by the outside observer of the language-game?'

Davidson is surely right that Quine 'saved philosophy of language as a serious subject' by getting rid of the analytic-synthetic distinction.[13] Quine's best argument for doing so was that the distinction is of no use to the field linguist. Davidson follows upon this argument by pointing out that, *pace* Dummett and Quine himself,[14] the distinction between the physical objects the natives react to and their neural stimulations is of no use either. The linguist cannot start with knowledge of native meanings acquired prior to knowledge of native beliefs, nor with translations of native observation sentences which have been certified by matching them with stimulations. He must be purely coherentist in his approach, going round and round the hermeneutic circle until he begins to feel at home.

All the linguist has to go on is his observation of the way in which linguistic is aligned with non-linguistic behavior in the course of the native's interaction with his environment, an interaction which he takes to be guided by rules for action (Peirce's definition of 'belief'). He approaches this data armed with the regulative principle that most of the native's rules are the same as ours, which is to say that most of them are true. The latter formulation of the principle is an extension of Quine's remark that any anthropologist who claims to have translated a native utterance as '*p* and not-*p*' just shows that she has not yet put together a good translation manual. Davidson generalizes this: any translation which portrays the natives as denying most of the evident facts about their environment is automatically a bad one.

The most vivid example of this point is Davidson's claim that the best way to translate the discourse of a brain which has always lived in a vat will be as referring to the vat-cum-computer environment the brain is actually in.[15] This will be the analogue of construing most native remarks as about, e.g., rocks and diseases rather than about trolls and demons. In Davidson's words:

What stands in the way of global skepticism of the senses is, in my view, the fact that we must, in the plainest and methodologically most basic cases, take the objects of a belief to be the causes of that belief. And what we, as interpreters, must take them to be is what they in fact are. Communication begins where causes converge: your utterance means what mine does if belief in its truth is systematically caused by the same events and objects.[16]

---

13 'A Coherence Theory . . .', p. 313.

14 See 'A Coherence Theory . . .', p. 313: 'Quine and Dummett agree on a basic principle, which is that whatever there is to meaning must be traced back somehow to experience, the given, or patterns of sensory stimulation, something intermediate between belief and the usual objects our beliefs are about. Once we take this step, we open the door to skepticism . . . When meaning goes epistemological in this way, truth and meaning are necessarily divorced.'

15 As far as I know, Davidson has not used this example in print. I am drawing upon unpublished remarks at a colloquium with Quine and Putnam, Heidelberg, 1981.

16 'A Coherence Theory . . .', pp. 317–318. This line of argument – together with Davidson's account of reference as fallout from translation (as at *Inquiries*, pp. 219ff., 236ff.) – is my chief textual evidence for imputing (2) to Davidson.

In this passage, Davidson weds the Kripkean claim that causation must have *something* to do with reference to the Strawsonian claim that you figure out what somebody is talking about by figuring out what object most of his beliefs are true of. The wedding is accomplished by saying that Strawson is right if construed holistically – if one prefaces his claim with Aristotle's phrase 'on the whole and for the most part'. You cannot, however, use Strawson's criterion for individual cases and be sure of being right. But if *most* of the results of your translation-scheme, and consequent assignment of reference, do not conform to Strawson's criterion, then that scheme must have something terribly wrong with it. The mediating element between Strawson and Kripke is the Quinean insight that knowledge *both* of causation *and* of reference is (equally) a matter of coherence with the field linguist's own beliefs.

Thesis (2) above can be construed in either a Kripkean or a Davidsonian way. On the former, building-block, approach to reference, we want to trace causal pathways from objects to individual speech-acts. This approach leaves open the possibility that speakers may get these pathways all wrong (e.g., by being largely wrong about what there is) and thus that they may never know to what they are referring. This allows the possibility of a wholesale divorce between referents and intentional objects – just the kind of scheme-content gap which Davidson warns us against. By contrast, Davidson is suggesting that we maximize coherence and truth first, and then let reference fall out as it may.

This guarantees that the intentional objects of lots of beliefs – what Davidson calls 'the plainest cases' – will be their causes. Kripkean slippage (e.g., the Gödel-Schmidt case) must be the exception. For if we try to imagine that a split between entities referred to and intentional objects is the rule we shall have drained the notion of 'reference' of any content. That is: we shall have made it, like 'analytic', a notion which the field linguist has no use for. The linguist can communicate with the natives if he knows most of their intentional objects (i.e., which objects most of their rules for action are good for dealing with, which objects most of their beliefs are true of). But he can make as little sense of the skeptical claim that this is not 'really' communication (but just accidentally felicitous cross-talk) as of the suggestion that the 'intended interpretation' of some platitudinous native utterance is 'There are no rocks.'

Davidson's application of this view of the job of the field linguist to epistemological skepticism is as follows. Unless one is willing to postulate some intermediary between the organism and its environment (e.g., 'determinate meanings', 'intended interpretations', 'what is before the speaker's mind', etc.) then radical interpretation begins at home. So, like all other natives, we turn out to have mostly true beliefs. The argument is neat, but does it *answer* the skeptic, as the idealist and the physicalist want to do? Or does it simply tell the skeptic that his question, 'Do we ever represent reality as it is in itself?' was a bad one, as the Jamesian pragmatist does?

A skeptic is likely to reply to Davidson that it would take a lot more than an account of the needs of the field linguist to show that belief is, as Davidson says, 'in its nature veridical'.[17] He will think that Davidson has shown no more than that the field linguist must assume that the natives believe mostly what we do, and that the question of whether most of *our* beliefs are true is still wide open. Davidson can only reply, once again, that radical interpretation begins at home – that if we want an outside view of our own language-game, the only one available is that of the field linguist. But that is just what the skeptic will not grant. He thinks that Davidson has missed the philosophical point. He thinks that Davidson's outside standpoint is not, so to speak, far enough outside to count as philosophical.

As far as I can see, the only rejoinder readily available to Davidson at this point is to remark on the intuitive appeal of (2): the naturalistic thesis, which he shares with Kripke, that there is nothing more to be known about the relation between beliefs and the rest of reality than what we learn from an empirical study of causal transactions between organisms and their environment. The relevant result of this study is the field linguist's translation-manual-cum-ethnographic-report.[18] Since we already have (in dictionaries) a translation manual for ourselves, as well as (in encyclopedias) an auto-ethnography, there is nothing more for us to know *about our relation to reality* than we already know. There is no further job for philosophy to do. This is just what the pragmatist has been telling the skeptic all the time. Both the pragmatist and Davidson are saying that if 'correspondence' denotes a relation between beliefs and the world which can vary though nothing else varies – even if all the causal relations remain the same – then 'corresponds' cannot be an explanatory term. So if truth is to be thought of as 'correspondence', then 'true' cannot be an explanatory term. Pressing (2) to the limit, and freeing it from the atomistic presuppositions which Kripkean 'building-block' theories of reference add to it, results in (1).

Thus Davidson's strategy with the skeptic would seem to give him reason to subscribe to (1) as well as to (2). Whereas the physicalist invokes (2) with an eye to finding something for 'correspondence' to refer to, Davidson takes the absence of such a thing in the field linguist's results as a reason for thinking that there is nothing to look for. Like Dewey's (and unlike Skinner's) his is a *non-reductive* naturalism, one which does not assume that every important semantical term must describe a physical relationship.[19] He thinks that there will be lots of terms used by theorists who study causal relations (e.g., field linguists, particle physicists) which do not themselves denote causal relations.

---

17 'A Coherence Theory . . .', p. 314.
18 That such a manual cannot be separated from such a report is entailed by the Quine-Davidson argument that you cannot figure out beliefs and meanings independently of one another.
19 Davidson's 'Mental Events' illustrates his strategy of combining identity-with-the-physical with irreducibility-to-the-physical.

On my interpretation, then, Davidson joins the pragmatist in saying that 'true' has no explanatory use.[20] His contribution to pragmatism consists in pointing out that it has a disquotational use in addition to the normative uses seized upon by James. The traditional philosophical attempt to conflate these two kinds of use, and to view them both as explained by the use of 'true' to denote a non-causal relation called 'correspondence', is, on this account, a confused attempt to be inside and outside the language-game at the same time.

My interpretation, however, must deal with the fact that Davidson, unlike the pragmatist, does not present himself as repudiating the skeptic's question, but as answering it. He says that 'even a mild coherence theory like mine must provide a skeptic with a reason for supposing coherent beliefs are true.'[21] Again, he says 'the theory I defend is not in competition with a correspondence theory, but depends for its defense on an argument that purports to show that coherence yields correspondence.'[22] This sounds as if Davidson were not only adopting something like (D) above, but claiming to deduce (D) from (B), in the manner of idealism and Peircean pragmatism. In wanting 'correspondence without confrontation', he shows that he shares with these latter 'isms' the view that we cannot compare a belief with a non-belief to see if they match. But what does Davidson suppose is left of correspondence after confrontation is taken away? What is it that he thinks the skeptic wants? What is it that he proposes to give the skeptic by making coherence yield it?

Davidson says that the skeptical question he wishes to answer is: 'how, given that we "cannot get outside our beliefs and our language so as to find some test other than coherence" we nevertheless can have knowledge and talk about an objective public world which is not of our making?'[23] But this does not help us much. Only if one held some view which made it mysterious that there could be such knowledge and such talk (e.g., one which required ontological homogeneity between beliefs and non-beliefs, or one which thought that there was an intermediary 'scheme' which 'shaped' the non-beliefs before they became talkable-about), would this be a challenging question. If there is to be a problem here, it must be because the skeptic has been allowed to construe 'objective' in such a way that the

20 One might object, as Alan Donagan has suggested to me, that the fact that both the linguist's and the native's beliefs are mostly true is an explanation of the fact that they are able to communicate with one another. But this sort of explanation does not invoke a causally efficacious property. It is like explaining the fact of communication by saying that the two inhabit the same space-time continuum. We do not know what it would be like for them not to, any more than we know what it would be like for one or the other to have mostly false beliefs. The only candidates for causally efficacious properties are properties which we can imagine away.

21 'A Coherence Theory . . .', pp. 309–310.

22 'A Coherence Theory . . .', p. 307.

23 'A Coherence Theory . . .', p. 310. Davidson correctly says, in this passage, that I do not think this is a good question. I am here trying to explain what is wrong with it, and why I think Davidson too should regard it as a bad question.

connection between coherence and objectivity has become unperspicuous.[24] What sense of 'correspondence' will both preserve this lack of perspicuity and yet be such that Davidson can argue that coherence will yield it?

To make a start, we can note that Davidson thinks 'correspondence' is not, as correspondence-to-*fact* theorists believe, a relation between a sentence and a chunk of reality which is somehow isomorphic to that sentence. In 'True to the Facts', he agrees with Strawson that facts – sentence-shaped chunks of the world – are *ad hoc* contrivances which do not answer to the skeptic's needs. What does, he thinks, is the more complex notion of correspondence made intelligible by Tarski's notion of satisfaction. Rather than thinking of the correspondence of language to reality as symbolized by the relation between two sides of a T-sentence, Davidson says, we should attend to word–world rather than sentence–world mappings, and in particular to the constraints on such mappings required for 'the elaboration of a nontrivial theory capable of meeting the test of entailing all those neutral snowbound trivialities' (viz., the T-sentences).[25]

These constraints are what guide the field linguist who tries to guess the causes of the native's behavior, and then goes around the hermeneutic circle long enough to come up with T-sentences which maximize the truth of the native's beliefs. The eventual theory will link native words with bits of the world by the satisfaction-relation, but these links will not be the basis for the translations. Rather, they will be fallout from the translations. Going around this circle means not attempting (in the manner of building-block theories of reference) to start with some 'secure' links, but rather going back and forth between guesses at translations of occasion-sentences and of standing sentences until something like Rawlsian 'reflective equilibrium' emerges.

The correspondence between words and objects provided by the satisfaction-relations incorporated in a T-theory are thus irrelevant to the sort of correspondence which was supposed to be described by 'true of', and which is supposed to be revealed by 'philosophical analysis', culminating in a 'theory of truth'. So whatever the skeptic's desired correspondence may be, it is not something which is captured in Tarski's account of satisfaction. For 'true' does not offer material for analysis. As Davidson says,

> Truth is beautifully transparent compared to belief and coherence and I take it as primitive. Truth, as applied to utterances of sentences, shows the disquotational feature enshrined in Tarski's Convention T, and that is enough to fix its domain of application.[26]

---

24 I think that Davidson may be worrying, in this passage, about the sort of identification of criterial and causal relations for which I criticized Plantinga in note 11 above. This is the sort of identification which is characteristic of idealism, and which generates fear that coherence theories will result in human beings having 'constituted the world'. On my interpretation, he has already disposed of that identification, and thus of the need for worry.

25 *Inquiries*, p. 51.

26 'A Coherence Theory . . .', p. 308.

So we cannot define 'true' in terms of satisfaction, nor of anything else. We can only explain our sense that, as Davidson says, 'the truth of an utterance depends on just two things, what the words mean and how the world is arranged' by explaining how we go about finding out these two things, and by pointing out that these two inquiries cannot be conducted independently.

I think Davidson should be interpreted as saying that the plausibility of the thesis just cited – that there is no third thing relevant to truth besides meanings of words and the way the world is – is the best explanation we are going to get of the intuitive force of (D): the idea that 'truth is correspondence with reality.' This thesis is all there is to the 'realistic' intuition which idealists, physicalists, and Peirceans have been so concerned to preserve. But, so construed, (D) makes the merely *negative* point that we need not worry about such *tertia* as, in Davidson's words, 'a conceptual scheme, a way of viewing things, a perspective' (or a transcendental constitution of consciousness, or a language, or a cultural tradition). So I think that Davidson is telling us, once again, that less is more: we should not ask for more detail about the correspondence relation, but rather realize that the *tertia* which have made us have skeptical doubts about whether most of our beliefs are true are just not there.

To say that they are not there is to say, once again, that the field linguist does not need them – and that therefore philosophy does not need them either. Once we understand how radical interpretation works, and that the interpreter can make no good use of notions like 'determinate meaning', 'intended interpretation', 'constitutive act of the transcendental imagination', 'conceptual scheme', and the like, then we can take the notion of 'correspondence to reality' as trivial, and not in need of analysis. For this term has now been reduced to a stylistic variant of 'true'.

If this is indeed what Davidson is saying, then his answer to the skeptic comes down to: you are only a skeptic because you have these intentionalistic notions floating around in your head, inserting imaginary barriers between you and the world. Once you purify yourself of the 'idea idea' in all its various forms, skepticism will never cross your enlightened mind. If this *is* his response to the skeptic, then I think he is making exactly the right move, the same move which James and Dewey were trying, somewhat more awkwardly, to make. But I also think Davidson was a bit misleading in suggesting that he was going to show us how coherence yields correspondence. It would have been better to have said that he was going to offer the skeptic a way of speaking which would prevent him from asking his question, than to say that he was going to answer that question. It would have been better to tell him that when confrontation goes, so does representation, and thus the picture which made possible both the fears of the skeptic and the hopes of the physicalist, the idealist and the Peircean.

Davidson's favorite characterization of the picture which the skeptic should abjure is 'the dualism of scheme and content'. A common feature of all the forms of this dualism which Davidson lists is that the relations between the two sides of the dualism are non-causal. Such *tertia* as a 'conceptual framework' or an 'intended interpretation' are non-causally related to the things which they organize or intend. They vary independently of the rest of the universe, just as do the skeptic's relations of 'correspondence' or 'representation'. The moral is that if we have no such *tertia*, then we have no suitable items to serve as representations, and thus no need to ask whether our beliefs represent the world accurately. We still have beliefs, but they will be seen from the outside as the field linguist sees them (as causal interactions with the environment) or from the inside as the pre-epistemological native sees them (as rules for action). To abjure *tertia* is to abjure the possibility of a third way of seeing them – one which somehow combines the outside view and the inside view, the descriptive and the normative attitudes. To see language in the same way as we see beliefs – not as a 'conceptual framework' but as the causal interaction with the environment described by the field linguist, makes it impossible to think of language as something which may or may not (how could we ever tell?) 'fit the world'. So once we give up *tertia*, we give up (or trivialize) the notions of representation and correspondence, and thereby give up the possibility of formulating epistemological skepticism.

If my understanding of Davidson is right, then – apart from his appeal to physicalistic unified science, the appeal formulated in the pragmatist's (2) – his only arguments for the claim that the philosophy of language of the field linguist is all we need will be the arguments offered in 'On the Very Idea of a Conceptual Scheme' to the effect that various 'confrontationalist' metaphors are more trouble than they are worth. All that we might add would be further arguments to the same point drawn from the history of philosophy – illustrations of the impasses into which the attempts to develop those metaphors drew various great dead philosophers. It will not be an empirical or a metaphysical discovery that there is no *tertium quid* relevant to the truth of assertions, nor a result of 'analysis of the meaning' of 'true' or 'belief' or any other term. So, like James (though unlike Peirce) Davidson is not giving us a new 'theory of truth'. Rather, he is giving us reasons for thinking that we can safely get along with less philosophizing about truth than we had thought we needed. On my interpretation, his argument that 'coherence yields correspondence' comes down to saying the following: From the field linguist's point of view, none of the notions which might suggest that there was more to truth than the meaning of words and the way the world is are needed; if you are willing to assume this point of view you will have no more skeptical doubts about the intrinsic veridicality of belief.

4. Davidson as non-reductive physicalist

Before turning to a well-known set of objections to the claim that the philosophy of the field linguist is all the philosophy of language we need – those of Michael Dummett – it will be useful to compare Davidson with a philosopher to whom he is, beneath a few superficial differences in rhetoric, very close: Hilary Putnam. Putnam is a proponent of many familiar pragmatist doctrines. He makes fun, as James and Dewey did, of the attempt to get an outside view – a 'God's-eye-view' of the sort which the traditional epistemologist, and the skeptic, have tried for. But when he confronts disquotationalist theories of truth he is troubled. They smell reductionist to him, and he sees them as symptoms of a lingering positivism, a 'transcendental Skinnerianism'. Putnam says:

> If a philosopher says that *truth* is different from *electricity* in precisely this way: that there is room for a theory of electricity but *no room* for a theory of truth, that knowing the assertibility conditions is *all there is to know* about truth, then, in so far as I understand him at all, he is denying that there is a *property* of truth (or a property of rightness or correctness), not just in the realist sense, but in *any* sense. But this is to deny that our thoughts and assertions are *thoughts* and *assertions*.[27]

Putnam is here assuming that the only reason why one might disclaim the need for a theory of the nature of X is that one has discovered that Xs are 'nothing but' Ys, in good reductivist fashion. So he thinks that Davidson's abjuration of 'an account of what it is for an assertion to be correct and what it is for it to be incorrect' must be made on the basis of a reduction of true assertions to conventionally accepted noises.[28] On this view, to assume the point of view of the field linguist is to reduce actions to movements. But Davidson is not saying that assertions are nothing but noises. Rather he is saying that truth, unlike electricity, is not an explanation of anything.

The idea that the property of truth can serve as an explanation is a product of the misleading picture which engenders the idea that its presence requires an explanation. To see this, notice that it would be a mistake to think of 'true' as having an explanatory use on the basis of such examples as 'He found the correct house because his belief about its location was true' and 'Priestley failed to understand the nature of oxygen because his beliefs about the nature of combustion were false.' The quoted sentences are not explanations but promissory notes for explanations. To get them cashed, to get real explanations, we need to say things like 'He found the correct house because he believed that it was located at . . .' or 'Priestley failed because he thought that phlogiston . . .'. The explanation of success and failure is given by the details about what was true or what was false, not by the truth or falsity itself – just as the explanation of the praiseworthiness of an action is not 'it was the right thing to do' but the details of the circumstances in which it was done.[29]

27 Hilary Putnam, *Realism and Reason* (Cambridge University Press, Cambridge, 1983), p. xv.
28 Ibid., p. xiv.
29 The line of argument I have been employing in this paragraph may also be found in Michael Levin, 'What Kind of Explanation is Truth?' (in *Scientific Realism*, ed. Jarrett Leplin [University of California Press, Berkeley, 1984], pp. 124–39) and in Michael Williams, 'Do We (Epistemologists) Need a Theory of Truth?', *Philosophical Topics*, 1986.

If truth *itself* is to be an explanation of something, that explanandum must be of something which can be caused by truth, but not caused by the content of true beliefs. The function of the *tertia* which Davidson wishes to banish was precisely to provide a mechanism outside the causal order of the physical world, a mechanism which could have or lack a quasi-causal property with which one might identify truth. Thus to say that our conceptual scheme is 'adequate to the world', is to suggest that some cogs and gears are meshing nicely – cogs and gears which are either non-physical or which, though physical, are not mentioned in the rest of our causal story. To suggest, with the skeptic, that our language-game may have nothing to do with the way the world is, is to call up a picture of a gear-wheel so out of touch with the rest of the mechanism as to be spinning idly.[30]

Given his distaste for intentionalist notions, Putnam should have no relish for such pictures, and thus no inclination to regard truth as an explanatory notion. But because he still retains the idea that one should give an 'account of what it is for an assertion to be correct', he demands more than Davidson is in a position to give. He retains this idea, I think, because he is afraid that the inside point of view on our language-game, the point of view where we use 'true' as a term of praise, will somehow be weakened if it receives no support from 'a philosophical account'. Consider the following passage:

If the cause-effect-description [of our linguistic behavior qua production of noises] is complete from a philosophical as well as from a behavioral-scientific point of view; if all there is to say about language is that it consists in the production of noises (and subvocalizations) according to a certain causal pattern; *if the causal story is not to be and need not be supplemented by a normative story* . . . then there is no way in which the noises we utter . . . are more than mere 'expressions of our subjectivity'. . .[31]

The line I have italicized suggests that disquotationalist theorists of truth think that there is only one story to be told about people: a behavioristic one. But why on earth should such theorists not allow for, and indeed insist upon, supplementing such stories with 'a normative story'? Why should we take the existence of the outside point of view of the field linguist as a recommendation never to assume the inside point of view of the earnest seeker after truth? Putnam, I think, still takes a 'philosophical account of *X*' to be a synoptic vision which will somehow synthesize every other possible view, will somehow bring the outside and the inside points of view together.

It seems to me precisely the virtue of James and of Dewey to insist that we cannot have such a synoptic vision – that we cannot back up our norms by 'grounding' them in a metaphysical or scientific account of the world. Pragma-

---

30 Davidson's position, as Alan Donagan has pointed out to me, is the same as Wittgenstein's: no gears are necessary, for the sentences in which our beliefs are expressed touch the world directly. See *Tractatus Logico-Philosophicus*. 2.1511–2.1515.

31 Hilary Putnam, 'On Truth', in *How Many Questions*, ed. Leigh S. Cauman et al. (Hackett, Indianapolis, 1983), p. 44.

tism, especially in the form developed by Dewey, urges that we not repeat Plato's mistake of taking terms of praise as the names of esoteric things – of assuming, e.g., we would do a better job of being good if we could get more theoretical knowledge of The Good. Dewey was constantly criticized, from the Platonist right, for being reductionist and scientistic, inattentive to our needs for 'objective values'. This is the kind of criticism Davidson is currently getting from Putnam. He was also constantly criticized, from the positivist left, for a light-minded relativistic instrumentalism which paid too little attention to 'hard facts', and for trivializing the notion of 'truth' by this neglect.[32] This is the kind of criticism Davidson gets from physicalists such as Field.

Attack from both sides is the usual reward of philosophers who, like Dewey and Davidson, try to stop the pendulum of philosophical fashion from swinging endlessly back and forth between a tough-minded reductionism and a high-minded anti-reductionism. Such philosophers do so by patiently explaining that norms are one thing and descriptions another. In Davidson's case, this comes down to saying that the understanding you get of how the word 'true' works by contemplating the possibility of a Tarskian truth-theory for your language is utterly irrelevant to the satisfaction you get by saying that you know more truths today than you did yesterday, or that truth is great, and will prevail. Putnam's insistence that there is more to truth than disquotationalism can offer is not based on having looked at 'true', or at the language-games we play, and having seen more than Davidson saw. Rather, it is based on a hope that there is more to the notion of a 'philosophical account' than Dewey or Davidson think there can be.

This parallel between Dewey and Davidson seems to me reinforced by Stephen Leeds' formulation of what he calls 'Naturalistic Instrumentalism': the Quine-like combination of the view that 'the only goal relative to which our methods of theory construction and revision fall into place as a rational procedure is the goal of prediction observations'[33] with the claim that the world is, really and truly *is*, made up of the entities of current science. As Leeds says, this new 'ism' may sound like an oxymoron (as a similar 'ism' did to Dewey's critics). But it only sounds that way if, as Leeds says, one thinks that 'a theory of truth is needed to explain why our theories work'[34] – if one thinks that 'truth' can be an explanatory notion. Leeds and Arthur Fine[35] have pointed out the circularity of attempts to use semantics to explain our predictive successes. Such circularity is the natural consequence of trying to be both outside our inquiries and inside them at the same time – to describe them both as motions and as actions. As Davidson has

---

32 So, simultaneously, was Neurath – who is beginning to get a better press these days.

33 Stephen Leeds, 'Theories of Reference and Truth', *Erkenntnis*, 13 (1978), p. 117.

34 Dewey would not have restricted theory construction and revision to the sciences which aim at prediction and control, but this difference between Dewey and Leeds is not relevant to the point at hand.

35 In his 'The Natural Ontological Attitude', in *Essays on Scientific Realism*, ed. J. Leplin.

reiterated in his writings on the theory of action, there is no need to choose between these two descriptions: there is only a need to keep them distinct, so that one does not try to use both at once.

5. Davidson and Dummett

The question of whether 'truth' is an explanatory property encapsulates the question of whether the philosophy of the field linguist is philosophy of language enough or whether (as Michael Dummett thinks) we need a philosophy of language which links up with epistemology, and with traditional metaphysical issues. Dummett says that a theory of meaning should tell us how:

an implicit grasp of the theory of meaning, which is attributed to a speaker, issues in his employment of the language and hence . . . in the content of the theory. Holism in respect of how one might, starting from scratch, arrive at a theory of meaning for a language, on the other hand, has no such implications, and is, as far as I can see, unobjectionable and almost banal. It is certain that Davidson intends his holism as a doctrine with more bite than this.[36]

Dummett thinks that what you get out of Davidsonian radical interpretation does not include 'the content' of a theory of meaning – 'the specific senses speakers attach to the words of the language'. But on the interpretation of Davidson I have been offering, what Dummet calls a 'sense' is just the sort of *tertium quid* which Davidson wants us to forget about. So the bite of Davidson's theory is not the sort Dummett wants. Dummett wants a theory that bites down on the problems which he thinks can only be formulated when one has a theory of 'sense' – e.g., epistemological and metaphysical issues. Davidson wants a theory of meaning which will serve the field linguists' purposes and to which such problems are irrelevant.

Dummett's argument that more is needed than Davidson gives us is that somebody could know the ensemble of truth-conditions produced by a Davidsonian interpreter without knowing the content of the right-hand, metalinguistic, portions of the T-sentences. He thinks that 'a T-sentence for which the metalanguage contains the object-language is obviously unexplanatory' and that if this is so then 'a T-sentence for an object-language disjoint from the metalanguage is equally unexplanatory.'[37] Davidson will reply that no single T-sentence – no single 'neutral snowbound triviality' – will tell you what it is to understand any of the words occurring on the left-hand sides, but that the whole

---

36 Michael Dummett, 'What Is a Theory of Meaning?' in *Mind and Language,* ed. Samuel Guttenplan (Oxford University Press, Oxford, 1975), p. 127.

37 Ibid., p. 108. Dummett actually says 'M-sentence' (i.e., a sentence of the form ' " – – " means – – ') rather than 'T-sentence'. I have changed the quotation for the sake of perspicuity. As Dummett rightly says, for Davidson's purposes the two sorts of sentence are interchangeable.

body of such sentences tells you *all* there is to know about this. Dummett regards that reply as an admission of defeat. He says:

> On such an account, there can be no answer to the question what constitutes a speaker's understanding of any one word or sentence: one can say only that the knowledge of the entire theory of truth issues in an ability to speak the language, and, in particular, in a propensity to recognize sentences of it as true under conditions corresponding, by and large, to the T-sentences.[38]

And again:

> No way is provided, even in principle, of segmenting his ability to use the language as a whole into distinct component abilities.[39]

Now it is of the essence of Davidson's position, as of the positions of Wittgenstein and Sellars, that there are no such distinct component abilities.[40] For when you get rid of such *tertia* as 'determinate meanings', 'intended interpretations', 'responses to stimuli', and the like, you are left with nothing to split up the overall know-how into component bits – nothing to reply to 'How do you know that that's called "red"?' save Wittgenstein's: 'I know English.' Davidson has to insist that the individual T-sentences do not replicate any inner structures, and that any attempt to provide such structures will pay the price of reintroducing *tertia*, entities which will get between our words and the world.

Dummett notes that Davidson tries 'to make a virtue of necessity', but insists that doing so 'is an abnegation of what we are entitled to expect from a theory of meaning.'[41] For Dummett thinks that we are entitled to a theory of meaning which will preserve the traditional notions of empiricist epistemology. He thinks that any such theory must grant that 'an ability to use a given sentence in order to give a report of observation may reasonably be taken, as a knowledge of what has to be the case for that sentence to be true.'[42]

Dummett's paradigm case of grasping the content of an expression is what you do when you observe that something is red. He thinks that the contrast between 'That's red!' and cases like 'Caesar crossed the Rubicon', 'Love is better than hate', and 'There are transfinite cardinals' is something which any adequate philosophy

38 Ibid., p. 115.
39 Ibid., p. 116.
40 A similar position is adopted by Ernest Tugendhat in his *Traditional and Analytical Philosophy* (Cambridge University Press, Cambridge, 1983). Tugendhat thinks of this position as the only alternative to the 'objectualist' account of the understanding of language which has dominated the philosophical tradition up through Husserl and Russell.
41 Dummett, 'What Is a Theory of Meaning?', p. 117. Some of the complaints about Davidson I have been citing from Dummett are modified in the appendix to 'What is a Theory of Meaning?' (pp. 123ff.). But the insistence on the point that Davidson 'can make no sense of knowing part of the language' (p. 138) and the unargued-for presumption that philosophy of language must preserve an unQuinean language-fact distinction (p. 137) remain.
42 Dummett, 'What Is a Theory of Meaning? (II)' in Gareth Evans and John McDowell (eds.), *Truth and Meaning* (Oxford University Press, Oxford, 1976), p. 95.

of language must preserve. But for Davidson's and Wittgenstein's holism there simply is no contrast. On their view, to grasp the content is, in *all* these cases, to grasp the inferential relationships between these sentences and the other sentences of the language.[43]

The same point can be made in reference to Dummett's presentation of the issue about realism and anti-realism in terms of bivalence. Dummett seems to think that the question of bivalence, of whether statements are 'determinately true or false, independently of our knowledge or our means of knowing'[44] arises only for statements made by means of sentences 'belonging to the less primitive strata of our language.'[45] He has no doubt that for the 'lower storeys' – e.g., for statements like 'That's red!' – bivalence obtains. Our inarticulable knowledge of what it is for such a statement to be true, presumably, is enough to make us realists about redness. For these types of statements we can have a strong sense of 'correspondence to reality' – 'strong' in that we are confident that what makes the statement true is 'reality' rather than merely ourselves. Here we have the empiricist picture, shared by Quine and Dummett, according to which language stands as a veil between us and reality, with reality punching its way through (or being known to punch its way through) only at the tips of a few sensory receptors. The farther into the upper storeys we get, on the other hand, the more doubt there is that we are in touch with the world, and the more temptation to be an 'anti-realist' in regard to certain entities – that is, to adopt a theory of meaning which explains the truth of such statements 'in terms of our capacity to recognize statements as true, and not in terms of a condition which transcends human capacities'.[46]

By contrast, if one follows Davidson, one will not know what to make of the issue between realist and anti-realist. For one will feel in touch with reality *all the time*. Our language – conceived as the web of inferential relationships between our uses of vocables – is not, on this view, something 'merely human' which may hide something which 'transcends human capacities'. Nor can it deceive us into thinking ourselves in correspondence with something like that when we really are not. On the contrary, using those vocables is as direct as contact with reality can

---

43 Dummett thinks that Wittgenstein's view that 'acceptance of any principle of inference contributes to determining the meaning of words' – a view which Davidson shares – is unacceptably holistic. (See 'What Is A Theory of Meaning? (II)', p. 105). Elsewhere Dummett has said that this sort of holism leads to the view that 'a systematic theory of meaning for a language is an impossibility' and thus to the view that philosophy 'seeks to remove, not ignorance or false beliefs, but conceptual confusion, and therefore has nothing positive to set in place of what it removes' (*Truth and Other Enigmas* [Harvard University Press, Cambridge, Mass., 1978], p. 453). By 'a systematic theory of meaning for a language' Dummett means one which gives him 'what we are entitled to expect', viz., a handle on traditional philosophical problems. But he begs the question against Davidson when he rebuts the holism shared by Davidson and Wittgenstein on the ground that it leads to the therapeutic approach to traditional problems shared by Dewey and Wittgenstein.

44 'What Is a Theory of meaning?' (II), p. 101.

45 Ibid., p. 100.

46 'What Is a Theory of Meaning?' (II), p. 116.

get (as direct as kicking rocks, e.g.). The fallacy comes in thinking that the relationship between vocable and reality has to be piecemeal (like the relation between individual kicks and individual rocks), a matter of discrete component capacities to get in touch with discrete hunks of reality.

If one thinks that, one will, for example, agree with Plato and Dummett that there is an important philosophical question about whether there really are moral values 'out there'. For Davidson, on the other hand, there is goodness out there in exactly the same trivial sense in which there is redness out there. The relevant sense is explicated by saying that the field linguist will come up with a T-sentence whose right-hand side is 'that's morally right' in just the same manner as he comes up with one whose right-hand side is 'that's red'. He will assume that insofar as the natives fail to find the same things red, or morally right, as we do, our disagreements with them will be explicable by various differences in our respective environments (or the environments of our respective ancestors).

I conclude that for Dummett no philosophy of language is adequate which does not permit the perspicuous reformulation of the epistemological and metaphysical issues discussed by the philosophical tradition. For Davidson this ability is not a desideratum. For James and Dewey, the *in*ability to formulate such issues was a desideratum. I should like to attribute this latter, stronger, view to Davidson, but I have no good evidence for doing so. I commend it to him, because I think that his only recourse in arguing with those who think they have a right to expect more philosophy of language than he offers is to adopt this therapeutic stance. More specifically, all he can do is point out that Dummett's expectations stem from the habit of construing correspondence as confrontation, and then exhibit the unhappy history of this construal, a history which stretches from Plato through Locke to Quine. In the end, the issue is going to be decided on a high metaphilosophical plane − one from which we look down upon the philosopical tradition and judge its worth.

6. *Davidson, realism and anti-realism*

If the argument of the preceding section is right, then Davidson has been put in a false position by Dummett's attempts to place him on the 'realist' side of a distinction between realism and anti-realism. That distinction, stated in terms of a distinction between truth-conditions and assertibility-conditions, will seem a plausible way of classifying philosophical doctrines only if one accepts what Michael Devitt has called Dummett's 'propositional assumption': the assumption that 'an L-speaker's understanding of a sentence of L consists in his knowing that the sentence is true-in-L in such and such circumstances.'[47] Davidson, however, thinks it hopeless to isolate such circumstances. His holism makes him reject the idea of such knowledge. Yet Dummett gives an account of Davidsonian 'truth-conditions' which is radically non-holistic. As Devitt rightly says, Dummett tries to infer from

47 Michael Devitt, 'Dummett's Anti-Realism', *Journal of Philosophy*, 80 (1983), p. 84.

'X knows the meaning of S' and 'The meaning of S = the truth-conditions of X' to 'S knows that the truth-conditions of X are TC', an inference which only goes through if we construe 'X knows the meaning of S' as 'there exists an entity which is the meaning of S and X is acquainted with it.'[48] The latter construal will be made only by someone who accepts the propositional assumption.

Davidson would not accept it,[49] and therefore cannot be seen as a theorist of 'truth-conditions' in Dummett's sense. Davidson thinks that one great advantage of his view is that it gives you a theory of meaning without countenancing such things as 'meanings'. Since he agrees with Quine that a theory of meaning for a language is what comes out of empirical research into linguistic behavior, Davidson would be the first to agree with Devitt, against Dummett, that 'any propositional knowledge of a language that a person has is something over and above his competence, something gained from theorizing about the language.'[50] If we bear Davidson's holism and behaviorism in mind, he will seem the last philosopher to believe that users of S are typically able to envisage acquaintance with sets of circumstances which would conclusively verify S.

Dummett misconstrues Davidson because he himself believes that (in Devitt's words), 'The only sort of behavior that could manifest the speaker's understanding of S is that behavior which brings him into the position in which, if the condition obtains that conclusively justifies the assertion of S, he recognizes it as so doing.'[51] As Devitt says, this expresses Dummett's commitment to 'anti-holist epistemology'.[52] Dummett thinks that there are some familiar cases (e.g., so-called 'observation sentences') where there are indeed such conditions, and such acts of recognition. But for Davidson there are never any of either. So the contrast which Dummett draws between, e.g., realism about tables and anti-realism about values makes no sense for Davidson. For holists, so to speak, truth is *always* evidence-transcendent. But that is to say that X's understanding of S is *never* manifested in the kind of recognitional abilities which Dummett envisages.[53]

---

48 Ibid., p. 86.

49 Devitt disagrees. He says 'Davidson is open to [Dummett's] argument because he accepts the propositional assumption' (ibid., p. 90). This willingness to accept Dummett's description of Davidson seems to me a blemish in Devitt's incisive criticism of Dummett's attempt to semanticize metaphysics. (Though, as I say below, I also disagree with Devitt's claim that desemanticizing metaphysics restores the purity of that discipline. I think that doing so merely exposes its barrenness.) I suspect the reason why Devitt thinks of Davidson as accepting the propositional assumption is that Davidson, in his earlier articles, identified a theory of meaning for L with what a speaker of L understands, an identification which suggests that the speaker *does* have 'distinct component abilities' corresponding to the various T-sentences. But this identification is, as far as I can see, either incompatible with the holism I have described in the previous section or as misleading a metaphor as that billiard balls have 'internalized' the laws of mechanics.

50 Ibid., pp. 89–90.

51 Ibid., p. 91.

52 Ibid., p. 92.

53 See Paul Horwich, 'Three Forms of Realism', *Synthese*, 51 (1982), p. 199: '[Dummett's] inference from not being able to establish when *p* is true to not being able to manifest knowledge of its

Dummett takes the upshot of Frege's linguistification of philosophy to be that the only way to make sense of a metaphysical disagreement is by semantic ascent – jacking up the old metaphysical issue into a new semantical issue. Davidson, on my interpretation, thinks that the benefit of going linguistic is that getting rid of the Cartesian mind is a first step toward eliminating the *tertia* which, by seeming to intrude between us and the world, created the old metaphysical issues in the first place. We can take the final step, and dissolve those issues for good, by not letting philosophy of language recreate the factitious contrasts in terms of which those issues were formulated, e.g., the contrast between 'objective realities' and 'useful fictions', or that between the 'ontological status' of the objects of, respectively, physics, ethics and logic. For Davidson, Quine's idea of 'ontological commitment' and Dummett's idea of 'matter of fact' are both unfortunate relics of metaphysical thought; they are among the ideas which metaphysics wove together to form the scheme-content dualism.

These ideas form such a large, mutually reinforcing, network that it is hard to pick one out as crucial. But the best candidate for being at the center of this network may be the idea repudiated in the pragmatists' thesis (3): the idea that sentences can be 'made true'. Davidson says that 'all the evidence there is is just what it takes to make our sentences or theories true. Nothing, however, no thing makes sentences or theories true: not experience, not surface irritations, not the world, can make a sentence true.'[54] I interpret this passage as saying that the inferential relations between our belief that S and our other beliefs have nothing in particular to do with the aboutness relation which ties S to its objects. The lines of evidential force, so to speak, do not parallel the lines of referential direction. This lack of parallelism is the burden of epistemological holism. To know about the former lines is to know the language in which the beliefs are expressed. To know about the latter is to have an empirical theory about what the people who use that language mean by what they say – which is also the story about the causal roles played by their linguistic behavior in their interaction with their environment.

The urge to coalesce the justificatory story and the causal story is the old metaphysical urge which Wittgenstein helped us overcome when he told us to beware of entities called 'meanings' – or, more generally, of items relevant to the fixation of belief which are, in Davidson's words, 'intermediate between belief and

---

truth-conditions is not at all compelling. All it takes to know p's truth-conditions is to understand it; and all it takes to understand p is the ability to use it in accordance with community norms, implicit in linguistic practice, for judging in various circumstances, the degree of confidence it should be given.' Horwich's own suggestion that we combine what he calls 'semantic realism' (the claim that truth may extend beyond our capacity to recognize it) with a 'use theory of meaning and a redundancy account of truth' (p. 186) seems to me a succinct description of Davidson's strategy. (For an earlier statement of Horwich's anti-Dummett point, see P. F. Strawson's criticism of Crispin Wright: 'Scruton and Wright on Anti-Realism', *Proceedings of the Aristotelian Society*, 1977, p. 16.)

54 *Inquiries*, p. 194.

the usual objects which beliefs are about'.[55] For such entities are supposed to be *both* causes *and* justifications: entities (like sense-data or surface irritations or clear and distinct ideas) which belong both to the story which justifies me in believing that S and to the story which the observer of my linguistic behavior tells us about the causes of my belief that S. Devitt succumbs to this pre-Wittgensteinian urge when he follows Field in suggesting that we can explicate the 'intuitive idea of correspondence to a "world out there" ' by making truth dependent on 'genuine reference relations between words and objective reality'.[56] Dummett succumbs to it when he thinks of a given state of the world as capable of 'conclusively verifying' a belief. The latter notion embodies just the idea of bits of the world making a belief true which Davidson rejects.

Devitt is, I think, right in saying that, once we drop Dummett's anti-holism, the issue about 'realism' is de-semanticized. But it is also trivialized. For there is now nothing for 'realism' to name save the banal anti-idealist thesis which Devitt formulates as 'Common-sense physical entities objectively exist independently of the mental.'[57] Devitt thinks this an interesting and controversial thesis. It is an embarrassment for my interpretation of Davidson as a pragmatist that he apparently does too: witness his pledge of allegiance, cited above, to the idea of 'an objective public world which is not of our making'.[58] This formula strikes me as no more than out-dated rhetoric. For on my view the futile metaphysical struggle between idealism and physicalism was superseded, in the early years of this century, by a metaphilosophical struggle between the pragmatists (who wanted to dissolve the old metaphysical questions) and the anti-pragmatists (who still thought there was something first-order to fight about).[59] The latter struggle is *beyond* realism and anti-realism.[60]

55 'A Coherence Theory . . .', p. 313.

56 Devitt, p. 77.

57 Devitt, p. 76.

58 See also *Inquiries into Truth and Interpretation*, p. 198: 'In giving up the dualism of scheme and world, we do not give up the world, but re-establish unmediated touch with the familiar objects whose antics make our sentences and opinions true or false.' Yet surely these familiar objects are simply not the world which anti-idealist philosophers have tried to underwrite. The idealists had these objects too. The world which their opponents were concerned about was one which could vary independently of the antics of the familiar objects; it was something rather like the thing-in-itself. (I developed this distinction between two senses of 'world', the familiar objects on the one hand and the contrived philosophical counterpart of 'scheme' on the other, in an earlier [1972], and rather awkward, attempt to latch on to Davidson's arguments; see 'The World Well Lost', reprinted in *Consequences of Pragmatism*.)

59 I should try to account for this change by reference to (a) Hegel's demonstration that idealism eventually eats itself up (like the Worm Ouroboros) by deconstructing the mind-matter distinction which it started out with and (b) the disenchantment with that distinction brought about by the theory of evolution. Dewey's importance, I think, lies in having brought Hegel and Darwin together. But this is a long and controversial story.

60 Current debates about Heidegger's 'destruction of the Western metaphysical tradition' and Derrida's 'deconstruction of the metaphysics of presence' form another wing of the same struggle. For some connections between Davidson and Derrida, see Samuel Wheeler, 'Indeterminacy of French

So, despite his occasional pledges of realist faith, is Davidson.[61] On my version of the history of twentieth-century philosophy, logical empiricism was a reactionary development, one which took one step forward and two steps back. Davidson, by subverting the scheme-content dualism which logical empiricism took for granted, has, so to speak, kept the logic and dropped the empiricism (or better, kept the attention to language and dropped the epistemology). He has thus enabled us to use Frege's insights to confirm the holistic and pragmatist doctrines of Dewey. His work makes possible the kind of synthesis of pragmatism and positivism which Morton White foresaw as a possible 'reunion in philosophy'.[62] From the point of view of such a synthesis, the Peirce-Frege turn from consciousness to language (and from transcendental to formal logic) was a stage in the dissolution of such traditional problems as 'realism vs. anti-realism', rather than a step towards a clearer formulation of those problems.[63]

Interpretation: Derrida and Davidson',: *Truth and Interpretation*, ed. E. LePore, pp. 477–494. For parallels between Heidegger's attempt to get beyond both Plato and Nietzsche and Fine's and Davidson's attempts to get beyond realism and anti-realism see my 'Beyond Realism and Anti-Realism', *Wo steht die sprachanalytische Philosophie heute*, ed. Herta Nagl-Docekal et al. (Vienna: Oldenbourg, 1986), pp. 103–115.

61 Arthur Fine has offered the best recent account of why we ought to get beyond this struggle. See the anti-realist polemic of his 'The Natural Ontological Attitude' (cited in note 35 above) and the anti-anti-realist polemic of 'And Not Anti-Realism Either', *Nous*, 18 (1984), pp. 51–65. The latter paper (p. 54) makes the point that 'The anti-realism expressed in the idea of truth-as-acceptance is just as metaphysical and idle as the realism expressed by a correspondence theory.' On my interpretation of Davidson, his position pretty well coincides with Fine's 'Natural Ontological Attitude'.

Fréderick Stoutland ('Realism and Anti-Realism in Davidson's Philosophy of Language', Part I in *Critica* XIV (August, 1982) and Part II in *Critica* XIV (December, 1982)) has given excellent reasons for resisting attempts (by, e.g., John McDowell and Mark Platts) to construe Davidson as a realist. However, I think that he is wrong in construing him as an anti-realist who holds that 'sentences are not true in virtue of their extra-linguistic objects: they are true in virtue of their role in human practise' (Part I, p. 21). To repeat, Davidson thinks that we should drop the question 'In virtue of what are sentences true?' Therefore, as I said earlier, he does not wish to be associated with pragmatism, for too many people calling themselves 'pragmatists' (including myself) have said things like 'a sentence is true in virtue of its helping people achieve goals and realize intentions' (Stoutland, Part II, p. 36). Despite my disagreement with Stoutland, however, I am much indebted to his discussion. In particular, his remark (Part II, p. 22) that Davidson opposes the idea that it is the 'intentionality of *thoughts* – their being directed to objects, independently of whether they are true or false – which accounts for the relation of language to reality' seems to me an admirably clear and succinct expression of the difference between Davidson's holism and the 'building-block' approach common to Russell, Husserl, Kripke and Searle.

62 See Morton White, *Toward Reunion in Philosophy* (Harvard University Press, Cambridge, Mass., 1956).

63 I am very grateful to Robert Brandom, Alan Donagan and Arthur Fine for comments on the penultimate version of this paper. I made substantial changes as a result of their comments, but have not tried to acknowledge my indebtedness in every case.

Representation, social practise, and truth

Some years ago, Robert Brandom suggested that recent philosophy of language divides up into two schools. For the first, or representationalist, school (typified by Frege, Russell, Tarski and Carnap), Brandom says, "the essential feature of language is its capacity to represent the way things are."[1] Representationalists, he continues, "take truth to be the basic concept in terms of which a theory of meaning, and hence a theory of language, is to be developed." The second school (typified by Dewey and Wittgenstein) starts off from a conception of language as a set of social practises. Members of this school start off from assertibility, and then squeeze the notion of truth in as best they can.

As Brandom says, both the early Heidegger and Sellars are members of the latter school. There is, I think, a useful comparison to be made between the way in which those two social-practise theorists handle the distinction between assertibility and truth. The Heidegger of *Being and Time,* as Brandom says in a later article,[2] defends "the ontological primacy of the social" on the basis of "pragmatism concerning authority." For the Heidegger of this period, truth as accuracy of representation, as mere correctness [*Richtigkeit, adaequatio*], is identified with warranted assertibility, treated as a matter of conformity to current practise. He takes the traditional pseudo-problems of the relation of language to *beings,* problems engendered by representationalism, to be solved by the discovery of the primacy of the social. But he thinks that "truth" still names a central philosophical topic – viz., the relation between *Being* and changing "understandings of Being" [*Seinsverstaendnisse*]. So Heidegger distinguishes between correctness and disclosedness, between *Richtigkeit* and *Erschlossenheit* or *aletheia.* Disclosedness is a relation between vocabularies, conceptual systems, and Being – as opposed to the correctness relation which holds between sentences and beings.

Sellars makes the same sort of move. He takes the traditional representationalist problematic of the relation of language and thought to the world to be resolved by recognizing that, as he says in *Science and Metaphysics,* "semantical statements of the Tarski-Carnap variety do not assert relations between linguistic and extra-linguistic items."[3] Sellars spells out his social-practise construal of the notion of truth as follows: "for a proposition to be true is for it to be as-

1 'Truth and Assertibility', *Journal of Philosophy* LXXIII (1976), p. 137.
2 'Heidegger's Categories in *Being and Time*', *The Monist* 66 (1983), pp. 387–409.
3 *Science and Metaphysics*, p. 82.

sertible . . . correctly assertible, that is, in accordance with the relevant semantical rules and on the basis of such additional, though unspecified, information as
these rules may require. . . ."[4] His substitution of inference-tickets for assertions
of word-world correspondence is illustrated by his claim that a Tarskian T-
sentence is "a consequence of the above *intensional* definition of 'true' [as S-
assertibility], in the sense that the assertion of the right-hand side of the implication statement is a *performance* of the kind authorized by the truth statement on
the left."[5]

Like Heidegger, however, Sellars is not content to leave the matter at that.
After analyzing truth as S-assertibility, he goes on to discuss the question of what
happens when the semantical rules themselves change, when we have a change of
"framework." This is the point at which he introduces his notion of "adequacy of
picturing." Picturing is for Sellars what disclosedness is for Heidegger. It is the
extra dimension which relates social practises to something beyond themselves,
and thus recaptures the Greek problematic of humanity's relation to the nonhuman (of *nomos* vs. *physis*). In Sellars' case this non-human something is "the
world." In Heidegger's case it is "Being."

Many of those who owe their philosophical formation to Heidegger, notably
Derrida, see his desire to save this traditional problematic, and thus his talk of
Being and of disclosedness, as pious nostalgia, further evidence of the dominion
of Greece over Germany. They view that desire, and that kind of talk, as a slide
back into metaphysics. Many of us whose minds were formed by reading Sellars
think of Sellars' doctrine of picturing as an unfortunate slide back into
representationalism – a last-minute recrudescence of the pious hope that the
great problems formulated by the philosophical tradition (and, more particularly, by Kant) were not *altogether* illusory.

Are Heidegger or Sellars in fact backsliding? Or has one or the other, or both,
found a happy *via media* between the uncritical representationalism of the philosophical tradition and an overenthusiastic pragmatism which throws Being and
the World overboard? One way to get this question into better focus is to take a
look at Davidson. Davidson's disdain for the idea of "conceptual frameworks," as
relic of the analytic-synthetic distinction, is well known. His refusal to admit
questions about a relation between scheme and content – for example, about the
adequacy of some historically-given language-game to "the world" – is part of
this disdain. So Davidson seems a good candidate for the position of *non*-
backsliding "social practises" theorist.

Davidson, however, may seem to resist Brandom's classification. For, as I said
earlier, Brandom makes it a mark of representationalism to "take truth to be the
basic concept in terms of which a theory of meaning, and hence a theory of

4 Ibid., p. 101.
5 p. 101, italics added.

language, is to be developed." On a first reading of his "Truth and Meaning" (1967), Davidson seems an arch-representationalist. But, as I have argued elsewhere,[6] by the time Davidson has finished (in some twenty years' worth of subsequent articles) with the notion of truth, it is as little suited for representationalist purposes as it is when Sellars has finished with it. For what Davidson now calls his "coherence theory" of truth says that only evidence – that is, other beliefs, as opposed to experience, sensory stimulation, or the world – can make beliefs true. Since "making true" is the inverse of "representing," this doctrine makes it impossible for Davidson to talk about language representing the world – standing to it as scheme to content.

This contrast between "evidence" and "world" may seem to repeat Sellars' point that "true" does not name a word-world relation, but instead is to be analyzed as "S-assertible." But such an assimilation is blocked by Davidson's urging us to leave "true" *un*analyzed, to take it as primitive.[7] Davidson would resist Sellars' analysis because he wants to de-epistemologize the notion of truth – to keep it as separate from questions of justification as Sellars keeps the notion of picturing. He thinks that although truth is, indeed, "the basic concept in terms of which a theory of meaning is to be developed," only a de-epistemologized conception of truth will get that job done.

To clarify what such a concept of truth is like, consider the difference between the ways in which Sellars and Davidson handle the familiar anti-pragmatist point that a sentence can be assertible without being true. Sellars distinguishes two senses in which this point is sound. One is that there is a distinction between assertibility from the point of view of a finite individual user of a conceptual system and assertibility from the point of view of an omniscient user. Omniscient Jones makes only *correct* assertions, because he has all the additional information which the rules require him to have before opening his mouth. Finite Smith, by contrast, is justified in making incorrect assertions by his lack of world enough and time. So truth has to be defined as S-assertibility, assertibility by Jones, rather than ordinary assertibility by you, me, or Smith. The *second* sense in which this anti-pragmatist point is sound is that Jones, despite his omniscience, may be using a second-rate set of semantical rules. He may, for example, be a Neanderthal or an Aristotelian. So his assertions, though correct by his lights, are still, we moderns are inclined to say, false. That is why Sellars wants to bring in picturing as distinct from truth, to allow for ever better S-assertibilities.

By contrast, Davidson wants to describe the distinction between assertibility and truth without reference to semantical rules or conceptual systems. He regards these latter notions as arbitrary divisions of a seamless and endless process of reweaving webs of belief, a seamless process of altering criteria of assertibility. So

---

6 'Pragmatism, Davidson and Truth' in this volume.
7 Davidson, 'A Coherence Theory of Truth and Knowledge', in LePore (ed.), p. 308.

for him there is no way to construct a notion of "ideal" assertibility with which to identify truth, nor is there any need to worry about the difference between us and the Neanderthals, or us and the Galactics. On his view, truth and assertibility have *nothing* to do with one another. Truth is not the name of a property, and in particular not the name of a relational property which ties a statement to the world or to a set of semantical rules as followed by an omniscient being. Ascriptions of truth are to be treated disquotationally, or, more generally, anaphorically. As Brandom says in the article I cited at the beginning, you need a notion of truth as distinct from assertibility to do semantics – and in particular to handle inferences involving compound sentences – but you may not need it for anything else. Assertibility, for Davidson, *is* the name of a property, but it is always assertibility by some finite Smith (or group of Smiths) in some situation at some time – assertibility relative to some *given,* actual, finite web of beliefs.

This contrast between Sellars' and Davidson's strategy stands out in the following passage from Davidson:

> [the principle that] whatever there is to meaning must be traced back to experience, the given, or patterns of sensory stimulation, something intermediate between belief and the usual objects our beliefs are about . . . open[s] the door to skepticism. Trying to make meaning accessible has made truth inaccessible. When meaning goes epistemological in this way, truth and meaning are necessarily divorced. One can, of course, arrange a shotgun wedding by redefining truth as what we are justified in asserting. But this does not marry the original mates.[8]

Davidson's point is that one can epistemologize meaning by tying it to the given, or one can epistemologize truth by tying it to justification, but *either* tie-up will lead either to skepticism or to extravagantly complicated, ultimately unsuccessful, efforts to evade skepticism. Either will lead us back into the maze of blind alleys which is the representationalist tradition. So the thing to do is to marry truth and meaning to nothing and nobody but each other. The resulting marriage will be so intimate a relationship that a theory of truth will *be* a theory of meaning, and conversely. But that theory will be of no use to a representationalist epistemology, nor to any other sort of epistemology. It will be an explanation of what people *do,* rather than of a non-causal, representing, relation in which they stand to non-human entities. I suspect that Davidson would say that Sellars is still held captive by a representationalist picture. In this picture, Neanderthal or Aristotelian sentences have meaning – that is, are translatable by us – by virtue of their referring, albeit unperspicuously, to what really exists – viz., the objects referred to in the ideal, Peircian, conceptual system. For if Sellars were free of this picture, it would not seem of importance to him to set up the baroque Tractarian apparatus with the aid of which he tries to explicate "the concept of a domain of objects which are pictured in one way (less adequate) by one linguistic system,

8 Davidson, 'A Coherence Theory . . .', p. 313.

and in another way (more adequate) by another."[9] As with all other accounts of meaning which insist on a tie with the world as a condition of meaningfulness, Sellars opens the gates to skepticism. For now he has to give an account of the notion of "more adequate picturing" which will serve as what he calls "an Archimedean point outside the series of actual and possible beliefs."[10] But any such account will lead back to skepticism. For Sellars' very description of the picturing relation raises doubts of the sort associated with what Putnam has called "metaphysical realism." We begin to wonder how we could ever know whether our increasing success at predicting and controlling our environment as we moved from Neanderthal through Aristotelian to Newtonian was an index of a nonintentional "matter-of-factual" relation called "adequate picturing." Perhaps the gods see things otherwise. Perhaps they are amused by seeing us predicting better and better while picturing worse and worse.

This sort of skeptical doubt, Davidson will urge, can never be resolved. For Sellars himself has to admit that there is no super-language, neutral between the three conceptual schemes just mentioned, in which we can formulate a criterion of adequacy. His own principles force him to agree with the point which Putnam makes against Kripke: that you cannot *specify* a non-intentional Archimedean tie with the world, a point outside a series of beliefs. For the non-intentional relations you specify will be as theory-relative, as belief-relative, as everything else. So either "CS_j pictures more adequately than CS_i," just *means* "CS_j is better suited to our needs than CS_i," or it does not. If it does, then we can dispense with the Tractarian apparatus which is supposed to unite all such conceptual systems. If it does not, and if we cannot say anything more about what it *does* mean, then surely we can forgo talk of picturing altogether. As Rosenberg puts it, talk of correct picturing is "in a sense idle" because "the *sense* of such claims of ontological adequacy or absolute correctness is given only in terms of the notion of conceptual schemes and retrospective collective justifiabilities constitutive of the very diachronic process we have been describing."[11]

The difference between Sellars and Davidson here is the difference between somebody who takes seriously the question "Does what we are talking about really exist?" and somebody who does not. This difference in attitude toward the reality-appearance distinction accounts for two more differences between the two philosophers. The first is that Davidson, unlike both Quine and Sellars, has no special interest in physical science. He cares nothing for the relation of intentional or moral locutions to the disposition of elementary particles. He has no reductionist impulses, no preferred vocabulary in which to describe the world, no particular regard for the vocabulary of unified natural science. His attitude toward Eddington's two tables is the Deweyan one which Sellars thinks childish: he says

9 *Science and Metaphysics*, p. 140.
10 Ibid., p. 142.
11 Jay Rosenberg, *One World and Our Knowledge of It*, p. 186.

"both". This is also his attitude toward the difference between the manifest and the scientific image: use whatever image is handy for the purpose at hand, without worrying about which is closer to reality.

This absence of reductionist impulses leads to an insouciance about the analytic-synthetic distinction. It leads, in particular, to the view that philosophers' "conceptual analyses" are usually just remnants of what Davidson calls an "adventitious puritanism" (of, e.g., empiricism) or of the morbid scientistic fear (common in Vienna and Berlin during the 1920's) that one may be using seemingly referring expressions which in fact do not refer. It also leads to the view that, as I said earlier, nothing is gained by talking about "conceptual systems" that could not be had more easily by just talking about change in linguistic behavior – change which can be described *either* as change of meaning or as change of belief, depending upon whether (as Harman puts it) it seems more convenient to revise our encyclopedias or our dictionaries.

So much for the differences between Davidson and Sellars. The similarities are, I think, more important. For, at bottom, their anti-representationalist strategy is the same. This strategy consists in appealing to *what we do* as a resolution of familiar representationalist problems. More specifically, it consists in letting self-referential indexicals play a role in philosophical explanation. Sellars, to my mind, is the great pioneer in this area. He was the first analytic philosopher to break with the idea that philosophy must be done from what Putnam calls a "God's eye view." This traditional representationalist conception of objectivity was shattered when Sellars (in his early article "A Semantical Solution of the Mind-Body Problem") suggested that the reason why intentional discourse was irreducible to non-intentional discourse was simply that intentional discourse was token-reflexive discourse and non-intentional discourse was not. More specifically, Sellars suggested that we explain what it is to be a language by reference to what *we* do – not "we" in some vague generic sense in which it is equivalent to "humanity" but in the sense of what you and I are currently doing. As he said in "Being and Being Known," "the basic role of signification statements is to say that two expressions, at least one of which is in *our own* vocabulary, have the same use."[12]

This seems to me an epoch-making step, for it is the beginning of the end of what Rosenberg has called the Myth of Mind Apart. It opens the way for Sellars' habitual appeals to inference-tickets and patterns of practical reasoning – his appeals to what *we* do – to explicate the concept of truth, to vindicate induction, and to expound the moral point of view. For such appeals presuppose that a philosophical account of our practises need *not* take the form of descriptions of our relation to something not ourselves, but need *merely* describe our practises. The desired "relation to the world" which representationalists fear may be lacking is,

12 *Science, Perception and Reality*, p. 56; italics added.

Sellars was implying, *built into* the fact that these are *our* practises – the practises of real live human beings engaged in causal interaction with the rest of nature.

The claim that reference to the practises of real live people is all the philosophical justification anybody could want for anything, and the only defense against the skeptic anybody needs, is central to Davidson's philosophical strategy as well. To bring this out, let me take the slightly circuitous route of citing some exasperated criticisms made of Davidson by one of his most acute representationalist critics. Jonathan Bennett has said that Davidson is unable or unwilling to carry out what Bennett sees as "the philosopher's task" – viz., "to take warm, familiar aspects of the human condition and look at them coldly and with the eye of a stranger."[13]

What annoys Bennett most is Davidson's habit of acting as if Grice had lived in vain, as if there were no need to ask what makes a language a language, as if "he could just rely on the premise that *he speaks a language,* without subjecting that premise "to any kind of explanation or analytical scrutiny." Bennett goes on to say that "With one strange exception . . . he [Davidson] tells us nothing about what it is for a behavioral system to be a language, or for a sound or movement to be (a token of) a sentence." He continues: "Davidson seems willing to take that concept on trust, as something whose instances are dropped into our laps without the need for philosophical work."[14]

The "strange exception" which Bennett mentions is Davidson's claim that Convention T "makes essential use of the notion of translation into a language we know."[15] As Bennett goes on to say, Davidson holds that "each person's concept of truth brings in a particular language – or a particular small set of languages – because *each person's concept of truth is partly self-referential.*" Here, I think, Bennett gets to the core of Davidson's position. But it is also, as I have been saying, the core of Sellars' position. These two social-practise theorists share a willingness to do what Bennett thinks fantastic: to "explain *true* in terms of *language I know.*"[16]

Representationalists like Bennett construe as mysterious relations between the human and the non-human what social-practise theorists like Sellars and Davidson construe as elliptical descriptions of practises – practises which we humans have developed in the course of interacting with non-human things. So when Davidson says that most of our beliefs, most of Aristotle's beliefs, and most of your average Neanderthal's beliefs, were true, Bennett diagnoses what he calls "incurious parochialism." He would say the same of Sellars' account of intentional discourse as explicated by self-referential indexicals. For if this account is sufficient there will be no way of explicating the notion of "intending" without

---

13 'Critical Notice' of *Inquiries into Truth and Interpretation, Mind,* p. 619.
14 Ibid., p. 619.
15 Bennett, p. 626, citing *Inquiries,* p. 194f.
16 Bennett, p. 626.

reference to *our* own vocabulary. So there will be no way for Gricean speech-act theory to carry out its program.

If Sellars and Davidson are right in suggesting that philosophical explication is always going to lead back to self-referential indexicals, then there is something seriously wrong with Bennett's idea that philosophers can step back from warm, familiar aspects of the human condition and look at them with the eye of a stranger. Bennett's phrasing gets to the heart of the representationalist philosopher's motives. It also gets to the heart of the initial Greek attempt to distinguish *nomos* from *physis* – an attempt which Heidegger links to the beginnings of *Seinsvergessenheit*. Hegel, Sellars' early hero, was properly suspicious of the idea that philosophers can take this step back. He thought that the great mistake of the Kantians was to try to view knowledge as a medium, or as an instrument.[17] He insisted that the proper starting-point for philosophy was not an aloof transcendental standpoint but rather the particular point in world-history at which we find ourselves. It may be the great mistake of the kind of neo-Kantian philosophy of language which Bennett represents to think that we can treat language as a medium or an instrument – that we can *avoid* doing what Bennett rightly says Davidson does: "explaining *true* in terms of *language I know.*"[18]

The question of whether there is anything for philosophers to appeal to save the way *we* live now, what *we* do now, how *we* talk now – anything beyond *our* own little moment of world-history – is the decisive issue between representationalist and social-practise philosophers of language. More generally, it is the decisive issue between an approach to philosophy which takes for granted what Rosenberg calls "the Myth of Mind Apart" and one which assumes that something is, indeed, dropped into the philosopher's lap – namely, her own linguistic know-how, or more generally, her own patterns of practical reasoning, the ways in which her community copes with the world. The alternative to this assumption would seem to be that what was dropped into her lap was a gift from heaven called "clarity of thought" or "powerful analytic techniques" or "critical distance" – a heaven-sent ability to wrench one's mind free from one's community's practises, to turn away from *nomos* toward *physis*.

So much for what seems to me the common core of Davidson and Sellars, and the source of the bafflement with which both men's views are greeted by representationalists. Now let me turn back to the differences between their respective treatments of the notion of truth. I said earlier that Sellars tried to take the curse off his Deweyan identification of truth with assertibility by distinguishing, first,

---

17 Hegel, 'Introduction' to *The Phenomenology of Spirit*, trans. Miller (Oxford: Oxford University Press, 1977), p. 47. 'Should we not be concerned as to whether this fear of error is not just the error itself? Indeed, this fear takes something – a great deal, in fact – for granted as truth, supporting its scruples and inferences on what is itself in need of prior scrutiny to see if it is true. To be specific, it takes for granted certain ideas about cognition as an *instrument* and a *medium*, and assumes that there is a *difference between ourselves and this cognition*'.

18 Bennett, p. 626.

Omniscient Jones' use of our conceptual system (CSO) from finite Smith's use, and second, CSO from a sequence of CS_i's which lead up to the limit CS. This limit conceptual system, CSP, is the conceptual scheme used by speakers of Peircish at the ideal end of inquiry. By these distinctions, he hopes to grant the skeptic his point that we may be getting everything wrong while still maintaining that "true" does not name a word-world relation. By contrast, Davidson's way with the skeptic is much quicker and dirtier. It is summed up in the following passage:

In order to doubt or wonder about the provenance of his beliefs an agent must know what belief is. This brings with it the concept of objective truth, for the notion of a belief is the notion of a state that may or may not jibe with reality. But beliefs are also identified, directly and indirectly, by their causes. What an omniscient interpreter knows a fallible interpreter gets right enough if he understands a speaker, and this is just the complicated causal truth that makes us the believers we are, and fixes the contents of our beliefs. The agent has only to reflect on what a belief is to appreciate that most of his basic beliefs are true, and among his beliefs, those most securely held and that cohere with the main body of his beliefs are the most apt to be true.[19]

Notice, in this passage, the claim that all that omniscience could know about our relation to the world is "the complicated causal truth that makes us the believers we are." Davidson's point is that knowing *that* truth would automatically enable omniscience to translate our utterances and to recognize most of them as truths. If we bear Sellars' distinctions in mind, we may be tempted to ask whether the Omniscience in question is merely Omniscient Jones using CSO, or rather Omniscient Jones in glory, using CSP. Davidson will reply that it simply doesn't matter. The difference between CSO and CSP is, for him, philosophically insignificant. Davidson and Sellars agree that what shows us that life is not just a dream, that our beliefs are in touch with reality, is the *causal,* non-intentional, non-representational, links between us and the rest of the universe. But Sellars thinks that it takes a long time (all the way to the end of inquiry) for these causal links to whip us into properly correspondent shape, and that in the meantime we may be talking about what does not exist. In contrast, Davidson thinks that they had already whipped us into the relevant shape as soon as they made us language-users.

For Sellars, the primitive animists and the Aristotelians employed referring expressions most of which did not pick out entities in the world, and the same may be true of *us,* who have not yet reached CSP. For Davidson, everybody has always talked about mostly real things, and has made mostly true statements. The only difference between primitive animists and us, or us and the Galactics, is that the latecomers can make a few extra true statements which their ancestors did not know how to make (and avoid a few falsehoods). But these little extras — the

---

19 Davidson, 'A Coherence Theory . . .', pp. 318–319.

difference between wood-nymphs and microbiology, or between our microbiology and its successor in Galactic unified science – are just icing on the cake. A massive amount of true belief and successful picking-out was already in place when the first Neanderthal went metalinguistic and found words in which to explain to her mate that one of his beliefs was false. For the Neanderthal lived in the same world that the omniscient user of CSP lives in, and the same causal forces which led most of her and her mate's linguistic behavior to consist of true assertions will lead an omniscient user to say mostly what she said. The complicated causal story about how this happened goes much the same, whether told in Neanderthal, Newtonian or Peircish; the details just get a bit more complicated at each successive stage.

The difference between Sellars and Davidson parallels a difference between Sellars and Rosenberg, or, more exactly, between Sellars and early Rosenberg on the one hand and slightly later Rosenberg on the other. In the first book, *Linguistic Representation,* Rosenberg took chapter 5 of *Science and Metaphysics* at face value and developed an account of proto-correlational isomorphisms, Jumblese et al. He wanted, at that time, to preserve Sellars' notion of "one truth about the world" – the one told according to the semantic rules of CSP. But in his second book, *One World and our Knowledge of It,* from which I earlier quoted the passage about the "idleness" of the notion of "correct picturing," he drops the idea of "one truth" and settles for that of "one world." Now he says that the fact that a "successor conceptual scheme is more nearly (absolutely) correct than its predecessor *consists* in its adoption or espousal as a successor being warranted or justified."[20] That sentence closes off the skeptical "metaphysical realist" possibility which was left open in both *Science and Metaphysics* and *Linguistic Representation.* These books made picturing a matter-of-factual relation causally independent of social practises; so they left open the possibility that successive schemes might predict better and better by picturing worse and worse. The later Rosenberg precludes this possibility. For he has made "pictures more correctly than" mean something like "accepted (for good reasons, in a relatively domination-free communication situation) later than."

The only important difference between this latter Rosenbergian account and Davidson's is the residual scientism which Rosenberg shares with Sellars, and from which Davidson is free. This scientism makes Sellars and Rosenberg take the notion of "conceptual scheme" seriously, and its absence lets Davidson shrug it off. Scientism, in this sense, is the assumption that every time science lurches forward philosophy must redescribe the face of the whole universe. Scienticists think that every new discovery of micro-structure casts doubt on the "reality" of manifest macro-structure and of any intervening middle structures. If one takes this claim seriously, one may well feel torn between van Fraassen's instrumen-

---

20 *One World and Our Knowledge of It,* p. 117.

talism and Sellars' realism. If one does not, as Davidson does not, then one will simply not ask which of Eddington's two tables is real, and one will be baffled about the difference between van Fraassen's ready belief in tables and his more tentative attitude toward electrons.[21] One will (with Bain and Peirce) take beliefs as rules for actions rather than elements in a representational system, and say that it is well to have lots of different sets of rules for dealing with tables – in order to be prepared for the various different contexts in which one may encounter them (in the dining room, under the electron microscope, etc.). One will be as obstinately Oxonian about the word "real" as Austin was, able to wield it when distinguishing real diamonds from paste and real cream from non-dairy whitener, but not when distinguishing primary from secondary qualities.

One can think of scientism in the relevant sense as going back to the latter distinction. Philosophers like Locke thought that they heard from Newton and Boyle the language which Plato and St. Paul had hoped to hear beyond the grave: the language which specified clearly and distinctly what we had previously spoken of obliquely and confusedly. In our own century, enthusiastic readers of *The Encyclopedia of Unified Science* hoped that that language was now actually in sight. So they retained the representationalist problematic of modern philosophy which Locke had initiated by distinguishing between ideas which did and did not resemble their objects.[22] Sellars thinks that we must take this problematic seriously, and that we can use the results of social-practise philosophy of language to answer questions posed by representationalist philosophy of language. Like the early Heidegger, he thinks that we can pour new wine into old bottles, and write in a way which is continuous with the philosophical tradition – that we can combine what Brandom calls "pragmatism about authority" with something like traditional ontology. More radical social-practise theorists such as Derrida and Davidson think that one cannot, and that attempts to do so amount to backsliding.[23] Though my own leanings are obviously toward radicalism, I have not attempted to adjudicate the issue between Davidson's quick and dirty dissolution of the traditional problematic and Sellars' attempt at a happy *via media*. I have merely tried to get that issue into sharper focus.

21 On dissolving the issue between Stellars and van Fraassen, see Gary Gutting, 'Scientific Realism vs. Constructive Empiricism: A Dialogue' in *Images of Science: Essays on Realism and Empiricism*, (eds.) Paul M. Churchland and Clifford A. Hooker (Chicago: Univ. of Chicago Press, 1985).

22 Note that recent defenders of the primary-secondary quality distinction such as Thomas Nagel and Bernard Williams join Bennett in thinking that it is possible, and for some purposes useful, to step back from warm, familiar aspects of the human condition and view them with the eye of a stranger. That is why Nagel says that a full-fledged Wittgensteinian social-practise view of language is incompatible with realism. (See Nagel, *The View From Nowhere* (Oxford: Oxford University Press, 1986), p. 106.

23 For the convergence of Davidson and Derrida, see Samuel Wheeler, 'Indeterminacy of French Interpretation: Derrida and Davidson' in *Truth and Interpretation: Perspectives on the Philosophy of Donald Davidson*, (ed.) Ernest LePore (Oxford and New York: Basil Blackwell, 1986), pp. 477–494.

Unfamiliar noises:
Hesse and Davidson on metaphor

> We speak of one thing being like some other thing, when what we are really
> craving to do is to describe something that is like nothing on earth.
>
> Vladimir Nabokov

Philosophers of science like Mary Hesse have helped us realize that metaphor is
essential to scientific progress. This realization has encouraged Hesse and others
to argue for 'the cognitive claims of metaphor'.[1] She is concerned to give metaphorical sentences truth and reference – to find worlds for them to be about;
"imaginative symbolic worlds that have relations with natural reality other than
those of predictive interest . . . utopias, fictional exposés of the moral features of
this world by caricature and other means, and all kinds of myths symbolic of our
understanding of nature, society and the gods'.[2] Like many other philosophers of
this century (e.g., Cassirer, Whitehead, Heidegger, Gadamer, Habermas, Goodman, Putnam) she sees over-attention to the natural sciences as having distorted
modern philosophy. Following Habermas, Hesse sees cognition as wider than the
satisfaction of our 'technical interest' and as extending to 'the practical interest of
personal communication and the emancipatory interest of critique of ideology'. In
discourse which satisfies these interests, Hesse says, 'metaphor remains the necessary mode of speech'.[3] So she believes that metaphor 'poses a radical challenge to
contemporary philosophy' and that we need 'a revised ontology and theory of
knowledge and truth' in order to do justice to metaphor as an instrument of
cognition.[4]

I agree with Hesse that over-attention to natural science has skewed philosophy, but I do not think that her strategy is sufficiently radical to let us correct the
error. For one way in which this skewing is evident is that we philosophers still
tend to take 'cognition' as the highest compliment we can pay to discourse. We
take 'cognitive claims' as the most important claims which can be made for a
given sort of language. Were we not concerned to raise the rest of discourse to the
level of science, we would not be so concerned to broaden our use of terms like
'truth', 'refers to a world' and 'meaning' so as to make them relevant to metaphor.

To correct the error of the tradition, to help ourselves see natural science as
simply an instrument of prediction and control rather than as a standard-setting
area of culture, we need instead to restrict the applicability of these semantical
terms. We need to see that the applicability of such terms is not a measure of the

---

1 This is the title of Hesse's article in *Metaphor and Religion,* ed. J. P. Van Noppen (Brussels, 1984).
2 Hesse, op. cit., p. 39.
3 Ibid., p. 40.
4 See ibid., p. 41.

cultural importance of a use of language, but merely of the extent to which language-use can be predicted and controlled on the basis of presently-available, widely-shared, theory. We should see semantical notions as applicable only to familiar and relatively uninteresting uses of words, and 'cognition' as the positivists saw it: confined to familiar and relatively uninteresting uses of language, to discourses for which there are generally accepted procedures for fixing belief. We should find other compliments to pay other sorts of discourse rather than trying to 'broaden' either semantic or epistemic notions.

In particular, we should follow Davidson rather than (as Hesse does) Black in our account of metaphor. For, by putting metaphor outside the pale of semantics, insisting that a metaphorical sentence has no meaning other than its literal one, Davidson lets us see metaphors on the model of unfamiliar events in the natural world – *causes* of changing beliefs and desires – rather than on the model of *representations* of unfamiliar worlds, worlds which are 'symbolic' rather than 'natural'. He lets us see the metaphors which make possible novel scientific theories as causes of our ability to know more about the world, rather than expressions of such knowledge. He thereby makes it possible to see other metaphors as causes of our ability to do lots of other things – e.g., be more sophisticated and interesting people, emancipate ourselves from tradition, transvalue our values, gain or lose religious faith – without having to interpret these latter abilities as functions of increased *cognitive* ability. Not the least of the advantages of Davidson's view, I shall be arguing, is that it gives us a better account of the role played in our lives by metaphorical expressions which are not sentences – scraps of poetry which send shivers down our spine, non-sentential phrases which reverberate endlessly, change our selves and our patterns of action, without ever coming to express belief or desires.

The issue between Black and Davidson has struck many people as factitious. Both philosophers insist that metaphors are unparaphrasable, and also that they are not merely ornamental. But Black thinks that a defence of these claims requires the notion of 'metaphorical meaning' and Davidson denies this. Clearly they are using 'meaning' in different ways, and so it is easy to suspect that the issue is verbal. But we can see that something important is at stake by looking at Black's claims that Davidson is 'fixated' on 'the explanatory power of standard sense' and that his account gives us 'no insight into how metaphors work.'[5] These assertions show that Black and Davidson differ not just about how to use the term 'meaning' but about the ends which a theory of meaning should serve, about the point and reach of semantics.

Davidson is, indeed, 'fixated' on the explanatory power of standard sense. But this is because he thinks that semantical notions like 'meaning' have a role only

---

5 Max Black, 'How metaphors work: a reply to Donald Davidson' in *On Metaphor*, ed. Sheldon Sacks (Chicago, University of Chicago Press, 1979), pp. 189, 191.

within the quite narrow (though shifting) limits of regular, predictable, linguistic behaviour – the limits which mark off (temporarily) the literal use of language. In Quine's image, the realm of meaning is a relatively small 'cleared' area within the jungle of use, one whose boundaries are constantly being both extended and encroached upon.[6] To say, as Davidson does, that 'metaphor belongs exclusively to the domain of use'[7] is simply to say that, because metaphors (while still alive) are unparaphrasable, they fall outside the cleared area. By contrast, if one regards meaning and use as co-extensive, one will be inclined to adopt what Hesse calls a 'network view of language' – one according to which, as she says, 'the use of a predicate in a new situation in principle shifts, however little, the meaning of every other word and sentence in the language'.[8]

Davidson's resistance to this 'network' view can be put in terms of an analogy with dynamics. In the case of the gravitational effects of the movements of very small and faraway particles (a phenomenon to which Hesse analogizes the insensible but continuous process of meaning-change), physicists must simply disregard insensible perturbations and concentrate on relatively conspicuous and enduring regularities. So it is with the study of language-use. The current limits of those regularities fix the current limits of the cleared area called 'meaning'.[9] So where 'the explanatory power of standard sense' comes to an end, so does semantics.

If one holds a different conception of the limits of semantics and of philosophical explanation, as Black and Hesse do, this is probably because one has a different conception of the reach of philosophy. Davidson's metaphilosophical approach differs from theirs as Newton's metascientific approach to dynamics differed from Leibniz's; the one is an approach which describes regularities without venturing on hypotheses about the underlying forces at work, while the other tries to go further in the direction of what Leibniz called 'metaphysics'. Hesse's demand for a

6 See Quine, 'A Postscript on Metaphor' in *On Metaphor,* ed. Sacks, cited above, p. 160: 'Metaphor, or something like it, governs both the growth of language and our acquisition of it. What comes as a subsequent refinement is rather cognitive discourse itself, at its most dryly literal. The neatly worked out inner stretches of science are an open space in the tropical jungle, created by clearing tropes away'.

7 Davidson, "What Metaphors Mean,' *Inquiries into Truth and Interpretation* (Oxford, Clarendon Press, 1984), p. 247.

8 Hesse, op. cit., p. 31.

9 Akeel Bilgrami puts this point as follows: '[O]ne should not go away with the impression that there is no more to the study of meaning than a specification of the assertions (or other speech-acts) that different sentences can be used to effect. If we were under this impression, the simple fact that a sentence can be used to effect any number of assertions in different contexts is a fact that would threaten the possibility of theorizing systematically about meaning. . . . [L]inguistic meaning is a *theoretical* core that is indispensable in the explanation of our use of language – and so, unsurprisingly, manifest in it . . . The point of the method of radical interpretation is to distill or abstract out of the assent behaviour of an agent (via a combination of observation of the world around the agent and an application of the constraint of charity) this theoretical core.' ('Meaning, Holism and Use', *Truth and Interpretation: Perspectives on the Philosophy of Donald Davidson,* ed. Ernest LePore [Oxford, Blackwell, 1986], pp. 120–121).

new ontology, and her praise of Ricoeur as the only theorist of metaphor who 'recognizes an ontological foundation for metaphor other than the naturalistic one',[10] are indications of this difference.

The need to go further in a 'metaphysical' direction than Davidson wants to go is also felt by Michael Dummett, who denies that the task of the philosopher of language has been completed when we have described the process of constructing translation manuals, exhibited the ways in which we are able to predict (and, in some measure, control) linguistic behaviour. Thus when Davidson says that 'the ability to communicate by speech consists in the ability to make oneself understood and to understand', and that this ability does not require 'shared grammar or rules' or 'a portable interpreting machine set to grind out the meaning of an arbitrary utterance', Dummett suggests that this is true only of the idiosyncratic features of idiolects.[11] When Davidson says that 'we should give up the attempt to illuminate how we communicate by appeal to conventions',[12] Dummett replies that 'Conventions, whether they be expressly taught or picked up piecemeal, are what constitutes a social practice; to repudiate the role of convention is to deny that a language is in this sense a practice'.[13]

This exchange brings out the fact that, whereas Davidson is content with an outside view, with discovering the sort of behavioural regularities in which a radical interpreter would be interested, Dummett wants to take up, so to speak, a position inside the speaker or the speaker's community. He wants to discover the rules or conventions which form the program of an interpreting machine. For only if there is something like that to find, Dummett thinks, can one 'throw light on what meaning is'.[14] Dummett thinks that if we follow Davidson in jettisoning the notion of 'a language', then 'our theories of meaning have no subject-matter'.[15] Davidson, by contrast, thinks that there is nothing called 'meaning' whose nature is mysterious, and that philosophy of language need no more offer theories about the nature of such a mysterious thing than Newton's *Principia* needed to offer a theory about the nature of gravity. Gravity was not the subject-matter of that book, but rather various regular motions; meaning is not the subject-matter either of a radical interpreter's T-theory or of philosophy of language, but rather behaviour.

To be sure, the behaviour in question is typically, but not necessarily, behaviour which is sufficiently regular among large numbers of people to give those

---

10 Hesse, op. cit., p. 38.
11 Dummett, 'A nice derangement of epitaphs: some comments on Davidson and Hacking' in *Truth and Interpretation*, ed. LePore, p. 474.
12 Davidson, 'A Nice Derangement of Epitaphs', in *Truth and Interpretation*, ed. LePore, cited above, pp. 445–446.
13 Dummett, op. cit., p. 474.
14 Dummett, op. cit., p. 464.
15 Dummett, op. cit., p. 469.

people a handle for notions like 'correctness', 'rule' and 'social practice'.[16] But the utility of such normative notions within a community for controlling and changing the members' linguistic behaviour is independent of the utility of translation manuals for predicting that behaviour. Only when there are sufficient regularities for the insider's normative notions to apply will there be sufficient for the outsider's interpretative, semantical, notions to apply. But this coextensiveness does not mean that the former notions 'ground' or 'explain' or 'complement' the latter, or that the two sets of notions are relevant to each other in any other way. So the job of the philosopher of language is, for Davidson, finished when the latter notions are explicated by reference to the radical interpreter's procedures.[17]

Only if one agrees with Dummett that what makes understanding possible is something like a portable interpreting machine will one be inclined to think Black's question 'how does metaphor work?' a good one. More specifically, only then will one assume that there is something called 'mastery of a language' which includes an ability to 'get the point' of metaphorical uses of bits of that language. Conversely, only if one thinks that there is such a thing as 'the point' of such a use will we be inclined to think of our ability to understand a metaphor as the result of the workings of such a machine. For only if one has already put irregular and unpredictable uses of language within the reach of notions like 'mastery of the language', will one think of reactions to metaphors as dictated by rules, or conventions, or the program of an interpreting machine. Only then will one think 'How do metaphors work?' a better question than 'What is the nature of the unexpected?' or 'How do surprises work?'

It is of course true that if you do not know English you will get no use out of such metaphors as 'Man is a wolf' or 'Metaphor is the dreamwork of language'. Your reaction to these metaphors will be as limited as your reactions to any other

16 See Ian Hacking, 'The parody of conversation', in *Truth and Interpretation*, ed. LePore, p. 458 for the point that we only have correctness where we have lots of people (not just two) exhibiting the same regularities in the behaviour. Davidson would, I think, have no difficulty accepting this 'anti-private language' point – since it leaves open the possibility of understanding (translating) noises regularly made only by one person, and takes away only the possibility of saying that this person has used a language correctly or incorrectly.

17 I have developed this notion of the 'outside' view of the field linguist, and the contrast between Davidson and Dummett's programs, in 'Pragmatism, Davidson and truth' in this volume. On my account of the matter, Davidson sees no need to supplement a T-theory for a language with what Dummett calls 'linking principles', principles which 'make the connection between the theoretical notions and what the speakers of the language say and do'. (Dummett, op. cit., p. 467). At p. 475 Dummett tells us that such linking principles 'will be very complex, since they have to describe an immensely complex social practice: they will treat, among other things, of the division of linguistic labour, of the usually ill-defined sources of linguistic authority, of the different modes of speech and the relations between the parent language and various dialects and slangs.' It is not clear to me how such descriptions can provide a criterion of correctness for a theory of meaning (in Davidson's sense), as Dummett says they can at p. 467. But it is apparent that Dummett thinks that there is some sort of criterion for the correctness of a translation manual other than its giving us what Quine calls the ability to 'bicker with the native like a brother', and that Davidson does not.

utterly unfamiliar noise. But it is one thing to say that the ability to grasp the literal meaning of an English sentence is causally necessary if you are to get something out of its metaphorical use and another to say that this ability insures that you will do so. If Davidson is right, *nothing* could insure that. The difference between a literal use and a metaphorical use of an English sentence is, on Davidson's view, precisely that 'knowing English' (that is, sharing the current theory about how to handle the linguistic behaviour of English-speakers) is sufficient to understand the former. That is just why we call the use 'literal'. But nothing in existence prior to the metaphor's occurrence is sufficient to understand the metaphorical use. That is just why we call it 'metaphorical'. If 'understanding' or 'interpreting' means 'bringing under an antecedent scheme', then metaphors cannot be understood or interpreted. But if we extend these two notions to mean something like 'making use of' or 'coping with', then we can say that we come to understand metaphors in the same way that we come to understand anomalous natural phenomena. We do so by revising our theories so as to fit them around the new material. We interpret metaphors in the same sense in which we interpret such anomalies — by casting around for possible revisions in our theories which may help to handle the surprises.[18]

Davidson does, occasionally, say things which seem to support the view that metaphors have 'cognitive content'. For example: 'Metaphors often make us notice aspects of things we did not notice before; no doubt they bring surprising analogies and similarities to our attention. . . .'[19] But notice that the same can be said about anomalous non-linguistic phenomena like platypuses and pulsars. The latter do not (literally) *tell* us anything, but they do make us notice things and start looking around for analogies and similarities. They do not have cognitive content, but they are reponsible for a lot of cognitions. For if they had not turned up we should not have been moved to formulate and deploy certain sentences which do have such content. As with platypuses, so with metaphors. The only important difference is that the platypus does not *itself* come to express a literal truth, whereas the very same string of words which once formed a metaphorical utterance may, if the metaphor dies into literalness, come to convey such a truth. You may not have to kill the platypus to get a satisfactory theory of how it works, but you do have to kill off a metaphor to get a satisfactory theory of how *it* works.

18 See Davidson's 'A Nice Derangement of Epitaphs' for a parallel between metaphors and malapropisms. See also my 'Texts and Lumps' in this volume for suggestions on how to avoid Diltheyan distinctions between linguistic and non-linguistic surprises. Hesse has commented on the latter paper in her 'Texts Without Types and Lumps Without Laws', *New Literary History*, XVII (1985), pp. 31–48. In her paper she interprets Davidson as a 'reductionist' in regard to metaphor. My account of Davidson's view of metaphor in the present paper is an implicit reply to some of Hesse's criticisms of him in hers.

19 Davidson, 'What Metaphors Mean', p. 261. Davidson goes on to say that metaphors 'do provide a kind of lens or lattice, through which we view the relevant phenomenon'. I confess that I cannot see how to use Black's 'lens' and 'filter' metaphors in ways which fit in with Davidson's metaphors, so I am inclined to say that in this passage Davidson grants too much to the opposition.

For such a theory will give you a widely-accepted paraphrase, and a metaphor for which such a paraphrase is widely available is just what we mean by a dead metaphor.

I take Davidson to be saying that the positivists were on the right track both when they urged that meaning and cognitive content are coextensive, and when they deprived metaphor of cognitive content. They went wrong only when they failed to add that metaphors were necessary for gaining knowledge, even though they did not (while alive) express knowledge. If this interpretation is right, Davidson should deny what Black affirms: that to say, for example, 'Metaphor is the dreamwork of language' is to 'express a distinctive view of metaphor', a 'new *insight* into what metaphor is', to say something which a reader could 'understand or misunderstand', etc.[20] He should say that, when he began 'What Metaphors Mean' with that metaphor, he was instead inviting the reader to participate in a 'creative endeavour'.[21] As he puts it, if we 'give up the idea that the metaphor carries a message' then we can see that the various theories about 'how metaphors work' do not 'provide a method for deciphering an encoded content . . . [but] tell us (or try to tell us) something about the *effects* metaphors have on us'.[22] Davidson can cheerfully agree with the positivists that these effects are 'psychological' rather than 'logical'. But the acquisition of knowledge is, after all, a psychological matter.

One reason philosophers like Habermas and Hesse – philosophers who are suspicious of positivism – are likely to be suspicious of Davidson's attack on 'the thesis that associated with metaphor is a definite cognitive content that its author wishes to convey'[23] is that this seems to give the highest flights of genius the same metaphysical status as thunderclaps and birdsongs. It takes them out of the sphere of what Grice calls 'non-natural meaning' and reduces them to the level of mere stimuli, mere evocations. But such suspicion shows how many background assumptions Habermas and Hesse share with their positivist enemies. They share the Kantian presumption that there is some sort of inviolable 'metaphysical' break between the formal and the material, the logical and the psychological, the non-natural and the natural – between, in short, what Davidson calls 'scheme and content'.

For Davidson, the break between the realm of meaning and cognitive content (the realm in which it is useful to speak of norms and intentions), and the realm of 'mere' stimuli, is just the pragmatic and temporary break between stimuli whose occurrences are more or less predictable (on the basis of some antecedent theory) and stimuli which are not – a break whose location changes as theory changes and

20 See Black, op. cit., pp. 182–3.
21 Davidson, *Inquiries into Truth and Interpretation*, p. 245.
22 Ibid., p. 261.
23 Davidson, *Inquiries into Truth and Interpretation*, p. 262.

as, concomitantly, fresh new metaphors die off into literalness.[24] The genius who transcends the predictable thereby transcends the cognitive and the meaningful. This is not to the discredit of the genius, but, if to anybody's, to that of the sceptical 'man of reason'. For neither knowledge nor morality will flourish unless somebody uses language for purposes other than making predictable moves in currently popular language-games.[25] (Hesse goes too far in saying that metaphor is 'the necessary mode of speech' when fulfilling, e.g., Habermas' 'emancipatory interest'. Plain argumentative prose may, depending on circumstances, be equally useful. But it is certainly true that apt new metaphors have done a lot for radical emancipatory programs in morals and politics.)

One way to see why, if one repudiates Davidson's *bête noire* – the scheme-content view of meaning and cognition – one will want to analogize metaphor to birdsong is to note that traditional empiricism notoriously ran together the claim that sensory observation (of, e.g., birdsong) was a stimulus to knowledge and the claim that it *conveyed* knowledge. This confusion (exposed most thoroughly in Sellars' classic 'Empiricism and the Philosophy of Mind') was between the claim that overhearing, e.g., an unfamiliar noise *caused* you to acquire the belief that there was a quetzal in the forest and the claim that it 'conveyed the information' that there was a quetzal there. The empiricist slogan 'Nothing in the intellect that was not previously in the senses' traded on this confusion, on the ambiguity in 'source of knowledge' between 'cause of belief' and 'justification of belief'.

The same ambiguity arises in the case of 'metaphor is an indispensable source of knowledge'. If we accept the Black-Hesse-Searle view that metaphors convey information, they will be able to function as reasons for belief. On Davidson's view, by contrast, 'live' metaphors can justify belief only in the same metaphorical sense in which one may 'justify' a belief not by citing another belief but by using a non-sentence to stimulate one's interlocutor's sense organs – hoping thereby to cause assent to a sentence. (As when someone holds up a probative photograph and asks '*Now* do you believe?')

The relation between birdsong, poetic imagery (the poets' wood-notes wild)

---

24 Davidson's anti-Kantian naturalism is well expressed in a passage from 'A Nice Derangement of Epitaphs', pp. 445–446: '. . . we have erased the boundary between knowing a language and knowing our way around in the world generally'. Another way to put the point is to say that this boundary changes as metaphors pass over from the 'world' side to the 'language' side – pass from being evocative to being clichés. It is essential to Davidson's view that dead metaphors are not metaphors, just as it is essential for the opposing 'metaphysical' view, common to Black and Searle (and to the view of Hesse, Mark Johnson and George Lakoff that language is 'shot through' with metaphor), that dead metaphors still count as metaphors. See Searle, 'Metaphor' in Johnson, ed. *Philosophical Perspectives on Metaphor*, p. 225.

25 Davidson enlarges on this point at the end of his essay 'Paradoxes of Irrationality' in Richard Wollheim and James Hopkins, eds., *Philosophical Essays on Freud* (Cambridge, Cambridge University Press, 1982).

and the sort of metaphorical uses of sentences discussed by Black and Davidson may be clarified by considering the following spectrum of unfamiliar noises:

(1) A noise in the primeval forest, heard for the first time and eventually discovered to be the song of a bird hitherto unknown to science, the quetzal.
(2) The first utterance of an 'imagistic' and 'poetic' phrase – e.g., 'that dolphin-torn, that gong-tormented sea'.
(3) The first intentional use of an apparently false or pointless sentence – e.g., 'She set me ablaze', 'Metaphor is the dreamwork of language', 'Man is a wolf', 'No man is an island'.
(4) The first (startling, highly paradoxical) utterance of a sentence which, though still construed literally by reference to a theory which antedated it, comes eventually to be taken as truistic – e.g., 'No harm can come to a good man', 'Love is the only law', 'The earth whirls round the sun', 'There is no largest set', 'The heavens will fill with commerce', 'Meaning does not determine reference'.

Consider what happens as each of these unfamiliar noises becomes more and more integrated into our practices, better and better coped with. (1) Helps bring into existence a taxonomy of the avifauna of Central America. In time the call of the quetzal is one more occasion for the heavens filling with commerce, as wealthy bird-watchers fly in. The bird's call never acquires a non-natural meaning, but it does acquire a place in our causal stories about our interaction with the world. The question 'What does that noise mean?' now has answers (e.g., 'It means there is a quetzal around'; 'It means that our village can get in on the tourist industry').

The fragment of Yeats – (2) – also does not acquire a non-natural meaning. But it acquires a place in people's practices – not just in the Yeats industry but in the lives of all those who find themselves remembering it, being haunted by it. It becomes part of what such people are able to say (neither about gongs, dolphins, the sea or Byzantium, nor *about* anything else), but not part of what they know.[26] People's linguistic repertoires are thus enlarged, and their lives and actions changed in ways they cannot easily articulate. But they have not acquired any beliefs which these particular words express. They would not claim to have

26 There is a character in one of Charles Williams' novels for whom the most salient feature of the universe is Milton's line 'And thus the filial Godhead, answering, spake.' It is not that he cares about whether there is or could be such a thing as a filial Godhead. It is the noise itself which matters to him. This noise could not have had this effect, of course, unless he had been familiar with the role in the English language of noises like 'filial' and 'Godhead' (and, perhaps, with the use of similiar noises in Latin and German as well) nor unless he had some familiarity with Christian doctrine. But neither could the little phrase from Vinteuil's sonata have had its effect on Proust's narrator's life and actions if he had not previously listened to other pieces of music of roughly the same sort. The hair on the back of our neck would not stand up when it does if we had not lived the lives we have, but this is not to say that the noises which make them stand up have anything like non-natural meaning, even when these noises happen to be expressions of English, or notes on a musical scale.

acquired *information* from Yeats. Black's apparatus of 'filters' – which, in his 'Man is a wolf' example, are supposed to highlight the wolfish features of humanity – is irrelevant to this sort of non-sentential fragment, a fragment which lacks what Black calls a 'primary subject'. Yeats is not interested in making us notice something about the sea, nor about anything else which he or we can usefully put a finger on.

Between (2) and (3) we cross the fuzzy and fluctuating line between natural and non-natural meaning, between stimulus and cognition, between a noise having a place in a causal network and having, in addition, a place in a pattern of justification of belief. Or, more precisely, we begin to cross this line if and when these unfamiliar noises acquire familiarity and lose vitality through being not just mentioned (as the Yeats fragment was) but used: used in arguments, cited to justify beliefs, treated as counters within a social practice, employed correctly or incorrectly.

The difference between (3) and (4) is the difference between fresh metaphorical sentences and fresh paradoxes. These two blend into one another, but a rough sorting can be made by asking whether the first utterer of what seems a blatantly false remark can offer arguments for what he says. If he can, it is a paradox. If not, it is a metaphor. Both are the sort of noises which, on first hearing, 'make no sense'. But as metaphors get picked up, bandied about, and begin to die, and as paradoxes begin to function as conclusions, and later as premises, of arguments, both sorts of noises start to convey information. The process of becoming stale, familiar, unparadoxical and platitudinous is the process by which such noises cross the line from 'mere' causes of belief to reasons for belief.

Crossing this line is not the acquisition of a new metaphysical character, but simply the process of becoming, through increasingly predictable utterance, usefully describable in intentionalistic language – describable as an expression of belief. For a noise to become so describable is for it to assume a place in a pattern of justification of belief. This can, under propitious circumstances, happen to any noise; one can even imagine it happening to the examples I have placed under (1) and (2). It is pointless to ask what there is about the noise which brings about this double describability, as noise and as language. Whether it occurs is a matter of what is going on in the rest of the universe, not of something which lay deep within the noise itself.[27] This double describability (as cause and reason, noise and

---

27 Davidson says

It is no help in explaining how words work in metaphor to posit metaphorical or figurative meanings, or special kinds of poetic or metaphorical truth. Once we understand a metaphor we can call what we grasp the 'metaphorical truth' and (up to a point) say what the 'metaphorical meaning' is. But simply to lodge this meaning in the metaphor is like explaining why a pill puts you to sleep by saying it has a dormitive power.

I should prefer to say 'once the metaphor, or the paradox, ceases to seem metaphorical or paradoxical' rather than 'once we understand the metaphor'. Once we drop the idea of a meaning lodged deep within the metaphorical sentence, it is less misleading to say that we simultaneously

language) is brought about not by the unfolding of latent content (like a Leibnizian monad), but by unpredictable shifts in causal relations to other noises (like a Newtonian corpuscle). If it does come about, we can look back and explain what features of the noise suited it for this process of familiarization, but there is no way to do so prospectively. For similar reasons, there is no way of telling geniuses from eccentrics, or creativity from idle paradox-mongering, or poetry from babble, prior to seeing how utterances are, over the course of centuries, received. To ask "how metaphors work' is like asking how genius works. If we knew that, genius would be superfluous. If we knew how metaphors work they would be like the magician's illusions: matters of amusement, rather than (as Hesse rightly says they are) indispensable instruments of moral and intellectual progress.[28]

de-metaphorize the sentence and endow it with a use. We thus endow it with something to be understood – a new *literal* sense.

I take it that Davidson would regard Black's talk of a 'filter' (adopted by Hesse), Goodman's talk of a 'scheme', and Johnson and Lakoff's talk of a 'gestalt' as so many 'dormitive power' explanations of 'how metaphors work' – so many attempts to find something hidden inside the sentence, as opposed to something lying outside it, which accounts for the transition from an unfamiliar noise to a familiar counter in a social practice. But see n. 19 above.

28 Michael Levenson and Samuel Wheeler made very valuable criticisms of an earlier draft of this paper, and I have made many revisions in response.

PART III

The priority of democracy to philosophy

Thomas Jefferson set the tone for American liberal politics when he said "it does me no injury for my neighbor to say that there are twenty Gods or no God."[1] His example helped make respectable the idea that politics can be separated from beliefs about matters of ultimate importance – that shared beliefs among citizens on such matters are not essential to a democratic society. Like many other figures of the Enlightenment, Jefferson assumed that a moral faculty common to the typical theist and the typical atheist suffices for civic virtue.

Many Enlightenment intellectuals were willing to go further and say that since religious beliefs turn out to be inessential for political cohesion, they should simply be discarded as mumbo jumbo – perhaps to be replaced (as in twentieth-century totalitarian Marxist states) with some sort of explicitly secular political faith that will form the moral consciousness of the citizen. Jefferson again set the tone when he refused to go that far. He thought it enough to privatize religion, to view it as' irrelevant to social order but relevant to, and possibly essential for, individual perfection. Citizens of a Jeffersonian democracy can be as religious or irreligious as they please as long as they are not "fanatical." That is, they must abandon or modify opinions on matters of ultimate importance, the opinions that may hitherto have given sense and point to their lives, if these opinions entail public actions that cannot be justified to most of their fellow citizens.

This Jeffersonian compromise concerning the relation of spiritual perfection to public policy has two sides. Its absolutist side says that every human being, without the benefit of special revelation, has all the beliefs necessary for civic virtue. These beliefs spring from a universal human faculty, conscience – possession of which constitutes the specifically human essence of each human being. This is the faculty that gives the individual human dignity and rights. But there is also a pragmatic side. This side says that when the individual finds in her conscience beliefs that are relevant to public policy but incapable of defense on the basis of beliefs common to her fellow citizens, she must sacrifice her conscience on the altar of public expediency.

The tension between these two sides can be eliminated by a philosophical theory that identifies justifiability to humanity at large with truth. The Enlight-

[1] Thomas Jefferson, *Notes on the State of Virginia*, Query XVII, in *The Writings of Thomas Jefferson*, ed. A. A. Lipscomb and A. E. Bergh (Washington, D.C., 1905), 2: 217.

enment idea of "reason" embodies such a theory: the theory that there is a relation between the ahistorical essence of the human soul and moral truth, a relation which ensures that free and open discussion will produce "one right answer" to moral as well as to scientific questions.[2] Such a theory guarantees that a moral belief that cannot be justified to the mass of mankind is "irrational," and thus is not really a product of our moral faculty at all. Rather, it is a "prejudice," a belief that comes from some other part of the soul than "reason." It does not share in the sanctity of conscience, for it is the product of a sort of pseudoconscience – something whose loss is no sacrifice, but a purgation.

In our century, this rationalist justification of the Enlightenment compromise has been discredited. Contemporary intellectuals have given up the Enlightenment assumption that religion, myth, and tradition can be opposed to something ahistorical, something common to all human beings qua human. Anthropologists and historians of science have blurred the distinction between innate rationality and the products of acculturation. Philosophers such as Heidegger and Gadamer have given us ways of seeing human beings as historical all the way through. Other philosophers, such as Quine and Davidson, have blurred the distinction between permanent truths of reason and temporary truths of fact. Psychoanalysis has blurred the distinction between conscience and the emotions of love, hate, and fear, and thus the distinction between morality and prudence. The result is to erase the picture of the self common to Greek metaphysics, Christian theology, and Enlightenment rationalism: the picture of an ahistorical natural center, the locus of human dignity, surrounded by an adventitious and inessential periphery.

The effect of erasing this picture is to break the link between truth and justifiability. This, in turn, breaks down the bridge between the two sides of the Enlightenment compromise. The effect is to polarize liberal social theory. If we stay on the absolutist side, we shall talk about inalienable "human rights" and about "one right answer" to moral and political dilemmas without trying to back up such talk with a theory of human nature. We shall abandon metaphysical accounts of what a right is while nevertheless insisting that everywhere, in all times and cultures, members of our species have had the same rights. But if we swing to the pragmatist side, and consider talk of "rights" an attempt to enjoy the benefits of metaphysics without assuming the appropriate responsibilities, we shall still need something to distinguish the sort of individual conscience we respect from the sort we condemn as "fanatical." This can only be something relatively local and ethnocentric – the tradition of a particular community, the consensus of a particular culture. Accord-

---

2 Jefferson included a statement of this familiar Scriptural claim (roughly in the form in which it had been restated by Milton in *Areopagitica*) in the preamble to the Virginia Statute for Religious Freedom: "truth is great and will prevail if left to herself, . . . she is the proper and sufficient antagonist to error, and has nothing to fear from the conflict, unless by human interposition disarmed of her natural weapons, free argument and debate, errors ceasing to be dangerous when it is permitted freely to contradict them" (ibid., 2: 302).

ing to this view, what counts as rational or as fanatical is relative to the group to which we think it necessary to justify ourselves – to the body of shared belief that determines the reference of the word "we." The Kantian identification with a central transcultural and ahistorical self is thus replaced by a quasi-Hegelian identification with our own community, thought of as a historical product. For pragmatist social theory, the question of whether justifiability to the community with which we identify entails truth is simply irrelevant.

Ronald Dworkin and others who take the notion of ahistorical human "rights" seriously serve as examples of the first, absolutist, pole. John Dewey and, as I shall shortly be arguing, John Rawls serve as examples of the second pole. But there is a third type of social theory – often dubbed "communitarianism" – which is less easy to place. Roughly speaking, the writers tagged with this label are those who reject both the individualistic rationalism of the Enlightenment and the idea of "rights," but, unlike the pragmatists, see this rejection as throwing doubt on the institutions and culture of the surviving democratic states. Such theorists include Robert Bellah, Alasdair MacIntyre, Michael Sandel, Charles Taylor, early Roberto Unger, and many others. These writers share some measure of agreement with a view found in an extreme form both in Heidegger and in Horkheimer and Adorno's *Dialectic of Enlightenment*. This is the view that liberal institutions and culture either should not or cannot survive the collapse of the philosophical justification that the Enlightenment provided for them.

There are three strands in communitarianism that need to be disentangled. First, there is the empirical prediction that no society that sets aside the idea of ahistorical moral truth in the insouciant way that Dewey recommended can survive. Horkheimer and Adorno, for example, suspect that you cannot have a moral community in a disenchanted world because toleration leads to pragmatism, and it is not clear how we can prevent, "blindly pragmatized thought" from losing "its transcending quality and its relation to truth."[3] They think that pragmatism was the inevitable outcome of Enlightenment rationalism and that pragmatism is not a strong enough philosophy to make moral community possible.[4] Second, there is the moral judgment that the sort of human being who is

---

3 Max Horkheimer and Theodor W. Adorno, *Dialectic of Enlightenment* (New York: Seabury Press, 1972), p. xiii.
4 "For the Enlightenment, whatever does not conform to the rule of computation and utility is suspect. So long as it can develop undisturbed by any outward repression, there is no holding it. In the process, it treats its own ideas of human rights exactly as it does the older universals . . . Enlightenment is totalitarian" (ibid., p. 6). This line of thought recurs repeatedly in communitarian accounts of the present state of the liberal democracies; see, for example, Robert Bellah, Richard Madsen, William Sullivan, Ann Swidler, and Steven Tipton, *Habits of the Heart: Individualism and Commitment in American Life* (Berkeley: University of California Press, 1985): "There is a widespread feeling that the promise of the modern era is slipping away from us. A movement of enlightenment and liberation that was to have freed us from superstition and tyranny has led in the twentieth century to a world in which ideological fanaticism and political oppression have reached extremes unknown in previous history" (p. 277).

produced by liberal institutions and culture is undesirable. MacIntyre, for example, thinks that our culture – a culture he says is dominated by "the Rich Aesthete, the Manager, and the Therapist" – is a *reductio ad absurdum* both of the philosophical views that helped create it and of those now invoked in its defense. Third, there is the claim that political institutions "presuppose" a doctrine about the nature of human beings and that such a doctrine must, unlike Enlightenment rationalism, make clear the essentially historical character of the self. So we find writers like Taylor and Sandel saying that we need a theory of the self that incorporates Hegel's and Heidegger's sense of the self's historicity.

The first claim is a straightforward empirical, sociological-historical one about the sort of glue that is required to hold a community together. The second is a straightforward moral judgment that the advantages of contemporary liberal democracy are outweighed by the disadvantages, by the ignoble and sordid character of the culture and the individual human beings that it produces. The third claim, however, is the most puzzling and complex. I shall concentrate on this third, most puzzling, claim, although toward the end I shall return briefly to the first two.

To evaluate this third claim, we need to ask two questions. The first is whether there is any sense in which liberal democracy "needs" philosophical justification at all. Those who share Dewey's pragmatism will say that although it may need philosophical articulation, it does not need philosophical backup. On this view, the philosopher of liberal democracy may wish to develop a theory of the human self that comports with the institutions he or she admires. But such a philosopher is not thereby justifying these institutions by reference to more fundamental premises, but the reverse: He or she is putting politics first and tailoring a philosophy to suit. Communitarians, by contrast, often speak as though political institutions were no better than their philosophical foundations.

The second question is one that we can ask even if we put the opposition between justification and articulation to one side. It is the question of whether a conception of the self that, as Taylor says, makes "the community constitutive of the individual"[5] does in fact comport better with liberal democracy than does the Enlightenment conception of the self. Taylor summarizes the latter as "an ideal of disengagement" that defines a "typically modern notion" of human dignity: "the ability to act on one's own, without outside interference or subordination to outside authority." On Taylor's view, as on Heidegger's, these Enlightenment notions are closely linked with characteristically modern ideas of "efficacy, power, unperturbability."[6] They are also closely linked with the contemporary form of the doctrine of the sacredness of the individual conscience – Dworkin's claim that appeals to rights "trump" all other appeals. Taylor, like Heidegger, would like to

---

5 Charles Taylor, *Philosophy and the Human Sciences*, vol. 2 of *Philosophical Papers* (Cambridge: Cambridge University Press, 1985), p. 8
6 Ibid., p. 5.

substitute a less individualistic conception of what it is to be properly human – one that makes less of autonomy and more of interdependence.

I can preview what is to come by saying that I shall answer "no" to the first question about the communitarians' third claim and "yes" to the second. I shall be arguing that Rawls, following up on Dewey, shows us how liberal democracy can get along without philosophical presuppositions. He has thus shown us how we can disregard the third communitarian claim. But I shall also argue that communitarians like Taylor are right in saying that a conception of the self that makes the community constitutive of the self does comport well with liberal democracy. That is, if we *want* to flesh out our self-image as citizens of such a democracy with a philosophical view of the self, Taylor gives us pretty much the right view. But this sort of philosophical fleshing-out does not have the importance that writers like Horkheimer and Adorno, or Heidegger, have attributed to it.

Without further preface, I turn now to Rawls. I shall begin by pointing out that both in A *Theory of Justice* and subsequently, he has linked his own position to the Jeffersonian ideal of religious toleration. In an article called "Justice as Fairness: Political not Metaphysical," he says that he is "going to apply the principle of toleration to philosophy itself," and goes on to say:

> The essential point is this: as a practical political matter no general moral conception can provide the basis for a public conception of justice in a modern democratic society. The social and historical conditions of such a society have their origins in the Wars of Religion following the Reformation and the development of the principle of toleration, and in the growth of constitutional government and the institutions of large market economies. These conditions profoundly affect the requirements of a workable conception of political justice: such a conception must allow for a diversity of doctrines and the plurality of conflicting, and indeed incommensurable conceptions of the good affirmed by the members of existing democratic societies.[7]

We can think of Rawls as saying that just as the principle of religious toleration and the social thought of the Enlightenment proposed to bracket many standard theological topics when deliberating about public policy and constructing politi-

---

7   John Rawls, "Justice as Fairness: Political not Metaphysical," *Philosophy and Public Affairs* 14 (1985): 225. Religious toleration is a constantly recurring theme in Rawls's writing. Early in *A Theory of Justice* (Cambridge, Mass.: Harvard University Press, 1971), when giving examples of the sort of common opinions that a theory of justice must take into account and systematize, he cites our conviction that religious intolerance is unjust (p. 19). His example of the fact that "a well-ordered society tends to eliminate or at least to control men's inclinations to injustice" is that "warring and intolerant sects are much less likely to exist" (p. 247). Another relevant passage (which I shall discuss below) is his diagnosis of Ignatius Loyola's attempt to make the love of God the "dominant good": "Although to subordinate all our aims to one end does not strictly speaking violate the principles of rational choice . . . it still strikes us as irrational, or more likely as mad" (pp. 553–4).

cal institutions, so we need to bracket many standard topics of philosophical inquiry. For purposes of social theory, we can put aside such topics as an ahistorical human nature, the nature of selfhood, the motive of moral behavior, and the meaning of human life. We treat these as irrelevant to politics as Jefferson thought questions about the Trinity and about transubstantiation.

Insofar as he adopts this stance, Rawls disarms many of the criticisms that, in the wake of Horkheimer and Adorno, have been directed at American liberalism. Rawls can agree that Jefferson and his circle shared a lot of dubious philosophical views, views that we might now wish to reject. He can even agree with Horkheimer and Adorno, as Dewey would have, that these views contained the seeds of their own destruction. But he thinks that the remedy may be not to formulate better philosophical views on the same topics, but (for purposes of political theory) benignly to neglect these topics. As he says:

since justice as fairness is intended as a political conception of justice for a democratic society, it tries to draw solely upon basic intuitive ideas that are embedded in the political institutions of a democratic society and the public traditions of their interpretation. Justice as fairness is a political conception in part because it starts from within a certain political tradition. We hope that this political conception of justice may be at least supported by what we may call "overlapping consensus," that is, by a consensus that includes all the opposing philosophical and religious doctrines likely to persist and gain adherents in a more or less just constitutional democratic society.[8]

Rawls thinks that "philosophy as the search for truth about an independent metaphysical and moral order cannot . . . provide a workable and shared basis for a political conception of justice in a democratic society."[9] So he suggests that we confine ourselves to collecting, "such settled convictions as the belief in religious toleration and the rejection of slavery" and then "try to organize the basic intuitive ideas and principles implicit in these convictions into a coherent conception of justice."[10]

This attitude is thoroughly historicist and antiuniversalist.[11] Rawls can whole-

---

8 Rawls, "Justice as Fairness," pp. 225–6. The suggestion that there are many philosophical views that will *not* survive in such conditions is analogous to the Enlightenment suggestion that the adoption of democratic institutions will cause "superstitious" forms of religious belief gradually to die off.

9 Ibid., p. 230.

10 Ibid.

11 For Rawls's historicism see, for example, *Theory of Justice,* p. 547. There, Rawls says that the people in the original position are assumed to know "the general facts about society," including the fact that "institutions are not fixed but change over time, altered by natural circumstances and the activities and conflicts of social groups." He uses this point to rule out, as original choosers of principles of justice, those "in a feudal or a caste system," and those who are unaware of events such as the French Revolution. This is one of many passages that make clear (at least read in the light of Rawls's later work) that a great deal of knowledge that came late to the mind of Europe is present to the minds of those behind the veil of ignorance. Or, to put it another way, such passages make clear that those original choosers behind the veil exemplify a certain modern type of

heartedly agree with Hegel and Dewey against Kant and can say that the Enlightenment attempt to free oneself from tradition and history, to appeal to "Nature" or "Reason," was self-deceptive.[12] He can see such an appeal as a misguided attempt to make philosophy do what theology failed to do. Rawls's effort to, in his words, "stay on the surface, philosophically speaking" can be seen as taking Jefferson's avoidance of theology one step further.

On the Deweyan view I am attributing to Rawls, no such discipline as "philosophical anthropology" is required as a preface to politics, but only history and sociology. Further, it is misleading to think of his view as Dworkin does: as "rights-based" as opposed to "goal-based." For the notion of "basis" is not in point. It is not that we know, on antecedent philosophical grounds, that it is of the essence of human beings to have rights, and then proceed to ask how a society might preserve and protect these rights. On the question of priority, as on the question of the relativity of justice to historical situations, Rawls is closer to Walzer than to Dworkin.[13] Since Rawls does not believe that for purposes of political theory, we need think of ourselves as having an essence that precedes and antedates history, he would not agree with Sandel that for these purposes, we need

human being, not an ahistorical human nature. See also p. 548, where Rawls says, "Of course in working out what the requisite principles [of justice] are, we must rely upon current knowledge as recognized by common sense and the existing scientific consensus. We have to concede that as established beliefs change, it is possible that the principles of justice which it seems rational to choose may likewise change."

12 See Bellah et al., *Habits of the Heart*, p. 141, for a recent restatement of this "counter-Enlightenment" line of thought. For the authors' view of the problems created by persistence in Enlightenment rhetoric and by the prevalence of the conception of human dignity that Taylor identifies as "distinctively modern," see p. 21: "For most of us, it is easier to think about to get what we want than to know exactly what we should want. Thus Brian, Joe, Margaret and Wayne [some of the Americans interviewed by the authors] are each in his or her own way confused about how to define for themselves such things as the nature of success, the meaning of freedom, and the requirements of justice. Those difficulties are in an important way created by the limitations in the common tradition of moral discourse they – and we – share." Compare p. 290: "the language of individualism, the primary American language of self-understanding, limits the way in which people think."

To my mind, the authors of *Habits of the Heart* undermine their own conclusions in the passages where they point to actual moral progress being made in recent American history, notably in their discussion of the civil-rights movement. There, they say that Martin Luther King, Jr., made the struggle for freedom "a practice of commitment within a vision of America as a community of memory" and that the response King elicited "came from the reawakened recognition by many Americans that their own sense of self was rooted in companionship with others who, though not necessarily like themselves, nevertheless shared with them a common history and whose appeals to justice and solidarity made powerful claims on our loyalty" (p. 252). These descriptions of King's achievement seem exactly right, but they can be read as evidence that the rhetoric of the Enlightenment offers at least as many opportunities as it does obstacles for the renewal of a sense of community. The civil-rights movement combined, without much strain, the language of Christian fellowship and the "language of individualism," about which Bellah and his colleagues are dubious.

13 See Michael Walzer, *Spheres of Justice* (New York: Basic, 1983), pp. 312 ff.

have an account of "the nature of the moral subject," which is "in some sense necessary, non-contingent and prior to any particular experience."[14] Some of our ancestors may have required such an account, just as others of our ancestors required such an account of their relation to their putative Creator. But *we* – we heirs of the Enlightenment for whom justice has become the first virtue – need neither. As citizens and as social theorists, we can be as indifferent to philosophical disagreements about the nature of the self as Jefferson was to theological differences about the nature of God.

This last point suggests a way of sharpening up my claim that Rawls's advocacy of philosophical toleration is a plausible extension of Jefferson's advocacy of religious toleration. Both "religion" and "philosophy" are vague umbrella terms, and both are subject to persuasive redefinition. When these terms are broadly enough defined, everybody, even atheists, will be said to have a religious faith (in the Tillichian sense of a "symbol of ultimate concern"). Everybody, even those who shun metaphysics and epistemology, will be said to have "philosophical presuppositions."[15] But for purposes of interpreting Jefferson and Rawls, we must use narrower definitions. Let "religion" mean, for Jefferson's purposes, disputes about the nature and the true name of God – and even about his existence.[16] Let "philosophy" mean, for Rawls's purposes, disputes about the nature of human beings and even about whether there is such a thing as "human nature."[17] Using

14 Michael Sandel, *Liberalism and the Limits of Justice* (Cambridge: Cambridge University Press, 1982), p. 49.

15 In a recent, as yet unpublished, paper, Sandel has urged that Rawls's claim that "philosophy in the classical sense as the search for truth about a prior and independent moral order cannot provide the shared basis for a political conception of justice" presupposes the controversial metaphysical claim that there is no such order. This seems to me like saying that Jefferson was presupposing the controversial theological claim that God is not interested in the name by which he is called by human beings. Both charges are accurate, but not really to the point. Both Jefferson and Rawls would have to reply, "I have no arguments for my dubious theological-metaphysical claim, because I do not know how to discuss such issues, and do not want to. My interest is in helping to preserve and create political institutions that will foster public indifference to such issues, while putting no restrictions on private discussion of them." This reply, of course, begs the "deeper" question that Sandel wants to raise, for the question of whether we *should* determine what issues to discuss on political or on "theoretical" (for example, theological or philosophical) grounds remains unanswered.

16 Jefferson agreed with Luther that philosophers had muddied the clear waters of the gospels. See Jefferson's polemic against Plato's "foggy mind" and his claim that "the doctrines which flowed from the lips of Jesus himself are within the comprehension of a child; but thousands of volumes have not yet explained the Platonisms engrafted on them; and for this obvious reason, that nonsense can never be explained" (*Writings of Thomas Jefferson*, 14: 149).

17 I am here using the term "human nature" in the traditional philosophical sense in which Sartre denied that there was such a thing, rather than in the rather unusual one that Rawls gives it. Rawls distinguishes between a "conception of the person" and a "theory of human nature," where the former is a "moral ideal" and the latter is provided by, roughly, common sense plus the social sciences. To have a theory of human nature is to have "general facts that we take to be true, or true enough, given the state of public knowledge in our society," facts that "limit the feasibility of the ideals of person and society embedded in that framework" ("Kantian Constructivism in Moral Theory," *Journal of Philosophy* 88 [1980]: 534).

these definitions, we can say that Rawls wants views about man's nature and purpose to be detached from politics. As he says, he wants his conception of justice to "avoid . . . claims about the essential nature and identity of persons."[18] So presumably, he wants questions about the point of human existence, or the meaning of human life, to be reserved for private life. A liberal democracy will not only exempt opinions on such matters from legal coercion, but also aim at disengaging discussions of such questions from discussions of social policy. Yet it will use force against the individual conscience, just insofar as conscience leads individuals to act so as to threaten democratic institutions. Unlike Jefferson's, Rawls's argument against fanaticism is not that it threatens truth about the characteristics of an antecedent metaphysical and moral order by threatening free discussion, but *simply* that it threatens freedom, and thus threatens justice. Truth about the existence or nature of that order drops out.

The definition of "philosophy" I have just suggested is not as artificial and ad hoc as it may appear. Intellectual historians commonly treat "the nature of the human subject" as the topic that gradually replaced "God" as European culture secularized itself. This has been the central topic of metaphysics and epistemology from the seventeenth century to the present, and, for better or worse, metaphysics and epistemology have been taken to be the "core" of philosophy.[19] Insofar as one thinks that political conclusions require extrapolitical grounding – that is, insofar as one thinks Rawls's method of reflective equilibrium[20] is not good enough – one will want an account of the "authority" of those general principles.

If one feels a need for such legitimation, one will want either a religious or a philosophical preface to politics.[21] One will be likely to share Horkheimer and

---

18 Rawls, "Justice as Fairness," p. 223.

19 In fact, it has been for the worse. A view that made politics more central to philosophy and subjectivity less would both permit more effective defenses of democracy than those that purport to supply it with "foundations" and permit liberals to meet Marxists on their own, political, ground. Dewey's explicit attempt to make the central philosophical question "What serves democracy?" rather than "What permits us to argue for democracy?" has been, unfortunately, neglected. I try to make this point in "Philosophy as Science, as Metaphor, and as Politics" (in *Essays on Heidegger and Others*).

20 That is, give-and-take between intuitions about the desirability of particular consequences of particular actions and intuitions about general principles, with neither having the determining voice.

21 One will also, as I did on first reading Rawls, take him to be attempting to supply such legitimation by an appeal to the rationality of the choosers in the original position. Rawls warned his readers that the original position (the position of those who, behind a veil of ignorance that hides them from their life chances and their conceptions of the good, select from among alternative principles of justice) served simply "to make vivid . . . the restrictions that it seems reasonable to impose on arguments for principles of justice and therefore on those principles themselves" (*Theory of Justice*, p. 18).

      But this warning went unheeded by myself and others, in part because of an ambiguity between "reasonable" as defined by ahistorical criteria and as meaning something like "in accord with the moral sentiments characteristic of the heirs of the Enlightenment." Rawls's later work has, as I have said, helped us come down on the historicist side of this ambiguity; see, for example,

Adorno's fear that pragmatism is not strong enough to hold a free society to-gether. But Rawls echoes Dewey in suggesting that insofar as justice becomes the first virtue of a society, the need for such legitimation may gradually cease to be felt. Such a society will become accustomed to the thought that social policy needs no more authority than successful accommodation among individuals, individuals who find themselves heir to the same historical traditions and faced with the same problems. It will be a society that encourages the "end of ideology," that takes reflective equilibrium as the only method needed in discussing social policy. When such a society deliberates, when it collects the principles and intuitions to be brought into equilibrium, it will tend to discard those drawn from philosophical accounts of the self or of rationality. For such a society will view such accounts not as the foundations of political institutions, but as, at worst, philosophical mumbo jumbo, or, at best, relevant to private searches for perfection, but not to social policy.[22]

In order to spell out the contrast between Rawls's attempt to "stay on the surface, philosophically speaking" and the traditional attempt to dig down to "philosophical foundations of democracy," I shall turn briefly to Sandel's *Liberalism and the Limits of Justice*. This clear and forceful book provides very elegant and cogent arguments against the attempt to use a certain conception of the self, a certain metaphysical view of what human beings are like, to legitimize liberal politics. Sandel attributes this attempt to Rawls. Many people, including myself, initially took Rawls's *A Theory of Justice* to be such an attempt. We read it as a continuation of the Enlightenment attempt to ground our moral intuitions on a conception of human nature (and, more specifically, as a neo-Kantian attempt to ground them

"Kantian Constructivism": "the original position is not an axiomatic (or deductive) basis from which principles are derived but a procedure for singling out principles most fitting to the conception of the person most likely to be held, at least implicitly, in a democratic society" (p. 572). It is tempting to suggest that one could eliminate all reference to the original position from *A Theory of Justice* without loss, but this is as daring a suggestion as that one might rewrite (as many have wished to do) Kant's *Critique of Pure Reason* without reference to the thing-in-itself. T. M. Scanlon has suggested that we can, at least, safely eliminate reference, in the description of the choosers in the original position, to an appeal to self-interest. ("Contractualism and Utilitarianism," in *Utilitarianism and Beyond*, ed. Bernard Williams and Amartya Sen [Cambridge: Cambridge University Press, 1982]). Since justifiability is, more evidently than self-interest, relative to historical circumstance, Scanlon's proposal seems to be more faithful to Rawls's overall philosophical program than Rawls's own formulation.

22 In particular, there will be no principles or intuitions concerning the universal features of human psychology relevant to motivation. Sandel thinks that since assumptions about motivation are part of the description of the original position, "what issues at one end in a theory of justice must issue at the other in a theory of the person, or more precisely, a theory of the moral subject" (*Liberalism and the Limits of Justice*, p. 47). I would argue that if we follow Scanlon's lead (note 21) in dropping reference to self-interest in our description of the original choosers and replacing this with reference to their desire to justify their choices to their fellows, then the only "theory of the person" we get is a sociological description of the inhabitants of contemporary liberal democracies.

on the notion of "rationality"). However, Rawls's writings subsequent to *A Theory of Justice* have helped us realize that we were misinterpreting his book, that we had overemphasized the Kantian and underemphasized the Hegelian and Deweyan elements. These writings make more explicit than did his book Rawls's metaphilosophical doctrine that "what justifies a conception of justice is not its being true to an order antecedent to and given to us, but its congruence with our deeper understanding of ourselves and our aspirations, and our realization that, *given our history and the traditions embedded in our public life,* it is the most reasonable doctrine *for us.*"[23]

When reread in the light of such passages, *A Theory of Justice* no longer seems committed to a philosophical account of the human self, but only to a historico-sociological description of the way we live now.

Sandel sees Rawls as offering us "deontology with a Humean face" – that is, a Kantian universalistic approach to social thought without the handicap of Kant's idealistic metaphysics. He thinks that this will not work, that a social theory of the sort that Rawls wants requires us to postulate the sort of self that Descartes and Kant invented to replace God – one that can be distinguished from the Kantian "empirical self" as choosing various "contingent desires, wants and ends," rather than being a mere concatenation of beliefs and desires. Since such a concatenation – what Sandel calls a "radically situated subject"[24] – is all that Hume offers us, Sandel thinks that Rawls's project is doomed.[25] On Sandel's account, Rawls's doctrine that "justice is the first virtue of social institutions" requires backup from the metaphysical claim that "teleology to the contrary, what is most essential to our personhood is not the ends we choose but our capacity to choose them. And this capacity is located in a self which must be prior to the ends it chooses."[26]

But reading *A Theory of Justice* as political rather than metaphysical, one can see that when Rawls says that "the self is prior to the ends which are affirmed by it,"[27] he need not mean that there is an entity called "the self" that is something distinct from the web of beliefs and desires that that self "has." When he says that "we should not attempt to give form to our life by first looking to the good

23 Rawls, "Kantian Constructivism," p. 519. Italics added.
24 Sandel, *Liberalism and the Limits of Justice,* p. 21. I have argued for the advantages of thinking of the self as just such a concatenation in chapter 2 of *Contingency, Irony, and Solidarity* (Cambridge: Cambridge University Press, 1989). When Sandel cites Robert Nozick and Daniel Bell as suggesting that Rawls "ends by dissolving the self in order to preserve it" (*Liberalism and the Limits of Justice,* p. 95), I should rejoin that it may be helpful to dissolve the metaphysical self in order to preserve the political one. Less obliquely stated: It may be helpful, for purposes of systematizing our intuitions about the priority of liberty, to treat the self as having no center, no essence, but *merely* as a concatenation of beliefs and desires.
25 "Deontology with a Humean face either fails as deontology or recreates in the original position the disembodied subject it resolves to avoid" (ibid., p. 14).
26 Ibid., p. 19.
27 Rawls, *Theory of Justice,* p. 560.

independently defined,"[28] he is not basing this "should" on a claim about the nature of the self. "Should" is not to be glossed by "because of the intrinsic nature of morality"[29] or "because a capacity for choice is the essence of personhood," but by something like "because *we* – we modern inheritors of the traditions of religious tolerance and constitutional government – put liberty ahead of perfection."

This willingness to invoke what *we* do raises, as I have said, the specters of ethnocentrism and of relativism. Because Sandel is convinced that Rawls shares Kant's fear of these specters, he is convinced that Rawls is looking for an " 'Archimedean point' from which to assess the basic structure of society" – a "standpoint neither compromised by its implication in the world nor dissociated and so disqualified by detachment."[30] It is just this idea that a standpoint can be "compromised by its implication in the world" that Rawls rejects in his recent writings. Philosophically inclined communitarians like Sandel are unable to envisage a middle ground between relativism and a "theory of the moral subject" – a theory that is not about, for example, religious tolerance and large market economies, but about human beings as such, viewed ahistorically. Rawls is trying to stake out just such a middle ground.[31] When he speaks of an "Archimedian

28 Ibid.

29 It is important to note that Rawls explicitly distances himself from the idea that he is analyzing the very idea of morality and from conceptual analysis as the method of social theory (ibid., p. 130). Some of his critics have suggested that Rawls is practicing "reductive logical analysis" of the sort characteristic of "analytic philosophy"; see, for example, William M. Sullivan, *Reconstructing Public Philosophy* (Berkeley: University of California Press, 1982), pp. 94ff. Sullivan says that "this ideal of reductive logical analysis lends legitimacy to the notion that moral philosophy is summed up in the task of discovering, through the analysis of moral rules, both primitive elements and governing principles that must apply to any rational moral system, *rational* here meaning 'logically coherent' " (p. 96). He goes on to grant that "Nozick and Rawls are more sensitive to the importance of history and social experience in human life than were the classic liberal thinkers" (p. 97). But this concession is too slight and is misleading. Rawls's willingness to adopt "reflective equilibrium" rather than "conceptual analysis" as a methodological watchword sets him apart from the epistemologically oriented moral philosophy that was dominant prior to the appearance of *A Theory of Justice*. Rawls represents a reaction against the Kantian idea of "morality" as having an ahistorical essence, the same sort of reaction found in Hegel and in Dewey.

30 Sandel, *Liberalism and the Limits of Justice*, p. 17.

31 ". . . liberty of conscience and freedom of thought should not be founded on philosophical or ethical skepticism, nor on indifference to religious and moral interests. The principles of justice define an appropriate path between dogmatism and intolerance on the one side, and a reductionism which regards religion and morality as mere preferences on the other" (Rawls, *Theory of Justice*, p. 243). I take it that Rawls is identifying "philosophical or ethical skepticism" with the idea that everything is just a matter of "preference," even religion, philosophy, and morals. So we should distinguish his suggestion that we "extend the principle of toleration to philosophy itself" from the suggestion that we dismiss philosophy as epiphenomenal. That is the sort of suggestion that is backed up by reductionist accounts of philosophical doctrines as "preferences" or "wish fulfillments" or "expressions of emotion" (see Rawls's criticism of Freudian reductionism in ibid., pp. 539ff.). Neither psychology nor logic nor any other theoretical discipline can supply non-question-begging reasons why philosophy should be set aside, any more than philosophy can supply such reasons why theology should be set aside. But this is compatible with saying that the general course of historical experience may lead us to neglect theological topics and bring us to the point at which, like Jefferson, we find a theological vocabulary

point," he does not mean a point outside history, but simply the kind of settled social habits that allow much latitude for further choices. He says, for example,

The upshot of these considerations is that justice as fairness is not at the mercy, so to speak, of existing wants and interests. It sets up an Archimedean point for assessing the social system without invoking a priori considerations. The long range aim of society is settled in its main lines irrespective of the particular desires and needs of its present members. . . . There is no place for the question whether men's desires to play the role of superior or inferior might not be so great that autocratic institutions should be accepted, or whether men's perception of the religious practices of others might not be so upsetting that liberty of conscience should not be allowed.[32]

To say that there is no place for the questions that Nietzsche or Loyola would raise is not to say that the views of either are unintelligible (in the sense of "logically incoherent" or "conceptually confused"). Nor is it to say that they are based on an incorrect theory of the self. Nor is it *just* to say that our preferences conflict with theirs.[33] It is to say that the conflict between these men and us is so great that "preferences" is the wrong word. It is appropriate to speak of gustatory or sexual preferences, for these do not matter to anybody but yourself and your immediate circle. But it is misleading to speak of a "preference" for liberal democracy.

Rather, we heirs of the Enlightenment think of enemies of liberal democracy like Nietzsche or Loyola as, to use Rawls's word, "mad." We do so because there is no way to see them as fellow citizens of our constitutional democracy, people whose life plans might, given ingenuity and good will, be fitted in with those of other citizens. They are not crazy because they have mistaken the ahistorical nature of human beings. They are crazy because the limits of sanity are set by

"meaningless" (or, more precisely, useless). I am suggesting that the course of historical experience since Jefferson's time has led us to a point at which we find much of the vocabulary of modern philosophy no longer useful.

32 Ibid., pp. 261–2.

33 The contrast between "mere preference" and something less "arbitrary," something more closely related to the very nature of man or of reason, is invoked by many writers who think of "human rights" as requiring a philosophical foundation of the traditional sort. Thus my colleague David Little, commenting on my "Solidarity or Objectivity?" (above), says "Rorty appears to permit criticism and pressure against those societies [the ones we do not like] *if we happen to want to* criticize and pressure them in pursuit of some interest or belief we may (at the time) have, and for whatever ethnocentric reasons we may happen to hold those interests or beliefs" ("Natural Rights and Human Rights: The International Imperative," in *National Rights and Natural Law: The Legacy of George Mason,* ed. Robert P. Davidow [Fairfax, Va.: George Mason University Press, 1986], pp. 67–122; italics in original). I would rejoin that Little's use of "happen to want to" presupposes a dubious distinction between necessary, built-in, universal convictions (convictions that it would be "irrational" to reject) and accidental, culturally determined convictions. It also presupposes the existence of such faculties as reason, will, and emotion, all of which the pragmatist tradition in American philosophy and the so-called existentialist tradition in European philosophy try to undercut. Dewey's *Human Nature and Conduct* and Heidegger's *Being and Time* both offer a moral psychology that avoids oppositions between "preference" and "reason."

what *we* can take seriously. This, in turn, is determined by our upbringing, our historical situation.[34]

If this short way of dealing with Nietzsche and Loyola seems shockingly ethnocentric, it is because the philosophical tradition has accustomed us to the idea that anybody who is willing to listen to reason – to hear out all the arguments – can be brought around to the truth. This view, which Kierkegaard called "Socratism" and contrasted with the claim that our point of departure may be simply a historical event, is intertwined with the idea that the human self has a center (a divine spark, or a truth-tracking faculty called "reason") and that argumentation will, given time and patience, penetrate to this center. For Rawls's purposes, we do not need this picture. We are free to see the self as centerless, as a historical contingency all the way through. Rawls neither needs nor wants to defend the priority of the right to the good as Kant defended it, by invoking a theory of the self that makes it more than an "empirical self," more than a "radically situated subject." He presumably thinks of Kant as, although largely right about the nature of justice, largely wrong about the nature and function of philosophy.

More specifically, he can reject Sandel's Kantian claim that there is a "distance between subject and situation which is necessary to any measure of detachment, is essential to the ineliminably *possessive* aspect of any coherent conception of the self."[35] Sandel defines this aspect by saying, "I can never fully be constituted by my attributes . . . there must always be some attributes I *have* rather than am." On the interpretation of Rawls I am offering, we do not need a categorical distinction between the self and its situation. We can dismiss the distinction between an attribute of the self and a constituent of the self, between the self's accidents and its essence, as "merely" metaphysical.[36] If we are inclined to philosophize, we shall want the vocabulary offered by Dewey, Heidegger, Davidson, and Derrida, with its built-in cautions against metaphysics, rather than that offered

34 "Aristotle remarks that it is a peculiarity of men that they possess a sense of the just and the unjust and that their sharing a common understanding of justice makes a polis. Analogously one might say, in view of our discussion, that a common understanding of justice as fairness makes a constitutional democracy" (Rawls, *Theory of Justice*, p. 243). In the interpretation of Rawls I am offering, it is unrealistic to expect Aristotle to have developed a conception of justice as fairness, since he simply lacked the kind of historical experience that we have accumulated since his day. More generally, it is pointless to assume (with, for example, Leo Strauss) that the Greeks had already canvassed the alternatives available for social life and institutions. When we discuss justice, we cannot agree to bracket our knowledge of recent history.

35 Sandel, *Liberalism and the Limits of Justice*, p. 20.

36 We can dismiss other distinctions that Sandel draws in the same way. Examples are the distinction between a voluntarist and a cognitive account of the original position (ibid., p. 121), that between "the identity of the subject" as the "product" rather than the "premise" of its agency (ibid., p. 152), and that between the question "Who am I?" and its rival as "the paradigmatic moral question," "What shall I choose?" (ibid., p. 153). These distinctions are all to be analyzed away as products of the "Kantian dualisms" that Rawls praises Hegel and Dewey for having overcome.

by Descartes, Hume, and Kant.[37] For if we use the former vocabulary, we shall be able to see moral progress as a history of making rather than finding, of poetic achievement by "radically situated" individuals and communities, rather than as the gradual unveiling, through the use of "reason," of "principles" or "rights" or "values."

Sandel's claim that "the concept of a subject given prior to and independent of its objects offers a foundation for the moral law that . . . powerfully completes the deontological vision" is true enough. But to suggest such a powerful completion to Rawls is to offer him a poisoned gift. It is like offering Jefferson an argument for religious tolerance based on exegesis of the Christian Scriptures.[38] Rejecting the assumption that the moral law needs a "foundation" is just what distinguishes Rawls from Jefferson. It is just this that permits him to be a Deweyan naturalist who needs neither the distinction between will and intellect nor the distinction between the self's constituents and its attributes. He does not *want* a "complete deontological vision," one that would explain *why* we should give justice priority over our conception of the good. He is filling out the consequences of the claim that it is prior, not its presuppositions.[39] Rawls is not interested in conditions for the identity of the self, but only in conditions for citizenship in a liberal society.

Suppose one grants that Rawls is not attempting a transcendental deduction of American liberalism or supplying philosophical foundations for democratic institutions, but simply trying to systematize the principles and intuitions typical of American liberals. Still, it may seem that the important questions raised by the

---

37 For some similarities between Dewey and Heidegger with respect to anti-Cartesianism, see my "Overcoming the Tradition," in Richard Rorty, *Consequences of Pragmatism* (Minneapolis: University of Minnesota Press, 1982).

38 David Levin has pointed out to me that Jefferson was not above borrowing such arguments. I take this to show that Jefferson, like Kant, found himself in an untenable halfway position between theology and Deweyan social experimentalism.

39 Sandel takes "the primacy of the subject" to be not only a way of filling out the deontological picture, but also a necessary condition of its correctness: "If the claim for the primacy of justice is to succeed, if the right is to be prior to the good in the interlocking moral and foundational sense we have distinguished, then some version of the claim for the primacy of the subject must succeed as well" (*Liberalism and the Limits of Justice*, p. 7). Sandel quotes Rawls as saying that "the essential unity of the self is already provided by the conception of the right" and takes this passage as evidence that Rawls holds a doctrine of the "priority of the self" (ibid., p. 21). But consider the context of this sentence. Rawls says: "The principles of justice and their realization in social forms define the bounds within which our deliberations take place. The essential unity of the self is already provided by the conception of right. Moreover, in a well-ordered society this unity is the same for all; everyone's conception of the good as given by his rational plan is a sub-plan of the larger comprehensive plan that regulates the community as a social union of social unions" (*Theory of Justice*, p. 563). The "essential unity of the self," which is in question here, is simply the system of moral sentiments, habits, and internalized traditions that is typical of the politically aware citizen of a constitutional democracy. This self is, once again, a historical product. It has nothing to do with the nonempirical self, which Kant had to postulate in the interests of Enlightenment universalism.

critics of liberalism have been begged. Consider the claim that we liberals can simply dismiss Nietzsche and Loyola as crazy. One imagines these two rejoining that they are quite aware that their views unfit them for citizenship in a constitutional democracy and that the typical inhabitant of such a democracy would regard them as crazy. But they take these facts as further counts against constitutional democracy. They think that the kind of person created by such a democracy is not what a human being should be.

In finding a dialectical stance to adopt toward Nietzsche or Loyola, we liberal democrats are faced with a dilemma. To refuse to argue about what human beings should be like seems to show a contempt for the spirit of accommodation and tolerance, which is essential to democracy. But it is not clear how to argue for the claim that human beings ought to be liberals rather than fanatics without being driven back on a theory of human nature, on philosophy. I think that we must grasp the first horn. We have to insist that not every argument need to be met in the terms in which it is presented. Accommodation and tolerance must stop short of a willingness to work within any vocabulary that one's interlocutor wishes to use, to take seriously any topic that he puts forward for discussion. To take this view is of a piece with dropping the idea that a single moral vocabulary and a single set of moral beliefs are appropriate for every human community everywhere, and to grant that historical developments may lead us to simply *drop* questions and the vocabulary in which those questions are posed.

Just as Jefferson refused to let the Christian Scriptures set the terms in which to discuss alternative political institutions, so we either must refuse to answer the question "What sort of human being are you hoping to produce?" or, at least, must not let our answer to this question dictate our answer to the question "Is justice primary?"[40] It is no more evident that democratic institutions are to be measured by the sort of person they create than that they are to be measured against divine commands. It is not evident that they are to be measured by anything more specific than the moral intuitions of the particular historical community that has created those institutions. The idea that moral and political controversies should always be "brought back to first principles" is reasonable if it means merely that we should seek common ground in the hope of attaining agreement. But it is misleading if it is taken as the claim that there is a natural order of premises from which moral and political conclusions are to be inferred — not to mention the claim that some particular interlocutor (for example, Nietzsche or Loyola) has already discerned that order. The liberal response to the communitarians' second claim must be, therefore, that even if the typical character types of liberal democracies *are* bland, calculating, petty, and unheroic, the prevalence of such people may be a reasonable price to pay for political freedom.

40 This is the kernel of truth in Dworkin's claim that Rawls rejects "goal-based" social theory, but this point should not lead us to think that he is thereby driven back on a "rights-based" theory.

The spirit of accommodation and tolerance certainly suggests that we should seek common ground with Nietzsche and Loyola, but there is no predicting where, or whether, such common ground will be found. The philosophical tradition has assumed that there are certain topics (for example, "What is God's will?," "What is man?," "What rights are intrinsic to the species?") on which everyone has, or should have, views and that these topics are prior in the order of justification to those at issue in political deliberation. This assumption goes along with the assumption that human beings have a natural center that philosophical inquiry can locate and illuminate. By contrast, the view that human beings are centerless networks of beliefs and desires and that their vocabularies and opinions are determined by historical circumstance allows for the possibility that there may not be enough overlap between two such networks to make possible agreement about political topics, or even profitable discussion of such topics.[41] We do not conclude that Nietzsche and Loyola are crazy because they hold unusual views on certain "fundamental" topics; rather, we conclude this only after extensive attempts at an exchange of political views have made us realize that we are not going to get anywhere.[42]

One can sum up this way of grasping the first horn of the dilemma I sketched earlier by saying that Rawls puts democratic politics first, and philosophy second. He retains the Socratic commitment to free exchange of views without the Platonic commitment to the possibility of universal agreement — a possibility underwritten by epistemological doctrines like Plato's Theory of Recollection[43] or Kant's theory of the relation between pure and empirical concepts. He disengages the question of whether we ought to be tolerant and Socratic from the question of whether this strategy will lead to truth. He is content that it should lead to whatever intersubjective reflective equilibrium may be obtainable, given the contingent make-up of the subjects in question. Truth, viewed in the Platonic

41 But one should not press this point so far as to raise the specter of "untranslatable languages." As Donald Davidson has remarked, we would not recognize other organisms as actual or potential language users — or, therefore, as persons — unless there were enough overlap in belief and desire to make translation possible. The point is merely that efficient and frequent communication is only a necessary, not a sufficient, condition of agreement.

42 Further, such a conclusion is *restricted* to politics. It does not cast doubt on the ability of these men to follow the rules of logic or their ability to do many other things skillfully and well. It is thus not equivalent to the traditional philosophical charge of "irrationality." That charge presupposes that inability to "see" certain truths is evidence of the lack of an organ that is essential for human functioning generally.

43 In Kierkegaard's *Philosophical Fragments*, to which I have referred earlier, we find the Platonic Theory of Recollection treated as the archetypal justification of "Socratism" and thus as the symbol of all forms (especially Hegel's) of what Bernard Williams has recently called "the rationalist theory of rationality" — the idea that one is rational only if one can appeal to universally accepted criteria, criteria whose truth and applicability all human beings can find "in their heart." This is the philosophical core of the Scriptural idea that "truth is great, and will prevail," when the idea is dissociated from the idea of "a New Being" (in the way that Kierkegaard refused to dissociate it).

way, as the grasp of what Rawls calls "an order antecedent to and given to us," is simply not relevant to democratic politics. So philosophy, as the explanation of the relation between such an order and human nature, is not relevant either. When the two come into conflict, democracy takes precedence over philosophy.

This conclusion may seem liable to an obvious objection. It may seem that I have been rejecting a concern with philosophical theories about the nature of men and women on the basis of just such a theory. But notice that although I have frequently said that Rawls *can be content* with a notion of the human self as a centerless web of historically conditioned beliefs and desires, I have not suggested that he *needs* such a theory. Such a theory does not offer liberal social theory a *basis*. If one *wants* a model of the human self, then this picture of a centerless web will fill the need. But for purposes of liberal social theory, one can do without such a model. One can get along with common sense and social science, areas of discourse in which the term "the self" rarely occurs.

If, however, one has a taste for philosophy – if one's vocation, one's private pursuit of perfection, entails constructing models of such entities as "the self," "knowledge," "language," "nature," "God," or "history," and then tinkering with them until they mesh with one another – one *will* want a picture of the self. Since my own vocation is of this sort, and the moral identity around which I wish to build such models is that of a citizen of a liberal democratic state, I commend the picture of the self as a centerless and contingent web to those with similar tastes and similar identities. But I would not commend it to those with a similar vocation but dissimilar moral identities – identities built, for example, around the love of God, Nietzschean self-overcoming, the accurate representation of reality as it is in itself, the quest for "one right answer" to moral questions, or the natural superiority of a given character type. Such persons need a more complex and interesting, less simple-minded model of the self – one that meshes in complex ways with complex models of such things as "nature" or "history." Nevertheless, such persons may, for pragmatic rather than moral reasons, be loyal citizens of a liberal democratic society. They may despise most of their fellow citizens, but be prepared to grant that the prevalence of such despicable character types is a lesser evil than the loss of political freedom. They may be ruefully grateful that their private senses of moral identity and the models of the human self that they develop to articulate this sense – the ways in which they deal with their aloneness – are not the concern of such a state. Rawls and Dewey have shown how the liberal state can ignore the difference between the moral identities of Glaucon and of Thrasymachus, just as it ignores the difference between the religious identities of a Catholic archbishop and a Mormon prophet.

There is, however, a flavor of paradox in this attitude toward theories of the self. One might be inclined to say that I have evaded one sort of self-referential paradox only by falling into another sort. For I am presupposing that one is at liberty to rig up a model of the self to suit oneself, to tailor it to one's politics, one's religion, or one's private sense of the meaning of one's life. This, in turn, presupposes that there is no "objective truth" about what the human self is *really* like. That, in turn, seems a claim that could be justified only on the basis of a metaphysico-epistemological view of the traditional sort. For surely if anything is the province of such a view, it is the question of what there is and is not a "fact of the matter" about. So my argument must ultimately come back to philosophical first principles.

Here I can only say that if there were a discoverable fact of the matter about what there is a fact of the matter about, then it would doubtless be metaphysics and epistemology that would discover that meta-fact. But I think that the very idea of a "fact of the matter" is one we would be better off without. Philosophers like Davidson and Derrida have, I think, given us good reason to think that the *physis–nomos, in se–ad nos,* and objective–subjective distinctions were steps on a ladder that we can now safely throw away. The question of whether the reasons such philosophers have given for this claim are themselves metaphysico-epistemological reasons, and if not, what sort of reasons they are, strikes me as pointless and sterile. Once again, I fall back on the holist's strategy of insisting that reflective equilibrium is all we need try for – that there is no natural order of justification of beliefs, no predestined outline for argument to trace. Getting rid of the idea of such an outline seems to me one of the many benefits of a conception of the self as a centerless web. Another benefit is that questions about whom we need justify ourselves to – questions about who counts as a fanatic and who deserves an answer – can be treated as just further matters to be sorted out in the course of attaining reflective equilibrium.

I can, however, make one point to offset the air of light-minded aestheticism I am adopting toward traditional philosophical questions. This is that there is a moral purpose behind this light-mindedness. The encouragement of light-mindedness about traditional philosophical topics serves the same purposes as does the encouragement of light-mindedness about traditional theological topics. Like the rise of large market economies, the increase in literacy, the proliferation of artistic genres, and the insouciant pluralism of contemporary culture, such philosophical superficiality and light-mindedness helps along the disenchantment of the world. It helps make the world's inhabitants more pragmatic, more toler-ant, more liberal, more receptive to the appeal of instrumental rationality.

If one's moral identity consists in being a citizen of a liberal polity, then to encourage light-mindedness may serve one's moral purposes. Moral commitment, after all, does not require taking seriously all the matters that are, for moral reasons, taken seriously by one's fellow citizens. It may require just the opposite. It may require trying to josh them out of the habit of taking those topics so seriously. There may be serious reasons for so joshing them. More generally, we should not assume that the aesthetic is always the enemy of the moral. I should argue that in the recent history of liberal societies, the willingness to view matters aesthetically – to be content to indulge in what Schiller called "play" and to discard what Nietzsche called "the spirit of seriousness" – has been an important vehicle of moral progress.

I have now said everything I have to say about the third of the communitarian claims that I distinguished at the outset: the claim that the social theory of the liberal state rests on false philosophical presuppositions. I hope I have given reasons for thinking that insofar as the communitarian is a critic of liberalism, he should drop this claim and should instead develop either of the first two claims: the empirical claim that democratic institutions cannot be combined with the sense of common purpose predemocratic societies enjoyed, or the moral judgment that the products of the liberal state are too high a price to pay for the elimination of the evils that preceded it. If communitarian critics of liberalism stuck to these two claims, they would avoid the sort of terminal wistfulness with which their books typically end. Heidegger, for example, tells us that "we are too late for the gods, and too early for Being." Unger ends *Knowledge and Politics* with an appeal to a *Deus absconditus*. MacIntyre ends *After Virtue* by saying that we "are waiting not for a Godot, but for another – doubtless very different – St. Benedict."[44] Sandel ends his book by saying that liberalism "forgets the possibility that when politics goes well, we can know a good in common that we cannot know alone," but he does not suggest a candidate for this common good.

Instead of thus suggesting that philosophical reflection, or a return to religion, might enable us to re-enchant the world, I think that communitarians should stick to the question of whether disenchantment has, on balance, done us more harm than good, or created more dangers than it has evaded. For Dewey, communal and public disenchantment is the price we pay for individual and private spiritual liberation, the kind of liberation that Emerson thought characteristically American. Dewey was as well aware as Weber that there is a price to be paid, but he thought it well worth paying. He assumed that no good achieved by earlier societies would be worth recapturing if the price were a diminution in our ability to leave people alone, to let them try out their private visions of perfection in peace. He admired the American habit of giving democracy priority over philosophy by asking, about any vision of the meaning of life, "Would not acting out this vision interfere with the ability of others to work out their own salvation?" Giving priority to that question is no more "natural" than giving priority to, say, MacIntyre's question "What sorts of human beings emerge in the culture of liberalism?" or Sandel's question "Can a community of those who put justice first ever be more than a community of strangers?" The

44 See Jeffrey Stout's discussion of the manifold ambiguities of this conclusion in "Virtue Among the Ruins: An Essay on MacIntrye," *Newe Zeitschrift für Systematische Theologie und Religionsphilosophie* 26 (1984): 256–73, especially 269.

question of which of these questions is prior to which others is, necessarily, begged by *everybody*. Nobody is being any more arbitrary than anybody else. But that is to say that nobody is being arbitrary at all. Everybody is just insisting that the beliefs and desires they hold most dear should come first in the order of discussion. That is not arbitrariness, but sincerity.

The danger of re-enchanting the world, from a Deweyan point of view, is that it might interfere with the development of what Rawls calls "a social union of social unions,"[45] some of which may be (and in Emerson's view, should be) very small indeed. For it is hard to be both enchanted with one version of the world and tolerant of all the others. I have not tried to argue the question of whether Dewey was right in this judgment of relative danger and promise. I have merely argued that such a judgment neither presupposes nor supports a theory of the self. Nor have I tried to deal with Horkheimer and Adorno's prediction that the "dissolvent rationality" of the Enlightenment will eventually cause the liberal democracies to come unstuck.

The only thing I have to say about this prediction is that the collapse of the liberal democracies would not, in itself, provide much evidence for the claim that human societies cannot survive without widely shared opinions on matters of ultimate importance – shared conceptions of our place in the universe and our mission on earth. Perhaps they cannot survive under such conditions, but the eventual collapse of the democracies would not, in itself, show that this was the

---

45 This is Rawls's description of "a well-ordered society (corresponding to justice as fairness)" (*Theory of Justice*, p. 527). Sandel finds these passages metaphorical and complains that "intersubjective and individualistic images appear in uneasy, sometimes unfelicitous combination, as if to betray the incompatible commitments contending within" (*Liberalism and the Limits of Justice*, pp. 150ff.). He concludes that "the moral vocabulary of community in the strong sense cannot in all cases be captured by a conception that [as Rawls has said his is] 'in its theoretical bases is individualistic.' " I am claiming that these commitments will look incompatible only if one attempts to define their philosophical presuppositions (which Rawls himself may occasionally have done too much of), and that this is a good reason for not making such attempts. Compare the Enlightenment view that attempts to sharpen up the theological presuppositions of social commitments had done more harm than good and that if theology cannot simply be discarded, it should at least be left as fuzzy (or, one might say, "liberal") as possible. Oakeshott has a point when he insists on the value of theoretical muddle for the health of the state.

Elsewhere Rawls has claimed that "there is no reason why a well-ordered society should encourage primarily individualistic values if this means ways of life that lead individuals to pursue their own way and to have no concern for the interest of others" ("Fairness to Goodness," *Philosophical Review* 84 [1975]: 550). Sandel's discussion of this passage says that it "suggests a deeper sense in which Rawls' conception is individualistic," but his argument that this suggestion is correct is, once again, the claim that "the Rawlsian self is not only a subject of possession, but an antecedently individuated subject" (*Liberalism and the Limits of Justice*, pp. 61 ff.). This is just the claim I have been arguing against by arguing that there is no such thing as "the Rawlsian self" and that Rawls does not want or need a "theory of the person." Sandel says (p. 62) that Rawls "takes for granted that every individual consists of one and only one system of desires," but it is hard to find evidence for this claim in the texts. At worst, Rawls simplifies his presentation by imagining each of his citizens as having only one such set, but this simplifying assumption does not seem central to his view.

case – any more than it would show that human societies require kings or an established religion, or that political community cannot exist outside of small city-states.

Both Jefferson and Dewey described America as an "experiment." If the experiment fails, our descendants may learn something important. But they will not learn a philosophical truth, any more than they will learn a religious one. They will simply get some hints about what to watch out for when setting up their next experiment. Even if nothing else survives from the age of the democratic revolutions, perhaps our descendants will remember that social institutions *can* be viewed as experiments in cooperation rather than as attempts to embody a universal and ahistorical order. It is hard to believe that this memory would not be worth having.

Postmodernist bourgeois liberalism

Complaints about the social irresponsibility of the intellectuals typically concern the intellectual's tendency to marginalize herself, to move out from one community by interior identification of herself with some other community – for example, another country or historical period, an invisible college, or some alienated subgroup within the larger community. Such marginalization is, however, common to intellectuals and to miners. In the early days of the United Mine Workers its members rightly put no faith in the surrounding legal and political institutions and were loyal only to each other. In this respect they resembled the literary and artistic avant-garde between the wars.

It is not clear that those who thus marginalize themselves can be criticized for social irresponsibility. One cannot be irresponsible toward a community of which one does not think of oneself as a member. Otherwise runaway slaves and tunnelers under the Berlin Wall would be irresponsible. If such criticism were to make sense there would have to be a supercommunity one *had* to identify with – humanity as such. Then one could appeal to the needs of that community when breaking with one's family or tribe or nation, and such groups could appeal to the same thing when criticizing the irresponsibility of those who break away. Some people believe that there is such a community. These are the people who think there are such things as intrinsic human dignity, intrinsic human rights, and an ahistorical distinction between the demands of morality and those of prudence. Call these people "Kantians." They are opposed by people who say that "humanity" is a biological rather than a moral notion, that there is no human dignity that is not derivative from the dignity of some specific community, and no appeal beyond the relative merits of various actual or proposed communities to impartial criteria which will help us weigh those merits. Call these people "Hegelians." Much of contemporary social philosophy in the English-speaking world is a three-cornered debate between Kantians (like Ronald Dworkin) who want to keep an ahistorical morality-prudence distinction as a buttress for the institutions and practices of the surviving democracies, those (like the post-Marxist philosophical left in Europe, Roberto Unger, and Alasdair MacIntyre) who want to abandon these institutions both because they presuppose a discredited philosophy and for other, more concrete, reasons, and those (like Michael Oakeshott and John Dewey) who want to preserve the institutions while abandoning their traditional Kantian backup. These last two positions take over Hegel's criticism of Kant's conception of moral agency, while either naturalizing or junking the rest of Hegel.

If the Hegelians are right, then there are no ahistorical criteria for deciding when it is or is not a responsible act to desert a community, any more than for deciding when to change lovers or professions. The Hegelians see nothing to be responsible to except persons and actual or possible historical communities; so they view the Kantians' use of 'social responsibility' as misleading. For that use suggests not the genuine contrast between, for example, Antigone's loyalties to Thebes and to her brother, or Alcibiades' loyalties to Athens and to Persia, but an illusory contrast between loyalty to a person or a historical community and to something "higher" than either. It suggests that there is a point of view that abstracts from any historical community and adjudicates the rights of communities vis-à-vis those of individuals.

Kantians tend to accuse of social irresponsibility those who doubt that there is such a point of view. So when Michael Walzer says that "A given society is just if its substantive life is lived in . . . a way faithful to the shared understandings of the members," Dworkin calls this view "relativism." "Justice," Dworkin retorts, "cannot be left to convention and anecdote." Such Kantian complaints can be defended using the Hegelians' own tactics, by noting that the very American society which Walzer wishes to commend and to reform is one whose self-image is bound up with the Kantian vocabulary of "inalienable rights" and "the dignity of man." Hegelian defenders of liberal institutions are in the position of defending, on the basis of solidarity alone, a society which has traditionally asked to be based on something more than mere solidarity. Kantian criticism of the tradition that runs from Hegel through Marx and Nietzsche, a tradition which insists on thinking of morality as the interest of a historically conditioned community rather than "the common interest of humanity," often insists that such a philosophical outlook is − if one values liberal practices and institutions − irresponsible. Such criticism rests on a prediction that such practices and institutions will not survive the removal of the traditional Kantian buttresses, buttresses which include an account of "rationality" and "morality" as transcultural and ahistorical.

I shall call the Hegelian attempt to defend the institutions and practices of the rich North Atlantic democracies without using such buttresses "postmodernist bourgeois liberalism." I call it "bourgeois" to emphasize that most of the people I am talking about would have no quarrel with the Marxist claim that a lot of those institutions and practices are possible and justifiable only in certain historical, and especially economic, conditions. I want to contrast bourgeois liberalism, the attempt to fulfill the hopes of the North Atlantic bourgeoisie, with philosophical liberalism, a collection of Kantian principles thought to justify us in having those hopes. Hegelians think that these principles are useful for *summarizing* these hopes, but not for justifying them. I use 'postmodernist' in a sense given to this term by Jean-François Lyotard, who says that the postmodern attitude is that of "distrust of metanarratives," narratives which describe or predict the activities of such entities as the noumenal self or the Absolute Spirit or the Proletariat. These metanarratives are stories which purport to justify loyalty to, or breaks with, certain contemporary communities, but which are neither historical narratives about what these or other communities have done in the past nor scenarios about what they might do in the future.

"Postmodernist bourgeois liberalism" sounds oxymoronic. This is partly because, for local and perhaps transitory reasons, the majority of those who think of themselves as beyond metaphysics and metanarratives also think of themselves as having opted out of the bourgeoisie. But partly it is because it is hard to disentangle bourgeois liberal institutions from the vocabulary that these institutions inherited from the Enlightenment – e.g., the eighteenth-century vocabulary of rights, which judges, and constitutional lawyers such as Dworkin, must use *ex officiis*. This vocabulary is built around a distinction between morality and prudence. In what follows I want to show how this vocabulary, and in particular this distinction, might be reinterpreted to suit the needs of us postmodernist bourgeois liberals. I hope thereby to suggest how such liberals might convince our society that loyalty to itself is morality enough, and that such loyalty no longer needs an ahistorical backup. I think they should try to clear themselves of charges of irresponsibility by convincing our society that it need be responsible only to its own traditions, and not to the moral law as well.

The crucial move in this reinterpretation is to think of the moral self, the embodiment of rationality, not as one of Rawls's original choosers, somebody who can distinguish her *self* from her talents and interests and views about the good, but as a network of beliefs, desires, and emotions with nothing behind it – no substrate behind the attributes. For purposes of moral and political deliberation and conversation, a person just *is* that network, as for purposes of ballistics she is a point-mass, or for purposes of chemistry a linkage of molecules. She is a network that is constantly reweaving itself in the usual Quinean manner – that is to say, not by reference to general criteria (e.g., "rules of meaning" or "moral principles") but in the hit-or-miss way in which cells readjust themselves to meet the pressures of the environment. On a Quinean view, rational behavior is just adaptive behavior of a sort which roughly parallels the behavior, in similar circumstances, of the other members of some relevant community. Irrationality, in both physics and ethics, is a matter of behavior that leads one to abandon, or be stripped of, membership in some such community. For some purposes this adaptive behavior is aptly described as "learning" or "computing" or "redistribution of electrical charges in neural tissue," and for others as "deliberation" or "choice." None of these vocabularies is privileged over against another.

What plays the role of "human dignity" on this view of the self? The answer is well expressed by Michael Sandel, who says that we cannot regard ourselves as Kantian subjects "capable of constituting meaning on our own," as Rawlsian choosers,

. . . without great cost to those loyalties and convictions whose moral force consists partly in the fact that living by them is inseparable from understanding ourselves as the particular people we are − as members of this family or community or nation or people, as bearers of this history, as sons and daughters of that revolution, as citizens of this republic.[1]

I would argue that the moral force of such loyalties and convictions consists *wholly* in this fact, and that nothing else has *any* moral force. There is no "ground" for such loyalties and convictions save the fact that the beliefs and desires and emotions which buttress them overlap those of lots of other members of the group with which we identify for purposes of moral or political deliberations, and the further fact that these are *distinctive* features of that group, features which it uses to construct its self-image through contrasts with other groups. This means that the naturalized Hegelian analogue of "intrinsic human dignity" is the comparative dignity of a group with which a person identifies herself. Nations or churches or movements are, on this view, shining historical examples not because they reflect rays emanating from a higher source, but because of contrast-effects − comparisons with other, worse communities. Persons have dignity not as an interior luminescence, but because they share in such contrast-effects. It is a corollary of this view that the moral justification of the institutions and practices of one's group − e.g., of the contemporary bourgeoisie − is mostly a matter of historical narratives (including scenarios about what is likely to happen in certain future contingencies), rather than of philosophical metanarratives. The principal backup for historiography is not philosophy but the arts, which serve to develop and modify a group's self-image by, for example, apotheosizing its heroes, diabolizing its enemies, mounting dialogues among its members, and refocusing its attention.

A further corollary is that the morality/prudence distinction now appears as a distinction between appeals to two parts of the network that is the self − parts separated by blurry and constantly shifting boundaries. One part consists of those beliefs and desires and emotions which overlap with those of most other members of some community with which, for purposes of deliberation, she identifies herself, and which contrast with those of most members of other communities with which hers contrasts itself. A person appeals to morality rather than prudence when she appeals to this overlapping, shared part of herself, those beliefs and desires and emotions which permit her to say "WE do not do this sort of thing." Morality is, as Wilfrid Sellars has said, a matter of "we-intentions." Most

---

1   *Liberalism and the Limits of Justice* (New York: Cambridge University Press, 1982), p. 179. Sandel's remarkable book argues masterfully that Rawls cannot naturalize Kant and still retain the meta-ethical authority of Kantian "practical reason."

moral dilemmas are thus reflections of the fact that most of us identify with a number of different communities and are equally reluctant to marginalize ourselves in relation to any of them. This diversity of identifications increases with education, just as the number of communities with which a person may identify increases with civilization.

Intra-societal tensions, of the sort which Dworkin rightly says mark our pluralistic society, are rarely resolved by appeals to general principles of the sort Dworkin thinks necessary. More frequently they are resolved by appeals to what he calls "convention and anecdote." The political discourse of the democracies, at its best, is the exchange of what Wittgenstein called "reminders for a particular purpose" – anecdotes about the past effects of various practices and predictions of what will happen if, or unless, some of these are altered. The moral deliberations of the postmodernist bourgeois liberal consists largely in this same sort of discourse, avoiding the formulation of general principles except where the situation may require this particular tactic – as when one writes a constitution, or rules for young children to memorize. It is useful to remember that this view of moral and political deliberation was a commonplace among American intellectuals in the days when Dewey – a postmodernist before his time – was the reigning American philosopher, days when "legal realism" was thought of as desirable pragmatism rather than unprincipled subjectivism.

It is also useful to reflect on why this tolerance for anecdote was replaced by a reattachment to principles. Part of the explanation, I think, is that most American intellectuals in Dewey's day still thought their country was a shining historical example. They identified with it easily. The largest single reason for their loss of identification was the Vietnam War. The War caused some intellectuals to marginalize themselves entirely. Others attempted to rehabilitate Kantian notions in order to say, with Chomsky, that the War not merely betrayed America's hopes and interests and self-image, but was *immoral,* one which we had had no *right* to engage in in the first place.

Dewey would have thought such attempts at further self-castigation pointless. They may have served a useful cathartic purpose, but their long-run effect has been to separate the intellectuals from the moral consensus of the nation rather than to alter that consensus. Further, Dewey's naturalized Hegelianism has more overlap with the belief-systems of the communities we rich North American bourgeois need to talk with than does a naturalized Kantianism. So a reversion to the Deweyan outlook might leave us in a better position to carry on whatever conversation between nations may still be possible, as well as leaving American intellectuals in a better position to converse with their fellow citizens.

I shall end by taking up two objections to what I have been saying. The first objection is that on my view a child found wandering in the woods, the remnant of a slaughtered nation whose temples have been razed and whose books have been burned, has no share in human dignity. This is indeed a consequence, but it does not follow that she may be treated like an animal. For it is part of the tradition of *our* community that the human stranger from whom all dignity has been stripped is to be taken in, to be reclothed with dignity. This Jewish and Christian element in our tradition is gratefully invoked by freeloading atheists like myself, who would like to let differences like that between the Kantian and the Hegelian remain "merely philosophical." The existence of human rights, in the sense in which it is at issue in this meta-ethical debate, has as much or as little relevance to our treatment of such a child as the question of the existence of God. I think both have equally little relevance.

The second objection is that what I have been calling "postmodernism" is better named "relativism," and that relativism is self-refuting. Relativism certainly is self-refuting, but there is a difference between saying that every community is as good as every other and saying that we have to work out from the networks we are, from the communities with which we presently identify. Postmodernism is no more relativistic than Hilary Putnam's suggestion that we stop trying for a "God's-eye view" and realize that "We can only hope to produce a more rational conception of rationality or a better conception of morality if we operate from within our tradition."[2] The view that every tradition is as rational or as moral as every other could be held only by a god, someone who had no need to use (but only to mention) the terms 'rational' or 'moral,' because she had no need to inquire or deliberate. Such a being would have escaped from history and conversation into contemplation and metanarrative. To accuse postmodernism of relativism is to try to put a metanarrative in the postmodernist's mouth. One will do this if one identifies "holding a philosophical position" with having a metanarrative available. If we insist on such a definition of "philosophy," then postmodernism is post-philosophical. But it would be better to change the definition.[3]

2 *Reason, Truth and History* (New York: Cambridge University Press, 1981), p. 216.
3 I discuss such redefinition in the Introduction to *Consequences of Pragmatism* (Minneapolis: Univ. of Minnesota Press, 1982).

On ethnocentrism: A reply to Clifford Geertz

In his provoctive paper on "The Uses of Diversity," Professor Geertz asserts that ethnocentrism relegates gaps and asymmetries between individuals or groups to "a realm of repressible or ignorable difference, mere unlikeness." This is a good description of how we treat people whom we think not worth understanding: those whom we regard as irredeemably crazy, stupid, base, or sinful. Such people are not viewed as possible conversational partners, but, at most, as means to ends. We think we have nothing to learn from such people, for we would rather die than share the beliefs which we assume are central to their self-identities. Some people think of Jews and atheists in these terms. Others think this way about Nazis and religious fundamentalists.

When we bourgeois liberals find ourselves thinking of people in this way — when, for example, we find ourselves reacting to the Nazis and the fundamentalists with indignation and contempt — we have to think twice. For we are exemplifying the attitude we claim to despise. We would rather die than be ethnocentric, but ethnocentrism is precisely the conviction that one would rather die than share certain beliefs. We then find ourselves wondering whether our own bourgeois liberalism is not just one more example of cultural bias.

This bemusement makes us susceptible to the suggestion that the culture of Western liberal democracy is somehow "on a par" with that of the Vandals and the Ik. So we begin to wonder whether our attempts to get other parts of the world to adopt our culture are different in kind from the efforts of fundamentalist missionaries. If we continue this line of thought too long we become what are sometimes called "wet" liberals. We begin to lose any capacity for moral indignation, any capacity to feel contempt. Our sense of selfhood dissolves. We can no longer feel pride in being bourgeois liberals, in being part of a great tradition, a citizen of no mean culture. We have become so open-minded that our brains have fallen out.

This collapse of moral self-confidence, what Geertz calls "the desperate tolerance of UNESCO cosmopolitanism," provokes a reaction in the direction of anti-anti-ethnocentrism — the direction exemplified by the passages from Lévi-Strauss and myself which Geertz cites. This in turn provokes Geertz' counter-reaction. He says, for example: "Any moral philosophy so afraid of becoming entangled in witless relativism or transcendental dogmatism that it can think of nothing better to do with other ways of going at life than make them look worse than our own is destined merely toward making the world safe for condescension." Geertz fears that if the anti-anti-ethnocentrist reaction goes too far we shall become content to think of human communities as "semantic monads, nearly windowless."

Some human communities are such monads, some not. Our bourgeois liberal culture is not. On the contrary, it is a culture which prides itself on constantly adding on more windows, constantly enlarging its sympathies. It is a form of life which is constantly extending pseudopods and adapting itself to what it encounters. Its sense of its own moral worth is founded on its tolerance of diversity. The heroes it apotheosizes include those who have enlarged its capacity for sympathy and tolerance. Among the enemies it diabolizes are the people who attempt to diminish this capacity, the vicious ethnocentrists. Anti-anti-ethnocentrism is not an attempt to change the habits of our culture, to block the windows up again. Rather, it is an attempt to cope with the phenomenon of wet liberalism by correcting our culture's habit of giving its desire for windows a philosophical foundation. Anti-anti-ethnocentrism does not say that we are trapped within our monad or our language, but merely that the well-windowed monad we live in is no more closely linked to the nature of humanity or the demands of rationality than the relatively windowless monads which surround us.

I shall enlarge on this latter point later, but first I should like to comment on Geertz' Case of the Drunken Indian and the Kidney Machine.[1] This Case looks different to me than it does to Geertz. So I shall begin by saying how I see it, and then comment on the way Geertz sees it.

My own reaction to the case as Geertz presents it is that it is not particularly depressing, but rather cheering. It shows our liberal institutions functioning well and smoothly. Geertz says that "queuing [for the kidney machine] was organized in terms of severity of need and order of application." So it should have been. Since, as he says, "the Indian was already on the machine by the time the problem became visible" the doctors "could not quite bring themselves" to take him off. He then adds, in parentheses, "Nor, I suppose, would they have been permitted." Indeed they would not, and this is what I find cheering. If they had tried to take him off the machine, the media and the malpractice lawyers would have been all over them the next day. The whole apparatus of the liberal democratic state, an apparatus to which the press is as central as are the officers of the court, insured that once that Indian had the sense to get into the queue early, he was going to have more years in which to drink than he would otherwise have had.

Geertz says that this was "a hard case and it ended in a hard way." From the

---

1 In this "Case," an alcoholic American Indian in the southwestern United States, having taken his place in line, was permitted to begin and continue treatment on a kidney machine even though he refused to heed the doctors' orders to stop his drinking. He died after a few years on the machine, presumably in part because of his drinking. Geertz used the case to illustrate the moral dilemma of doctors – and by extension "enlightened" society – confronted by values and behaviors hostile to their own "liberal" ones.

legal point of view, surely, it was not a hard case. Procedural justice was visibly done. Nor does it seem hard from a moral point of view. It is morally satisfying to think that life-or-death decisions are made on the basis of "severity of need and priority of application" – rather than, say, on the basis of political or financial clout, family membership, or the sympathies of those present. We take moral pride in the fact that our society hands such decisions over to the mechanisms of procedural justice.

Geertz goes on to say that he "cannot see that either more ethnocentrism, more relativism, or more neutrality would have made things any better (though more imagination might have.)" I agree that no philosophical position or strategy could have made things any better, but I am not sure what he thinks imagination could have made better, because I am not sure what needed improvement. I take it that Geertz means that the doctors might have been less upset by the Indian's failure to be a good patient if they had been able to put themselves in the Indian's shoes. But it is not clear that they had any business being so distraught in the first place. We do not really want doctors to differentiate between the values of the lives they are saving, any more than we want defense lawyers to worry too much about the innocence of their clients, or teachers to worry about which students will make the best use of the education they are offering. A society built around procedural justice needs agents who do not look too closely at such matters.

Geertz says that "nobody in this episode learned very much about either themselves or about anyone else," that "the whole thing took place in the dark." At the end of his paper he suggests that what the doctors lacked was "knowledge of the degree to which he [the Indian] has earned his views and the bitter sense that is therefore in them," and "comprehension of the terrible road over which he has had to travel to arrive at them and of what it is – ethnocentrism and the crimes it legitimates – that has made it so terrible." What Geertz has and the doctors presumably didn't have is some knowledge of what it was like to be a member of that Indian's tribe before, during and after the conquest of that tribe by the whites.

I want to make two points about this difference between Geertz and the doctors. First, the fact that lots of doctors, lawyers and teachers are unable to imagine themselves in the shoes of lots of their patients, clients and students does not show that anything is taking place in the dark. There is light enough for them to get their job done, and to do it right. The only sense in which something took place in the dark is the sense in which *all* human relations untouched by love take place in the dark. This is an extended sense of "in the dark" analogous to the extended sense of "alone" in which we mortal millions live alone. When we gun down the psychopath, or send the war criminal to the gallows, we are, in this extended sense, acting in the dark. For if we had watched the war criminal grow up, had traveled the road he had traveled, we might have had difficulty reconciling the demands of love and of justice. But it is well for society that in most cases our ignorance permits us to avoid this dilemma. Most of the time, justice has to be enough.

The second and more important point I want to make about Geertz and the doctors is that it is the signal glory of our liberal society that it entrusts power to people like Geertz and his fellow anthropologists as well as to people like the doctors. Anthropologists, and Geertz' other connoisseurs of diversity, are the people who are expected and empowered to extend the range of society's imagination, thereby opening the doors of procedural justice to people on whom they had been closed. Why is it, after all, that the Indian was ever allowed into the clinic? Why are drunken Indians, in Geertz' words, "as much a part of contemporary America" as yuppie doctors? Roughly, because anthropologists have made them so. Drunken Indians were more common in America a hundred years ago than now, but anthropologists less common. Because of the absence of sympathetic interpreters who could place their behavior in the context of an unfamiliar set of beliefs and desires, drunken Indians were not part of nineteenth-century America: that is, the vast majority of nineteenth-century Americans took no more notice of them than they did of criminal psychopaths or village idiots. The Indians, whether drunk or sober, were non-persons, without human dignity, means to our grandparents' ends. The anthropologists made it hard for us to continue thinking of them that way, and thereby made them into "part of contemporary America." To be part of a society is, in the relevant sense, to be taken as a possible conversational partner by those who shape that society's self-image. The media, prodded by the intellectuals in general and the anthropologists in particular, have been making such partners of the Indians. But if the anthropologists had not sympathized with, learned from, even sometimes loved, the Indians, Indians would have remained invisible to the agents of social justice. They would never have gotten into the queue in the first place.

Now let me draw some conclusions from what I have been saying about Geertz' Case. The principal one is that the moral tasks of a liberal democracy are divided between the agents of love and the agents of justice. In other words, such a democracy employs and empowers both connoisseurs of diversity and guardians of universality. The former insist that there are people out there whom society has failed to notice. They make these candidates for admission visible by showing how to explain their odd behavior in terms of a coherent, if unfamiliar, set of beliefs and desires – as opposed to explaining this behavior with terms like stupidity, madness, baseness or sin. The latter, the guardians of universality, make sure that once these people are admitted as citizens, once they have been shepherded into the light by the connoisseurs of diversity, they are treated just like all the rest of us.

Our society's device for resolving what Geertz calls "wrenching social issues centered around cultural diversity" is simply to keep lots of agents of love, lots of connoisseurs of diversity, on hand. Our society has, tacitly, given up on the idea that theology or philosophy will supply general rules for resolving such issues. It recognizes that moral progress has, in recent centuries, owed more to the specialists in particularity – historians, novelists, ethnographers, and muckraking journalists, for example – than to such specialists in universality as theologians and philosophers. The formulation of general moral principles has been less useful to the development of liberal institutions than has the gradual expansion of the imagination of those in power, their gradual willingness to use the term "we" to include more and more different sorts of people. Engels' *Condition of the Working Class in England* and the writings of people like Harriet Beecher Stowe, Fenellosa, and Malinowski, did more than Engels' *Dialectics of Nature*, or the writings of Mill and Dewey, to justify the existence of the weak outsiders to the powerful insiders.

So I am inclined to set aside the questions Geertz poses about the resolution of social issues created by cultural diversity by saying that we should simply keep doing what our liberal society is already in the habit of doing: lending an ear to the specialists in particularity, permitting them to fulfill their function as agents of love, and hoping that they will continue to expand our moral imagination. There is nothing incompatible with this hope in the sort of anti-anti-ethnocentrism Geertz describes.

Let me now return to an explicit defense of the anti-anti-ethnocentrism which I sketched earlier. This mini-movement should be seen neither as putting forward a large philosophical view about the nature of culture nor as recommending a social policy. Rather, it should be seen as an attempt to resolve a small, local, psychological problem. This psychological problem is found only within the souls of bourgeois liberals who have not yet gone postmodern, the ones who are still using the rationalist rhetoric of the Englightenment to back up their liberal ideas. These liberals hold on to the Enlightenment notion that there is something called a common human nature, a metaphysical substrate in which things called "rights" are embedded, and that this substrate takes moral precedence over all merely "cultural" superstructures. Preserving this idea produces self-referential paradox as soon as liberals begin to ask themselves whether their belief in such a substrate is itself a cultural bias. Liberals who are both connoisseurs of diversity and Enlightenment rationalists cannot get out of this bind. Their rationalism commits them to making sense of the distinction between rational judgment and cultural bias. Their liberalism forces them to call any *doubts* about human equality a result of such irrational bias. Yet their connoisseurship forces them to realize that most of the globe's inhabitants simply do not believe in human equality, that such a belief is a Western eccentricity. Since they think it would be shockingly ethnocentric to say "So what? We Western liberals *do* believe in it, and so much the better for us," they are stuck.

Anti-anti-ethnocentrists suggest that liberals should say exactly that, and that they should simply drop the distinction between rational judgment and cultural bias. The Enlightenment had hoped that philosophy would both justify liberal ideals and specify limits to liberal tolerance by an appeal to transcultural criteria of rationality. But philosophers in the Deweyan tradition no longer attempt this. They tell us that we are going to have to work out the limits case by case, by hunch or by conversational compromise, rather than by reference to stable criteria. So we postmodernist bourgeois liberals no longer tag our central beliefs and desires as "necessary" or "natural" and our peripheral ones as "contingent" or "cultural." This is partly because the anthropologists, novelists and historians have done such a good job of exhibiting the contingency of various putative necessities. In part it is because philosophers like Quine, Wittgenstein and Derrida have made us wary of the very idea of a necessary-contingent distinction.

These philosophers describe human life by the metaphor of a continual reweaving of a web of beliefs and desires. Insofar as we adopt this metaphor, we shall regard the web as seamless, in the sense that we shall no longer use epistemological distinctions to divide it. So we shall no longer think of ourselves as having reliable "sources" of knowledge called "reason" or "sensation," nor unreliable ones called "tradition" or "common opinion." We put aside such distinctions as "scientific knowledge vs. cultural bias," and "question of fact vs. question of value."

The latter distinctions were once used to mark off the beliefs that appeared notably clear and distinct from those that seemed relatively debatable, those about which we self-consciously tried to keep an open mind. But in their absence it is natural for us to look about for other terms which will serve to mark off – if only temporarily and for certain purposes – the center of our self from its perpiphery. Typically, the terms we fall back on are self-consciously ethnocentric: being a Christian, or an American, or a Marxist, or a philosopher, or an anthropologist, or a postmodernist bourgeois liberal. In adopting these self-characterizations we announce to our audience "where we are coming from," our contingent spatio-temporal affiliations.

To sum up, anti-anti-ethnocentrism should be seen as a protest against the persistence of Enlightenment rhetoric in an era in which our connoisseurship of diversity has made this rhetoric seem self-deceptive and sterile. It is not a reaction against love, or against justice, or against liberal institutions. It is just a bit of *ad hoc* philosophical therapy, an attempt to cure the cramps caused in liberals by what Bernard Williams calls "the rationalist theory of rationality" – the idea that you are being irrational, and probably viciously ethnocentric, whenever you cannot appeal to neutral criteria. It urges liberals to take with full seriousness the fact that the ideals of procedural justice and human equality are parochial, recent, eccentric cultural developments, and then to recognize that this does not mean they are any the less worth fighting for. It urges that ideals may be local and culture-bound, and neverthless be the best hope of the species.

I shall conclude these comments by turning to Geertz' claim that "we have come to such a point in the moral history of the world that we are obliged to think about [cultural] diversity rather differently than we have been used to thinking about it." He develops this point by saying that "we are living more and more in the midst of an enormous collage," that "the world is coming at each of its local points to look more like a Kuwaiti bazaar than like an English gentlemen's club." These latter descriptions seem right to me, but I do not see why Geertz thinks that we bourgeois liberals need to change our thinking about cultural diversity in order to deal with this situation. For this is just the sort of situation that the Western liberal ideal of procedural justice was *designed* to deal with. John Rawls has remarked that "the historical circumstances of the emergence of the Western liberal notion of justice" include "the development of the principle of [religious] toleration" and "the institutions of large market economies." Both sources, he says, "spring from and encourage the diversity of doctrines and the plurality of conflicting and indeed incommensurable conceptions of the good affirmed by the members of existing democratic societies."

The relevant point is that one does not have to accept much *else* from Western culture to find the Western liberal ideal of procedural justice attractive. The advantage of postmodernist liberalism is that it recognizes that in recommending that ideal one is not recommending a philosophical outlook, a conception of human nature or of the meaning of human life, to representatives of other cultures. All we should do is point out the practical advantages of liberal institutions in allowing individuals and cultures to get along together without intruding on each other's privacy, without meddling with each other's conceptions of the good. We can suggest that UNESCO think about cultural diversity on a world scale in the way our ancestors in the seventeenth and eighteenth century thought about religious diversity on an Atlantic scale: as something to be simply *ignored* for purposes of designing political institutions. We can urge the construction of a world order whose model is a bazaar surrounded by lots and lots of exclusive private clubs.

Like Geertz, I have never been in a Kuwaiti bazaar (nor in an English gentlemen's club). So I can give free rein to my fantasies. I picture many of the people in such a bazaar as preferring to die rather than share the beliefs of many of those with whom they are haggling, yet as haggling profitably away nevertheless. Such a bazaar is, obviously, not a community, in the strong approbative sense of "community" used by critics of liberalism like Alasdair MacIntyre and Robert Bellah. You cannot have an old-timey *Gemeinschaft* unless everybody pretty well agrees on who counts as a decent human being and who does not. But you *can* have a civil society of the bourgeois democratic sort. All you need is the ability to control your feelings when people who strike you as irredeemably different show up at City Hall, or the greengrocers, or the bazaar. When this happens, you smile a lot, make the best deals you can, and, after a hard day's haggling, retreat to your club. There you will be comforted by the companionship of your moral equals.

Wet liberals will be repelled by this suggestion that the exclusivity of the private club might be a *crucial* feature of an ideal world order. It will seem a betrayal of the Enlightenment to imagine us as winding up with a world of moral narcissists, congratulating themselves on neither knowing nor caring what the people in the club over on the other side of the bazaar are like. But if we forget about the Enlightenment ideal of the self-realization of humanity as such, we can disassociate liberty and equality from fraternity. If we attend rather to the reports of our agents of love, our connoisseurs of diversity, we may agree with Lévi-Strauss that such exclusivity is a necessary and proper condition of selfhood. By attending to the reports of our agents of justice, we can see how such strong, ethnocentric, exclusivist selves might cooperate in keeping the bazaar open, in keeping the institutions of procedural justice functioning. Putting the two sets of reports together, we realize that the Enlightenment should not have yearned for a world polity whose citizens share common aspirations and a common culture. Then we will not try for a society which makes assent to beliefs about the meaning of human life or certain moral ideals a requirement for citizenship. We will aim at nothing stronger than a commitment to Rawlsian procedural justice – a moral commitment when made by members of some clubs (e.g., ours) but a matter of expediency when made by members of others. The ultimate political synthesis of love and justice may thus turn out to be an intricately-textured collage of private narcissism and public pragmatism.

Cosmopolitanism without emancipation: A response to Jean-François Lyotard

In the form John Dewey gave it, pragmatism is a philosophy tailored to the needs of political liberalism, a way of making political liberalism look good to persons with philosophical tastes. It provides a rationale for nonideological, compromising, reformist muddling-through (what Dewey called "experimentalism"). It claims that categorical distinctions of the sort philosophers typically invoke are useful only so long as they facilitate conversation about what we should do next. Such distinctions, Dewey says, should be blurred or erased as soon as they begin to hinder such conversation – to block the road of inquiry.

Dewey thinks that muddle, compromise, and blurry syntheses are usually less perilous, politically, than Cartesian clarity. That is one reason why his books are so often thought bland and boring. For he neither erects an exciting new binary opposition in terms of which to praise the good and damn the bad, nor does he distinguish between bad binary oppositions and some wonderful new form of discourse which will somehow avoid using any such oppositions. He just urges us to be on our guard against using intellectual tools which were useful in a certain sociocultural environment after that environment has changed, to be aware that we may have to invent new tools to cope with new situations.

Dewey spent half his time debunking the very idea of "human nature" and of "philosophical foundations" for social thought. But he spent the other half spinning a story about universal history – a story of progress according to which contemporary movements for social reform within the liberal democracies are parts of the same overall movement as the overthrow of feudalism and the abolition of slavery. He offered a historical narrative in which American democracy is the embodiment of all the best features of the West, while at the same time making fun of what Jean-François Lyotard, in his *The Postmodern Condition,* has called "metanarratives."

Dewey thought that we could have a morally uplifting historical narrative without bothering to erect a metaphysical backdrop against which this narrative is played out, and without getting very specific about the goal toward which it tends. Followers of Dewey like myself would like to praise parliamentary democracy and the welfare state as very good things, but only on the basis of invidious comparisons with suggested concrete alternatives, not on the basis of claims that these institutions are truer to human nature, or more rational, or in better accord with the universal moral law, than feudalism or totalitarianism. Like Lyotard, we want to drop *meta*narratives. Unlike him, we keep on spinning edifying first-order narratives.

So the pragmatist answer to the question Lyotard raises in his "Universal history and cultural differences" – "Can we continue to organize the events which crowd in upon us from the human and nonhuman worlds with the help of the Idea of a universal history of humanity?"[1] – is that we can and should, as long as the point of doing so is to lift our spirits through utopian fantasy, rather than to gird our loins with metaphysical weapons. We Deweyans have a story to tell about the progress of our species, a story whose later episodes emphasize how things have been getting better in the West during the last few centuries, and which concludes with some suggestions about how they might become better still in the next few. But when asked about cultural differences, about what our story has to do with the Chinese or the Cashinahua, we can only reply that, for all we know, intercourse with these people may help modify our Western ideas about what institutions can best embody the spirit of Western social democracy.

We look forward, in a vague way, to a time when the Cashinahua, the Chinese, and (if such there be) the planets which form the Galactic Empire will all be part of the same cosmopolitan social democratic community. This community will doubtless have different institutions than those to which we are presently accustomed, but we assume that these future institutions will incorporate and enlarge the sorts of reforms which we applaud our ancestors for having made. The Chinese, the Cashinahua, and the Galactics will doubtless have suggestions about what further reforms are needed, but we shall not be inclined to adopt these suggestions until we have managed to fit them in with our distinctively Western social democratic aspirations, through some sort of judicious give-and-take.

This sort of ethnocentrism is, we pragmatists think, inevitable and unobjectionable. It amounts to little more than the claim that people can rationally change their beliefs and desires only by holding most of those beliefs and desires constant – even though we can never say in advance just which are to be changed and which retained intact. ("Rationally" here means that one can give a retrospective account of why one changed – how one invoked old beliefs or desires in justification of the new ones – rather than having to say, helplessly, "it just happened; somehow I got converted.") We cannot leap outside our Western social democratic skins when we encounter another culture, and we should not try. All we should try to do is to get inside the inhabitants of that culture long enough to get some idea of how we look to them, and whether they have any ideas we can

---

1 Jean-François Lyotard, "Histoire universelle et différences culturelles," *Critique* 41 (May 1985), p. 559. This issue of *Critique* includes a French translation of the original version of my response to Lyotard, as well as a paper by Vincent Descombes ("Les mots de la tribu") which comments on the exchange between us, as well as on my earlier paper "Habermas, Lyotard, and Post-Modernity," reprinted in volume 2 of these papers, *Essays on Heidegger and Others*. *Critique* 41 also includes the transcript of a brief conversational exchange between me and Lyotard.

use. That is also all they can be expected to do on encountering us. If members of the other culture protest that this expectation of tolerant reciprocity is a provincially Western one, we can only shrug our shoulders and reply that we have to work by our own lights, even as they do, for there is no supercultural observation platform to which we might repair. The only common ground on which we can get together is that defined by the overlap between their communal beliefs and desires and our own.

The pragmatist utopia is thus not one in which human nature has been unshackled, but one in which everybody has had a chance to suggest ways in which we might cobble together a world (or Galactic) society, and in which all such suggestions have been thrashed out in free and open encounters. We pragmatists do not think that there is a natural "moral kind" coextensive with our biological species, one which binds together the French, the Americans, and the Cashinahua. But we nevertheless feel free to use slogans like Tennyson's "The Parliament of Man, the Federation of the World!" For we want narratives of increasing cosmopolitanism, though not narratives of emancipation. For we think that there was nothing to emancipate, just as there was nothing which biological evolution emancipated as it moved along from the trilobites to the anthropoids. There is no human nature which was once, or still is, in chains.[2] Rather, our species has — ever since it developed language — been making up a nature for itself. This nature has been developed through ever larger, richer, more muddled, and more painful syntheses of opposing values.

Lately our species has been making up a particularly good nature for itself — that produced by the institutions of the liberal West. When we praise this development, we pragmatists drop the revolutionary rhetoric of emancipation and unmasking in favor of a reformist rhetoric about increased tolerance and decreased suffering. If we have an Idea (in the capitalized Kantian sense) in mind, it is that of Tolerance rather than that of Emancipation. We see no reason why either recent social and political developments or recent philosophical thought should deter us from our attempt to build a cosmopolitan world-society — one which embodies the same sort of utopia with which the Christian, Enlightenment, and Marxist metanarratives of emancipation ended.

Consider, in this light, Lyotard's claim that his question "Can we continue to organize the crowd of human events into a universal history of humanity?"

---

2 See Bernard Yack, *The Longing for Total Revolution: Philosophical Sources of Social Discontent from Rousseau to Marx and Nietzsche* (Princeton: Princeton University Press, 1986). Yack describes a tradition to which, as I see it, Foucault and Lyotard belong, but Dewey does not. It never occurred to Dewey that there was something inherently "repressive" about society as such, or something wrong with using bio-power to create subjects. He took over from Hegel the idea that you have to be socialized to be human, and that the important question is how you can maximize both richness of socialization and tolerance for individual eccentricity and deviance. That is a question which can be answered only by designing and performing a lot of painful and difficult social experiments, a lot more than we have so far envisaged.

presupposes that there "persists" a "we," and his doubt that we can preserve a sense for "we" once we give up the Kantian idea of emancipation.[3] My first reaction to such doubts is that we need not presuppose a *persistent* "we," a transhistorical metaphysical subject, in order to tell stories of progress. The only "we" we need is a local and temporary one: "we" means something like "us twentieth-century Western social democrats." So we pragmatists are content to embrace the alternative which Lyotard calls "secondary narcissism."[4] We think that, once we give up metaphysical attempts to find a "true self" for man, we can continue to speak as the contingent historical selves we find ourselves to be.

Lyotard thinks that adopting this alternative will land us pragmatic liberals in the same position as the Nazis were in: in renouncing unanimity we shall fall back on terror, on a kind of terror "whose rationale is not in principle accessible to everybody and whose benefits are not sharable by everybody."[5] Against this assimilation of the pragmatist's inevitable ethnocentrism to Nazism, I would insist that there is an important difference between saying "We admit that we cannot justify our beliefs or our actions to all human beings as they are at present, but we hope to create a community of free human beings who will freely share many of our beliefs and hopes," and saying, with the Nazis, "We have no concern for legitimizing ourselves in the eyes of others." There is a difference between the Nazi who says "We are good because we are the particular group we are" and the reformist liberal who says "We are good because, by persuasion rather than force, we shall eventually convince everybody else that we are." Whether such a "narcissistic" self-justification can avoid terrorism depends on whether the notion of "persuasion rather than force" still makes sense after we renounce the idea of human nature and the search for transcultural and ahistorical criteria of justification. If I have correctly understood Lyotard's line of thought, he would argue that the existence of incommensurable, untranslatable discourses throws doubt on this contrast between force and persuasion. He has suggested that the collapse of metaphysics diagnosed by Adorno can be seen as a recognition of the "multiplicity of worlds of names, the insurmountable diversity of cultures."[6] I take him to be saying that, because of this insurmountability, one culture cannot convert another by persuasion, but only by some form of "imperialist" force. When, for example, he says that "Nothing in a savage community disposes it to argue itself into a society of citizens [of Kant's cosmopolitan world-state],"[7] I interpret him to mean that when people from preliterate cultures go to mission schools and European universities they are not freely arguing themselves into cosmopolitanism but rather being "forcibly" changed, terrorized. I assume that he would also say that,

3 Lyotard, "Histoire universelle," pp. 560–1.
4 Ibid., p. 561.
5 Ibid., p. 562.
6 Ibid., p. 564.
7 . Ibid., p. 566.

when an anthropologist is so charmed by the tribe he studies that he abandons Europe and "goes native," he too has not been persuaded but has been, equally, "terrorized." Lyotard would be justified in these distressing claims if it were the case, as he says it is, that the anthropologist describes "the savage narrations and their rules according to cognitive rules, without pretending to establish any continuity between the latter and his own mode of discourse." But surely this is overstated. The anthropologist and the native agree, after all, on an enormous number of platitudes. They usually share beliefs about, for example, the desirability of finding waterholes, the danger of fondling poisonous snakes, the need for shelter in bad weather, the tragedy of the death of loved ones, the value of courage and endurance, and so on. If they did not, as Donald Davidson has remarked, it is hard to see how the two would ever have been able to learn enough of each other's languages to recognize the other as a language user.

This Davidsonian point amounts to saying that the notion of a language untranslatable into ours makes no sense, if "untranslatable" means "unlearnable." If I can learn a native language, then even if I cannot neatly pair off sentences in that language with sentences in English, I can certainly offer plausible explanations in English of why the natives are saying each of the funny-sounding things they say. I can provide the same sort of gloss on their utterances which a literary critic offers on poems written in a new idiom or a historian of the "barbarism" of our ancestors. Cultural differences are not different in kind from differences between old and ("revolutionary") new theories propounded within a single culture. The attempt to give a respectful hearing to Cashinahua views is not different in kind from the attempt to give a respectful hearing to some radically new scientific or political or philosophical suggestion offered by one of our fellow Westerners.

So I think it is misleading to say, as Lyotard does in an essay on Wittgenstein, that Wittgenstein has shown that "there is no unity of language, but rather islets of language, each governed by a system of rules untranslatable into those of the others."[8] We need to distinguish between the following two theses: (1) there is no single commensurating language, known in advance, which will provide an idiom into which to translate any new theory, poetic idiom, or native culture; and (2) there are unlearnable languages. The first of these theses is common to Kuhn, Wittgenstein, and the common sense of the anthropological profession. It is a corollary of the general pragmatist claim that there is no permanent ahistorical metaphysical framework into which everything can be fitted. The second thesis seems to me incoherent. I do not see how we could tell when we had come against a human practice which we knew to be linguistic and also knew to be so foreign that we must give up hope of knowing what it would be like to engage in it.

Whereas Lyotard takes Wittgenstein to be pointing out unbridgeable divisions

8   Jean-François Lyotard, *Tombeau de l'intellectuel* (Paris Éditions Galilée, 1984) p. 61.

between linguistic islets, I see him as recommending the constructions of causeways which will, in time, make the archipelago in question continuous with the mainland. These causeways do not take the form of translation manuals, but rather of the sort of cosmopolitan know-how whose acquisition enables us to move back and forth between sectors of our own culture and our own history – for example, between Aristotle and Freud, between the language-game of worship and that of commerce, between the idioms of Holbein and of Matisse. On my reading, Wittgenstein was not warning us against attempts to translate the untranslatable but rather against the unfortunate philosophical habit of seeing different languages as embodying incompatible systems of rules. If one does see them in this way, then the lack of an overarching system of metarules for pairing off sentences – the sort of system which metanarratives were once supposed to help us get – will strike one as a disaster. But if one sees language-learning as the acquisition of a skill, one will not be tempted to ask what metaskill permits such acquisition. One will assume that curiosity, tolerance, patience, luck, and hard work are all that is needed.

This difference between thinking of linguistic mastery as a grasping of rules and as an inarticulable technique may seem a long way from the question of the possibility of universal history. So let me now try to connect the two topics. I have been suggesting that Lyotard sees languages as divided from one another by incompatible systems of linguistic rules, and is thereby committed to what Davidson has called "the third, and perhaps last, dogma of empiricism: the distinction between scheme and content."[9] He is committed, in particular, to the claim that we can usefully distinguish questions of fact from questions of language, a claim attacked by Dewey and Quine. It seems to me that only with the help of that distinction can Lyotard cast doubt on the pragmatist attempt to see the history of humanity as the history of the gradual replacement of force by persuasion, the gradual spread of certain virtues typical of the democratic West. For only the claim that commensuration is impossible will provide philosophical grounds for ruling out this suggestion, and only the language–fact distinction will make sense of the claim that incommensurability is something more than a temporary inconvenience.

I can try to put this point in Lyotard's own vocabulary by taking up his distinctions between *litige* and *différend,* and between *dommage* and *tort.* He defines a *différend* as a case in which "a plaintiff is deprived of means of arguing, and so becomes a victim," one in which the rules of conflict resolution which apply to a case are stated in the idiom of one of the parties in such a way that the other party cannot explain how he has been injured.[10] By contrast, in the case of *litige,* where it is a question of *dommage* rather than *tort,* both sides agree on how to state the

9 Donald Davidson, "On the Very Idea of a Conceptual Scheme," in his *Inquiries into Truth and Interpretation* (Oxford: Oxford University Press, 1984), p. 189.
10 Jean-François Lyotard, *Le Différend* (Paris: Éditions Minuit, 1983), pp. 24–5.

issues and on what criteria are to be applied to resolve them. In a very interesting and enlightening synthesis of philosophical and political problems, Lyotard suggests that we can see everything from the semantic paradoxes of self-reference to anticolonialist struggles in terms of these contrasts. Using this vocabulary, Lyotard's doubts about universal history can be put by saying that the liberal-pragmatist attempt to see history as the triumph of persuasion over force tries to treat history as a long process of litigation, rather than a sequence of *différends*.

My general reply to these doubts is to say that political liberalism amounts to the suggestion that we try to substitute litigation for *différends* as far as we can, and that there is no *a priori* philosophical reason why this attempt must fail, just as (*pace* Christianity, Kant, and Marx) there is no *a priori* reason why it must succeed. But I also want to raise doubts about Lyotard's choice of terminology. It seems a bad idea – and indeed a suspiciously Kantian idea – to think of inquiry on the model of judicial proceedings. The philosophical tradition has pictured institutions or theories as being brought before the tribunal of pure reason. If this were the only model available, then Lyotard would have a point when he asks "what language do the judges speak?" But Dewey wanted to get rid of the idea that new ideas or practices could be judged by antecedently existing criteria. He wanted everything to be as much up for grabs as feasible as much of the time as feasible. He suggested that we think of rationality not as the application of criteria (as in a tribunal) but as the achievement of consensus (as in a town meeting, or a bazaar).

This suggestion chimes with Wittgenstein's suggestion that we think of linguistic competence not as the mastery of rules but as the ability to get along with other players of a language-game, a game played without referees. Both Dewey and Wittgenstein made the point which Stanley Fish has recently restated: that attempts to erect "rules" or "criteria" turn into attempts to hypostatize and eternalize some past or present practice, thereby making it more difficult for that practice to be reformed or gradually replaced with a different practice.[11] The Deweyan idea that rationality is not the application of criteria goes together with holism in the philosophy of language, and in particular with the claim that there are no "linguistic islets," no such things as "conceptual schemes" but only slightly different sets of beliefs and desires. *Pace* Lyotard's interpretation of Wittgenstein, it seems to me profoundly unWittgensteinian to say as he does that "there is no unity of language," or that "there is an irredeemable opacity at the heart of language."[12] For language no more has a nature than humanity does; both have

11 See Stanley Fish, "Consequences," in his *Doing What Comes Naturally: Change, Rhetoric, and the Practice of Theory in Literary and Legal Studies* (Durham, N.C.: Duke University Press, 1989). This essay was delivered as a contribution to the same symposium for which Lyotard's and my papers were written, and was published along with ours as "La théorie est sans conséquences" in *Critique* 41 (May 1985).

12 Lyotard, *Tombeau*, p. 84.

only a history. There is just as much unity or transparency of language as there is willingness to converse rather than fight. So there is as much of either as we shall make in the course of history. The history of humanity will be a universal history just in proportion to the amount of free consensus among human beings which is attained – that is, in proportion to the replacement of force by persuasion, of *différends* by litigation.

On the holistic view of language elaborated by Quine and Davidson, distinctions between cultures, theories, or discourses are just ways of dividing up the corpus of sentences so far asserted into clusters. These clusters are not divided from one another by incompatible linguistic rules, nor by reciprocally unlearnable grammars. They represent no more than differences of opinion – the sorts of differences which can get resolved by hashing things out. So when we say that Aristotle and Galileo, or the Greeks and the Cashinahua, or Holbein and Matisse, did not "speak the same language," we should not mean that they carried around different Kantian categories, or different "semantic rules," with which to organize their experiences. Rather, we should mean merely that they held such disparate beliefs that there would have been no simple, easy, quick way for either to convince the other to engage in a common project. This phenomenon of disagreement cannot be explained by saying that they speak different languages, for that is a *virtus dormitiva* sort of explanation – like explaining the fact that people do different things in different countries by pointing to the existence of different national customs.

I can put the disagreement between Lyotard and myself in another way by saying that what he calls the *défaillance* of modernity strikes me as little more than the loss of belief in the first of the two theses I distinguished earlier – a loss of faith in our ability to come up with a single set of criteria which everybody in all times and places can accept, invent a single language-game which can somehow take over all the jobs previously done by all the language-games ever played. But the loss of this theoretical goal merely shows that one of the less important sideshows of Western civilization – metaphysics – is in the process of closing down. This failure to find a single grand commensurating discourse, in which to write a universal translation manual (thereby doing away with the need to constantly learn new languages) does nothing to cast doubt on the possibility (as opposed to the difficulty) of peaceful social progress. In particular, the failure of metaphysics does not hinder us from making a useful distinction between persuasion and force. We can see the preliterate native as being persuaded rather than forced to become cosmopolitan just insofar as, having learned to play the language-games of Europe, he decides to abandon the ones he played earlier – without being threatened with loss of food, shelter, or *Lebensraum* if he makes the opposite decision.

It is, of course, rare for a native to have been granted this sort of free choice.

We Western liberals have had the Gatling gun, and the native has not. So typically we *have* used force rather than persuasion to convince natives of our own goodness. It is useful to be reminded, as Lyotard reminds us, of our customary imperialist hypocrisy. But it is also the case that we Western liberals have raised up generations of historians of colonialism, anthropologists, sociologists, specialists in the economics of development, and so on, who have explained to us in detail just how violent and hypocritical we have been. The anthropologists have, in addition, shown us that the preliterate natives have some ideas and practices that we can usefully weave together with our own. These reformist arguments, of a sort familiar to the tradition of Western liberalism, are examples of the ability of that tradition to alter its direction from the inside, and thus to convert *différends* into processes of litigation. One does not have to be particularly cheerful or optimistic about the prospects for such internal reform, nor about the likelihood of a final victory of persuasion over force, to think that such a victory is the only plausible political goal we have managed to envisage – or to see ever more inclusive universal histories as useful instruments for the achievement of that goal.

By "ever more inclusive" I mean such that one's conception of the goal of history – of the nature of the future cosmopolitan society – constantly changes to accommodate the lessons learned from new experiences (e.g., the sort of experiences inflicted by Attila, Hitler, and Stalin, the sort reported by anthropologists, and the sort provided by artists). This Deweyan program of constant, experimental reformulation means that (in Lyotard's phrase) "the place of the first person" is constantly changing. Deweyan pragmatists urge us to think of ourselves as part of a pageant of historical progress which will gradually encompass all of the human race, and are willing to argue that the vocabulary which twentieth-century Western social democrats use is the best vocabulary the race has come up with so far (by, e.g., arguing that the vocabulary of the Cashinahua cannot be combined with modern technology, and that abandoning that technology is too high a price to pay for the benefits the Cashinahua enjoy.) But pragmatists are quite sure that their own vocabulary will be superseded – and, from their point of view, the sooner the better. They expect their descendants to be as condescending about the vocabulary of twentieth-century liberals as they are about the vocabulary of Aristotle or of Rousseau. What links them to the inhabitants of the utopia they foresee is not the belief that the future will still speak as they speak, but rather the hope that future human beings will think of Dewey as "one of us," just as we speak of Rousseau as "one of us." Pragmatists hope, but have no metaphysical justification for believing, that future universal histories of humanity will describe twentieth-century Western social democrats in favorable terms. But they admit that we have no very clear idea what those terms will be. They only insist that, if these new terms have been adopted as a result of persuasion rather than force, they will be better than the ones we are presently using – for that is analytic of their meaning of "better."

Let me close by making a general remark about the relations between French and American philosophy, taking off from a remark of Lyotard's. He has written that contemporary German and American philosophers think of current French thought as "neo-irrationalist," instancing Habermas's lectures in Paris, lectures which Lyotard describes as "giving lessons in how to be progressive to Derrida and Foucault."[13] The Deweyan line I have been taking in these remarks is reminiscent of Habermas's "consensus theory of truth," and it may seem that I too have been offering "lessons in progressivism." But I think that Lyotard misstates the criticism which Habermasians and pragmatists are inclined to make of recent French thought. Given our noncriterial conception of rationality, we are not inclined to diagnose "irrationalism"; since for us "rational" merely means "persuasive," "irrational" can only mean "invoking force." We are not claiming that French thinkers resort to the lash and knout. But we *are* inclined to worry about their antiutopianism, their apparent loss of faith in liberal democracy. Even those who, like myself, think of France as the source of the most original philosophical thought currently being produced, cannot figure out why French thinkers are so willing to say things like "May 1968 refutes the doctrine of parliamentary liberalism."[14] From our standpoint, nothing could refute that doctrine except some better idea about how to organize society. No event – not even Auschwitz – can show that we should cease to work for a given utopia. Only another, more persuasive, utopia can do that.

More generally, we cannot figure out why philosophers like Lyotard are so inclined to take particular historical events as demonstrating the "bankruptcy" of long-term efforts at social reform. This willingness – which is, perhaps, an aftereffect of a long attempt to salvage something from Marxism, an attempt which has resulted in the retention of certain characteristically Marxist habits of thought – sets contemporary French philosophy apart from philosophy in Britain, America, and Germany. Such a willingness to interpret very specific political, economic, and technological developments as indications of decisive shifts in the course of history will, to be sure, make the idea of "the universal history of humanity" very dubious. Conversely, a willingness to see these as probably just more of the same old familiar vicissitudes is required to take the Dewey-Habermas line, to persist in using notions like "persuasion rather than force" and "consensus" to state one's political goals.

I find it strange, for example, that Lyotard should both drop the project of universal history and yet be willing to discover world-historical significance in,

13 Ibid., p. 81.
14 Lyotard, "Histoire universelle," p. 563.

for example, new technologies of information processing and new developments in the physical and biological sciences. The standard Anglo-Saxon assumption is that the determination of world-historical significance – deciding whether May 1968 or the development of the microchip was a decisive turning point or just more of the same – should be postponed until a century or so after the event in question has taken place. This hunch dictates a philosophical style which is very different from Lyotard's, one which does not try to make philosophical hay out of current events. The difference between that style and current French styles is, I think, the main reason for the frequent breakdowns of communication between American philosophers and their French colleagues.

Another way of formulating the difference between these two styles is to say that French philosophers specialize in trying to establish what Lyotard calls *maîtrise de la parole et du sens* by engaging in "radical critique" – that is, by inventing a new vocabulary which makes all the old political and philosophical issues obsolete. Anglo-Saxon philosophers, by contrast, often try to pretend that everybody has always spoken the same language, that questions of vocabulary are "merely verbal" and that what matters is *argument* – argument which appeals to "intuitions" statable in the universal vocabulary which everybody has always used. As long as we Anglo-Saxons affect this implausible view, we shall continue to resort to the clumsy and inapt epithet "irrationalist."

It is certainly the case that Anglo-Saxon philosophers would do better to renounce this epithet, to become a bit more "French," and to realize that a universal vocabulary has to be worked for rather than taken for granted. But we Anglo-Saxons suspect that French philosophy could profit from realizing that adopting a new vocabulary only makes sense if you can say something about the debilities of the old vocabulary from the inside, and can move back and forth, dialectically, between the old and the new vocabulary. It seems to us as if our French colleagues are too willing to find, or make, a linguistic islet and then invite people to move onto it, and not interested enough in building causeways between such islets and the mainland.

This difference between wanting new vocabularies and wanting new arguments is closely connected with the difference between revolutionary and reformist politics. Anglo-Saxon intellectuals take for granted that (in countries like France and the United States where the press and the elections remain free) "serious" politics is reformist. From this point of view, revolutionary politics in such countries can be no more than intellectual exhibitionism. By contrast, it seems to be taken for granted among French intellectuals that "serious" political thought is revolutionary thought, and that offering concrete suggestions, phrased in the current political idiom of the day, to the electorate or to elected leaders is beneath one's dignity – or, at best, something one does only in one's spare time. I suspect that the difference between what Lyotard gets out of Wittgenstein and what I get out of him, and also the difference between Lyotard's interpretation of "postmodernity" as a decisive shift which cuts right across culture and my view of it as merely the gradual encapsulation and forgetting of a certain philosophical tradition, reflect our different notions of how politically conscious intellectuals should spend their time.

Index of names

Adorno, Theodor W., 33, 177, 179–180, 184, 195, 214
Althusser, Louis, 33, 76
Anscombe, G. E. M., 114
Aristotle, 48–51, 69, 71–72, 85–88, 99, 105, 106n, 110, 134, 157, 188n, 216, 218–219
Augustine, Saint, 106
Austin, J. L., 71, 161

Bacon, Francis, 47
Bain, Alexander, 10, 93, 161
Bell, Daniel, 185n
Bellah, Robert, 177, 209
Bennett, Jonathan, 157–158, 161n
Bergson, Henri, 118
Berkeley, George, 59, 131
Bernstein, Richard, 15n
Bilgrami, Akeel, 164n
Black, Max, 163, 166, 167n, 168–171, 172n
Blake, William, 86
Bloom, Harold, 86, 90, 95
Blumenberg, Hans, 33n, 61n
Boyd, Richard, 51n, 53, 54, 86
Boyle, Robert, 161
Brandom, Robert, 4n, 128n, 150n, 151–152, 154, 161

Caputo, John, 96n
Carnap, Rudolph, 46, 64, 71–72, 75, 151
Cassirer, Ernst, 162
Cavell, Stanley, 95
Churchill, Winston, 29
Chomsky, Noam, 54n, 98n, 201
Clifford, William Kingdon, 66
Comay, Rebecca, 15n
Copernicus, N., 120

Darwin, Charles, 10, 17, 63, 149n
Davidson, Donald, 1, 3n, 6, 8–12, 15, 25–26, 32, 40, 50–51, 60, 81, 85, 88n, 91, 99n, 103–105, 107–109, 113–114, 116–117, 120, 123–126, 128–129, 132–150, 152–170, 171n–172n, 176, 188, 191n, 193, 215–216, 218
Deleuze, Giles, 29n
de Man, Paul, 90
Democritus, 118
Dennett, Daniel, 11n, 88n, 91, 98n, 99
Derrida, Jacques, 90, 94–96, 99n, 125, 149n, 152, 161, 188, 193, 208, 220
Descartes, René, 10, 67, 185, 189
Descombes, Vincent, 29n, 212n
Devitt, Michael, 130, 146–147, 149
Dewey, John, 1, 3–4, 10, 13–17, 23n, 34, 42–44, 47, 60, 61n, 63–66, 68–77, 79, 82–85, 90, 94, 96n, 103, 109, 113, 123, 126, 129, 132, 135, 138, 140–142, 146, 149n, 150–151, 177–181, 183n, 184, 186n–187n, 188, 189n, 192, 194–197, 201, 207, 211, 213n, 216–217, 219–220
Dilthey, Wilhelm, 1, 79, 90, 102, 118
Disraeli, Benjamin, 26
Donagan, Alan, 136n, 141n, 150n
Dreyfus, Herbert, 96n
Duchamp, Marcel, 89
Dummett, Michael, 3, 8, 12, 48–49, 51, 121, 128n, 133, 139, 143–149, 165–166
Dworkin, Ronald, 177–178, 181, 190n, 197–199, 201

Eddington, A. S., 155, 161
Eliot, T. S., 94
Emerson, Ralph Waldo, 64, 194–195
Engels, Friedrich, 130, 207

Euripides, 21
Evans, Gareth, 99

Fenellosa, E., 207
Feyerabend, Paul, 24–25, 27–28, 47, 89, 95
Fichte, J. G., 118
Field, Hartry, 10, 130, 149
Fine, Arthur, 8n, 48–49, 52–53, 142, 150n
Fish, Stanley, 80, 82, 84, 89, 91, 217
Fisk, Milton, 15n
Fodor, Jerry, 54n, 130–131
Foucault, Michel, 15, 24, 26–27, 33, 213n, 220
Fraser, Nancy, 15n
Frege, Gottlob, 148, 150–151
Freud, Sigmund, 85, 216

Gadamer, Hans-Georg, 28, 91, 102, 162, 176
Galileo, 17, 48–51, 81, 89, 106n, 218
Geach, P. T., 57
Geertz, Clifford, 95, 96n, 203–210
Giddens, Anthony, 97n
Gladstone, William, 26
Glymour, Clark, 38, 53, 64,
Goodman, Nelson, 40, 162, 172n
Grene, Marjorie, 63
Grice, H. P., 157, 168
Gutting, Gary, 161n

Habermas, Jürgen, 1, 23n, 28, 62n, 97n, 162, 168–169, 220
Hacking, Ian, 166n
Haeckel, Ernst Heinrich, 71
Hanson, Norwood, 95
Harman, Gilbert, 56, 156
Harré, Rom, 64
Hartman, Geoffrey, 79, 90–91
Heidegger, Martin, 1, 4, 12, 16, 28, 33, 61n, 70–75, 86, 88, 99, 103, 149n, 151–152, 158, 161–162, 176–179, 187n, 188, 189n, 194
Hegel, G. W. F., 61, 61n, 63, 71–72, 75, 79, 83, 90, 149n, 158, 178, 181, 186n, 188n, 191n, 197–198, 213n
Hempel, C. G., 46–48
Herodotus, 21
Hesse, Mary, 25, 27, 56–57, 64, 91,

102, 124, 131n, 162–165, 167n, 168–169, 172
Hirsch, E. D., 84–90
Hitler, Adolf, 219
Holbein, Hans, 216, 218
Hollinger, David, 64
Hook, Sidney, 17n, 64–72, 74–77
Horkheimer, Max, 177, 179–180, 183, 195
Horwich, Paul, 147n
Hume, David, 40, 42, 185, 189
Husserl, Edmund, 144n, 150n
Huxley, T. H., 61

Jaeger, Werner, 88
James, William, 3, 12, 13n, 22, 23n, 58, 63, 66, 75, 79, 83, 123, 126–128, 132, 138–141, 146
Jefferson, Thomas, 175, 176n, 180, 182–183, 186n–187n, 189–190, 196
Jesus Christ, 182n
Johnson, Mark, 169n, 172n

Kant, Immanuel, 82–83, 118, 123, 152, 181, 185, 188–189, 191, 197, 200n, 217
Kenny, Anthony, 114
Kierkegaard, Søren, 188, 191n
King, Martin Luther, 181n
Kripke, Saul, 10, 59, 86, 88n, 89, 134–135, 150n, 155
Krüger, Lorenz, 91
Kuhn, Thomas S., 24–25, 27, 37–41, 43, 47–48, 51, 64–65, 85, 86n, 91, 95, 106n, 215

Lakatos, Imré, 47
Lakoff, George, 169n, 172n
Leeds, Stephen, 142
Leibniz, G. W., 164
Lentricchia, Frank, 15n
Lepenies, Wolf, 91
Levenson, Michael, 172n
Levin, David, 189n
Levin, Michael, 55–56, 140n
Lévi-Strauss, Claude, 203
Lewis, C. I., 105
Lewis, David, 7–9, 11
Little, David, 187n
Locke, John, 146, 161

Lovibond, Sabina, 32
Loyola, Ignatius, 179n, 187–188, 190–191
Luther, Martin, 182n
Lyotard, Jean-François, 199, 211–221

McCarthy, Mary, 76
McCarthy, Thomas, 2n
Macaulay, Thomas, 47
McDowell, John, 150n
McGinn, Colin, 3n, 97n, 99
MacIntyre, Alasdair, 177–178, 194, 197, 209
McMullin, Ernan, 49, 51–53
Malinowski, Bronislaw, 207
Marcuse, Herbert, 64
Marx, Karl, 85, 198, 217
Matisse, Henri, 216, 218
Meinong, Alexius, 97
Micheals, Walter, 82
Mill, John Stuart, 34, 67, 207
Millikan, Ruth Garrett, 11n
Milton, John, 1, 176n
Moore, G. E., 127
Morgenbesser, Sidney, 48

Nabokov, Vladimir, 162
Nagel, Ernest, 48
Nagel, Thomas, 6–8, 9n, 12, 14, 56, 59, 97n, 99, 121n, 161n
Nehamas, Alexander, 95
Neurath, Otto, 29, 142n
Newton, Isaac, 57, 69, 161, 164–165
Newton-Smith, W. H., 47, 86n
Nietzsche, Friedrich, 13, 15, 32–33, 60, 61n, 87, 150n, 187–188, 190–191, 194, 198
Norris, Christopher, 15n
Nozick, Robert, 185n

Oakeshott, Michael, 25, 28, 195n, 197
Okrent, Mark, 96n

Paine, Tom, 64
Papineau, David, 9, 11
Parmenides, 105–106
Paul, Saint, 161
Peirce, Charles Sanders, 1, 10, 23n, 41, 59n, 63, 93, 98, 118, 120, 123, 127, 128n, 129–131, 133, 138–139, 161

Planck, Max, 108
Plantinga, Alvin, 131n
Plato, 21–22, 32, 46, 49, 51–52, 71–72, 74, 87, 106, 116–118, 124–125, 142, 146, 150n, 161, 182n, 191
Platts, Mark, 150n
Plotinus, 72, 74
Polanyi, Michael, 25, 64
Popper, Karl, 23n
Protagoras, 28n
Ptolemy, 120
Putnam, Hilary, 6–7, 11–12, 13n, 24–27, 32, 48, 50–51, 86n, 88n, 98n, 100n, 113, 123, 127, 131n, 133n, 140–142, 155–156, 162, 202
Putnam, Ruth Anna, 13n

Quine, Willard van Orman, 1, 6, 26, 40, 46–48, 51, 65, 90–91, 97n, 99, 103, 107–108, 116, 120, 123, 126, 132–134, 135n, 142, 145–148, 155, 164, 166n, 176, 208, 216, 218

Rawls, John, 30, 34, 177, 179–186, 188–189, 190n, 191–192, 195, 199, 200n, 209
Ricoeur, Paul, 165
Riemann, Georg Friedrich, 97
Rosenberg, Jay, 130, 155–156, 158, 160
Rousseau, Jean Jacques, 219
Russell, Bertrand, 63, 99, 105–106, 109, 144n, 150n, 151

Sandel, Michael, 30n, 177–178, 182n, 184–186, 188–189, 194, 195n, 200
Sartre, Jean-Paul, 64, 182n
Scanlon, T. M., 30n, 184n
Scheffler, Israel, 47
Schiller, F. C. S., 194
Schopenhauer, Arthur, 118
Searle, John, 88n, 99, 150n, 169
Sellars, Wilfred, 1, 52, 123, 144, 151–161, 169, 200
Shakespeare, William, 97
Skinner, B. F., 33, 54n, 109–110, 135, 140
Socrates, 21, 29, 33
Stalin, Joseph, 219
Staten, Henry, 60n
Stout, Jeffrey, 82n, 194n

Stoutland, Fredrick, 150n
Stowe, Harriet Beecher, 207
Strauss, Leo, 188n
Strawson, P. F., 134, 137, 148n
Stroud, Barry, 97n
Sullivan, William M., 186n

Tarski, Alfred, 128, 132, 137, 151
Taylor, Charles, 96n, 102–104, 106–
    110, 114, 177–179
Tennyson, Alfred Lord, 213
Tillich, Paul, 64, 69–71, 74–75
Toulmin, Stephen, 95
Tugendhat, Ernest, 144n

Unger, Roberto, 15, 177, 194, 197

van Fraasen, Bas, 48–49, 106n, 160–161
Vico, Giambattista, 87

Walzer, Michael, 181, 198
Weber, Max, 194
Wheeler, Samuel, 99, 125n, 149n, 161n,
    172n
White, Morton, 150
Whitehead, Alfred North, 13, 99, 162
Williams, Bernard, 4–5, 7–9, 30n–31n,
    48–49, 55–61, 161n, 191n, 208
Williams, Charles, 170n
Williams, Michael, 97n, 130n, 140n
Wittgenstein, Ludwig, 1, 3–4, 7, 16, 25,
    40, 46, 59–60, 85, 88, 105n, 144–
    145, 148, 151, 201, 208, 215–217,
    221
Wollheim, Richard, 84n
Wright, Crispin, 148n

Yack, Bernard, 213n
Yeats, W. B., 170–171

4895